Introduction

Today it is widely agreed across a broad spectrum of opinion that the resurrection of Jesus is the central claim in the Christian faith. This can be seen in New Testament writings, and most scholars recognize that it remains so today. Supported by these writings, many recent scholars have shown that other doctrines also take the resurrection as their departure point.

This book attempts to establish a resurrection theology that moves from this event to several other key Christian beliefs. I will map out several paths, including historical, philosophical, counseling, and experiential, in which the resurrection might serve as the foundation for these theological tenets. Some readers may resist a particular angle. Even so, one should still appreciate the richness of the resurrection, as well as other doctrines following from it.

Much of the interaction with contemporary scholarship in this volume comes from my two-year study of most of the published sources on Jesus's resurrection written in German, French, and English from 1975 to 2003.[1] The study included more than fourteen hundred scholarly texts. Just plotting the positions on the current spectrum took well over five hundred pages.

The Great Scholarly Divide

While scholars generally agree that the resurrection is at the center of Christianity and has application to other doctrines, at least two major issues cause widespread disagreement. (1) Was the resurrection an actual event of history? If not, did it still occur, perhaps in other than a strictly space–time manner?

(2) Is the relationship between this doctrine and other theological beliefs and practices formed by some sort of evidential argument? Or is the relationship between Jesus's resurrection and, say, the believer's life after death simply a matter of faith, evidential arguments aside?

Even if there is little initial agreement on these two questions, the various positions that relate the resurrection to other theological truths still share much common ground. Strangely enough, even critical theologians who believe that Jesus was not raised from the dead in any actual or historical sense usually think that there is still an important, perhaps even crucial, connection between the resurrection and other religious beliefs and actions.

My position is that Jesus's resurrection is best considered a historical event of the past. There are varying amounts of entailment between this event and other Christian doctrines or practices. Sometimes there is a fairly direct argument. On other occasions, though, I develop pastoral and other practical links between the resurrection and the beliefs and practices of believers. I will pursue both sorts of connections.

I wish to make it clear that one could hold to other stances on these two issues and still make much sense of this volume. For instance, one might think that Jesus really rose from the dead historically but that arguments for this event violate the nature of faith. Or, it might be held that Jesus rose from the dead, but he appeared in a less-than-bodily fashion. In either case, one could still gain from various connections between this crucial occurrence and other Christian beliefs and practices.

The Center of Christian Theology

Most critical scholars, whether conservative or liberal, agree that the resurrection of Jesus is the key to the Christian faith. We have said that most critical scholars, whether conservative or liberal, agree that the resurrection of Jesus is the key to the Christian faith. For example, Hans Küng contends: "Christianity begins with Easter. Without Easter there would be no gospel, not a single narrative, not a letter in the New Testament. Without Easter, Christendom would have no belief in Christ, no proclamation of Christ, nor any church, any divine worship, any mission."[2] Similarly, Reginald Fuller adds: "The resurrection of Jesus from the dead was the central claim of the church's proclamation. There was no period of time when this was not so."[3]

The chief indication of this centrality is the New Testament testimony. The writers repeatedly agree not only that the resurrection actually occurred, but that it ensured, illuminated, or is otherwise related to a variety of other beliefs and practices.

The key passage here is 1 Corinthians 15. Paul reminded his audience of the Gospel message that he preached to them (vv. 1–2). Then he cited an early Christian creed(s) that defines the Gospel content and lists a number of appearances of the resurrected Jesus. He added the appearance to himself (vv. 3–8). Due to the exceptionally early date at which Paul received this material and the importance of his own eyewitness testimony, as well as his proximity to some of the other witnesses, this text is virtually always viewed as containing the best testimony for the resurrection. I look briefly at this topic in chapter 1.

Beginning in verse 12, Paul turns to the significance of the resurrection. If Jesus was not raised from the dead, then the Christian faith and preaching are fallacious (κενὸν, 15:14). Then the apostles, who were eyewitnesses to the appearances (vv. 11, 14–15), would be in error in their affirmation that God raised Jesus (vv. 14–15).

Using another term (ματαία, 15:17), Paul repeats that the entire Christian faith would be ineffective if it were not for Jesus's resurrection. Without this event, there is no forgiveness of sins, and believers who have died have perished in vain (vv. 17–18). Apart from the fact of the resurrection, our only hope lies in this life. In sum, without eternal hope, Christians are to be pitied above all others (v. 19). We would be living a lie with mundane consequences.

After outlining this dismal picture of a spineless Christianity, Paul moves to a triumphant note. Since Christ *was* raised from the dead (v. 20), we now have a firm foundation for our faith. The resurrection of the dead is based on this event (vv. 21–23).

So all of Paul's earlier reservations are, in fact, reversed. Christian preaching is not useless, and faith in Christ is not in vain (v. 14). Proclaiming the truth about God raising Christ is not false testimony (vv. 14, 15). Since Christ has been raised, our faith is not in vain and forgiveness of sins can be a reality (v. 17). As a result, saints who have died in Christ indeed do have hope (v. 18). And life does have much meaning, both in this world and the future (v. 19).

In an incredible comment, Paul additionally applies this teaching to the Christian's behavior. If the dead are not raised (which he has already said depends on Jesus's resurrection), then we may as well embrace an alien ethic: "Let us eat and drink, for tomorrow we die" (15:32 RSV). So the truth of the resurrection makes a claim on our present actions, as well as our future existence. Both are integrated and meaningful in Christian theology and ethics.

Building on this foundation of Christ's resurrection, Paul goes on to develop his doctrine of the believer's resurrection body and immortality (15:35–58). He makes at least three important applications of this doctrine.

He thinks that the doctrine is the ultimate answer to the problem of pain and suffering. He taunts death, for it has lost its sting due to Jesus Christ's victory over the grave (vv. 54–57).

Paul ends this passage with two additional comments regarding the application of the belief in a resurrection body and immortality. He asserts that, because of the truth of Jesus Christ's resurrection, believers should stand firmly in their faith, allowing nothing to dissuade them. Further, they should commit themselves completely to the Lord's work, since their labor is well spent (15:58). In the very next verses, Paul calls on the Corinthians to provide an offering in order to assist poor believers in Jerusalem (16:1–4). We find out later that this was a successful plea (2 Cor 8:1–15); Paul moves all the way from the truth of the resurrection to contributing liberally to the needs of less–fortunate believers. It should never be said that this apostle's theology and faith were disjointed from his actions.

In 1 Corinthians 15 alone, Paul makes it clear that Jesus's death and resurrection provide the grounding for Christian hope and action, as well as the basis for some Christian doctrines. Clearly, the apostle thinks that there would be no recognizable Christian faith without it. Interestingly, after remarking earlier that the Christian faith would be in vain (κενὸν, 15:14) were it not for the resurrection, he uses the same term to conclude that, because Christ was raised, the believer's work is not in vain (κενὸς, 15:58).

Although 1 Corinthians 15 is the earliest and lengthiest application of the resurrection to Christian theology and practice, it is not the only New Testament witness to the centrality of this doctrine. A few other texts might briefly be mentioned. Taking these passages at face value, we learn much about the importance that was attached to this occurrence.

The Gospels claim that Jesus's resurrection had multiple applications. It was the sign that Jesus was who he claimed to be (Mt 12:38–42; 16:1–4). The truth of the resurrection not only ensured the believer's own resurrection (Jn 14:19), but was used to comfort those who were grieving over the death of a loved one (Jn 11:21–27). Later, we are told that the resurrected Jesus consoled his own grieving disciples (Lk 24:13–43; Jn 20:10–20).

Paul returns often to the importance of the resurrection. In Romans 1:3–4, the apostle cites another ancient tradition that encompasses a brief Christology. Jesus is said to be both God's Son and David's offspring (v. 3). Jesus's resurrection from the dead showed that he was both the Son of God and Lord (v. 4). Similarly, the early Christological formula "Jesus is Lord" and the salvation requirement of belief that Jesus was raised from the dead are interrelated (Rom 10:9; cf. 14:9). The power of the resurrection is available to believers, to help them live godly lives (Rom 6:5–14, 8:5–11; Phil 3:10–11).

There is a crucial difference between grieving with hope and grieving without hope, and for believers, the source of that hope is Jesus's resurrection (1 Thes 4:14–15).

Several New Testament writers assert that Jesus's resurrection, more than any other doctrine, ensures that Christians will likewise be raised from the dead. This is true of Paul (1 Cor 6:14; Phil 3:20–21; 1 Thes 4:14) as well as other writers (1 Jn 3:2; Acts 4:2). The resurrection also provides the assurance of eternal life, as well as a heavenly perspective in the present (2 Cor 4:14–5:8; 1 Pt 1:3–4).

Further, the Book of Acts reports several early Christian proclamations of the Gospel in which the resurrection plays a pivotal role.[4] Each of these contexts includes at least three doctrinal items: Jesus is given exalted titles like "Lord" and "Christ," his death is mentioned, and his resurrection is reported. It appears that at least some of these texts represent remnants of the earliest Christian teaching, providing insights into what was considered to be pivotal truth.[5] I look briefly at a few of these examples.

In Acts 2:22–24, we are told that Peter proclaimed that Jesus's resurrection served as God's approval or accreditation of Jesus and his message. This event, along with his other miracles, singled out Jesus as God's messenger.

Acts 13:26–39 is presented as the crux of a Pauline sermon in which the apostle challenged the people of Antioch. The historicity of the resurrection, including Jesus's appearances and a strongly implied empty tomb (vv. 28–37), formed the heart of the message. This was the basis of Paul's plea for his hearers to seek the forgiveness of sins and exercise faith in Jesus for salvation (vv. 38–39).

The best example in Acts of Jesus's resurrection providing the grounds for certain elements of Christian theology is found in Paul's Areopagus lecture in the city of Athens (17:22–34). Paul began by speaking of God and how he revealed himself through his creation (vv. 22–27). In a surprising move, Paul cited two Greek writers, Epimenides and Aratus (17:28), most likely in order to establish some common ground with his audience. Now, Paul said, God challenged everyone to repent in light of the coming judgment, in which Jesus would act as the judge. Paul concluded by stating that God had provided a guarantee (πίστιν παρασχὼν, 17:31) of the truth of this message by raising Jesus from the dead. So God's challenge of repentance, the prospect of judgment, and Jesus's role in this scenario were all verified by Jesus's resurrection (vv. 30–31).

Still other instances could be cited. But these examples are sufficient to illustrate that, in the early church, Jesus's resurrection was the chief basis for Christian theology and ethics. We are told that, without it, the Christian faith is vain. Discussions of the Gospel message were incomplete without a reference to this event, which was considered to be an essential part of the central message, a truth that one had to believe. Other doctrines, such as the believer's resurrection, were said to follow from the reality of this historical event. Further, defenses of the Christian faith—for instance, defenses of the truth of Jesus's teachings—were also based on the resurrection.

In the New Testament, even practicing the Christian life, in such ways as preaching and ministering to the grieving, followed from Jesus's resurrection. Assurance of eternal life, the forgiveness of sins, living victoriously, as well as one's commitment to both the Lord and the poor, are related to this truth. Even the final victory over suffering and evil, our future hope, finds its ultimate meaning in Jesus's victory over the grave.

So without the resurrection there would have been no faith, theology, or church. Christianity would be groundless and fruitless. In brief, Jesus Christ's victory was clearly thought to be indispensable.

The Relevance of the Resurrection Today

Other reasons, besides the resurrection of Jesus, corroborate the truth of Christian theology. This event should not be arbitrarily separated from these other evidences, or from theology. It is not a stand-alone event, but must be taken in the context of the entire Christian message. In this volume I am concentrating on avenues by which the special significance of the resurrection can be pursued, without claiming that it is the only path to theology and practice or that it should be isolated from related studies.

How can the resurrection continue to provide a strong foundation for Christian theology, ethics, ministry, and personal practice? How does it evidence the truth of the Christian faith? Are the New Testament teachings on this subject still helpful? Can they be adapted to today's intellectual climate?

The purpose of this book is to relate the resurrection to some of these theological and practical areas. I attempt to build a modest case for reestablishing the resurrection as the center of Christian theism. This includes asking what early believers meant by taking this event as the foundation for the Christian faith.

Briefly, the approach in part 1 is to ask whether the resurrection of Jesus is historical, and how it might provide a basis for the Gospel doctrine of salvation and eternal life. I pursue this in five steps, with one chapter being given to the development of each of the following major subjects. A sixth chapter attempts to track down a few of the implications of the message of the resurrection.

First, while space prohibits me from developing a detailed case for the historicity of the resurrection, I outline a very brief argument for the historical nature of this event. Throughout, the case will be built on data that can be established by critical standards.

The second step is to ask how an event like the resurrection might be related to the existence and activity of God. In what sense might it be said that God was involved in raising Jesus from the dead?

If God did resurrect Jesus, what would that say about Jesus and his teachings? This is my third topic. I argue that, if God raised Jesus from the dead, it makes the most sense to conclude that God approved of and vindicated Jesus's message.

As Jesus's central teaching, the Kingdom of God and its entrance requirements are of primary interest. This subject is treated in two parts. The fourth chapter addresses the difficult question regarding the concept of the Kingdom. Although the issue is by no means settled, I make some suggestions.

The fifth chapter investigates Jesus's call for a decision in light of the eternal life of God's Kingdom. I examine the Gospel message, as well as Jesus's teachings on total commitment. A sixth chapter treats the variety of ancient views on the nature of the afterlife and addresses some practical considerations based on this topic.

While evidential and doctrinal discussions can answer some crucial questions, they frequently fail to relate to our deepest existential needs. For this reason, part II turns from doctrinal to practical concerns. Four chapters address some areas in which the resurrection of Jesus informs our present life. They include topics like treating the most painful aspects of the fear of death, as well as an application of Jesus's resurrection to personal suffering. Further, I study the New Testament teaching that the Holy Spirit's testimony to believers provides a more foundational assurance of the Gospel than do evidences. Lastly, I reflect on how the authority of Scripture provides a basis for living the Christian life.

I developed this approach about thirty years ago and have taught it in many lectures since that time. Still, I make no claim that this is the best approach to the topics given here; other outlooks are certainly valid. Different approaches can also be used in conjunction with one other.

A Variety of Approaches

In the New Testament, both evidential and nonevidential approaches are used to present the teachings of Jesus Christ. The factor determining which approach is used might be the religious tradition, language, nationality, or other orientation of the recipients of the message. But something as simple as the personal preference of the recipients could also be the key. Perhaps Paul said it best. After noting some of these factors, he proclaimed that he was willing to use various methods to reach a variety of people in preaching the Gospel (1 Cor 9:19–22).

A host of New Testament texts note different methods of preaching. Often, a straightforward presentation of the Gospel was appropriate. This was Jesus's approach with Nicodemus (Jn 3:1–15). Jesus's talk with the woman at the well was similar (Jn 4:5–42). Peter's sermon at the house of Cornelius (Acts 10:34–48), the testimony of Paul and his company to Lydia (Acts 16:13–15), and the episode with Paul, Silas, and the Philippian jailer (Acts 16:23–34) include some differences but many similarities to Jesus's straightforward presentation.

However, on other occasions we are told that evidence was presented, often combined with debate and argumentation. The Book of Acts is a primer on these differences in approach. The author relates that Paul often spoke to audiences of both Jews and Gentiles, such as at Pisidian Antioch (13:26, 48) and at Athens (17:17–18). This was precisely the sort of situation that required different methods, and different methods are precisely what we find.

Sometimes straightforward preaching was the order of the day, as at Iconium (14:7) and Derbe (14:20–21). At Iconium (14:3) and Lystra (14:9–10), we are told that Paul performed miracles. When evidence was presented, he generally appealed either to Old Testament prophecy, used at Pisidian Antioch (13:23–29) and Thessalonica (17:1–4), or to Jesus's resurrection, used in Athens (17:18, 31) and before Agrippa and Festus (26:8, 12–19, 22–23). On most of the occasions on which he presented evidence, Paul used both Old Testament prophecy and Jesus's resurrection.

Paul was not shy about using sophisticated arguments whenever necessary or appropriate. We are told that he debated with his audiences in both Thessalonica (διελέξατο, 17:2) and Athens (διαλέγετο, 17:17). We have already remarked on the way Paul quoted Greek sources and used evidence (πίστιν παρασχών, 17:31) at Areopagus; his choice of terms in the speech make it reminiscent of a courtroom situation.

We read that these different methods frequently led to many of Paul's hearers becoming Christians. It would presumably surprise few that this would occur after Paul's preaching (14:20–21). But Paul's argumentation and his use of evidential presentations also led to many conversions, such as at Thessalonica (17:1–4) and Athens (17:22–34). On other occasions, like in Corinth (18:4–6) and Ephesus (19:8–9), Paul tried to win converts by these methods, but perhaps did not. Yet it is clear that many individuals were persuaded by the Holy Spirit to believe the Gospel after evidence was presented or even after debates took place. So it is mistaken to assert that such techniques never produce spiritual or other positive results.

Even from this brief overview, it should be apparent that, as the early church grew, various techniques were involved in communicating the Gospel. It makes sense that diverse methods are also appropriate today, and can still produce good results in teaching, counseling, living, and defending Christian theism.[6]

Surveying some of the material found in the Book of Acts is helpful, especially for its methodological variety. Oftentimes preaching, a quiet conversation, or a straightforward testimony is exactly what is needed. When someone is ready to consider the claims of the Gospel, the simplest approach is probably the best one. On the other hand, sometimes a more evidential approach is required.

My dual approach has already been identified. If the resurrection of Jesus occurred, much follows, both theoretically and practically. If I am correct that this event would indicate God's confirmation of Jesus's teachings, then it would seem to evidence some degree of entailment between this event and other Christian doctrines. There are also meaningful links between Jesus's resurrection and several practical concerns of Christian living.

What about those who oppose the use of evidences in the presentation of the Gospel message? It could be held, in spite of the examples in Acts, that only faith-based approaches ought to be attempted and that debate and evidence never have a place in Christian presentations. Many think that the issues presented in the Gospel are simply matters of faith, unrelated to any sort of argument.

Others conclude that the application of the Gospel message to more practical topics, to which I turn in part II, is often groundless. They argue that experiential considerations are too frequently open to charges of subjectivity and that we can never know if they represent only our personal feelings. Our faith needs to be grounded.

Those who prefer more evidential arguments respond that New Testament faith was grounded in strong arguments, so it is no crime for ours to be, as well. Rather, the question is whether or not our arguments are legitimate. If they are, then our faith stands on firm grounds. Those inclined to more practical considerations may respond that our personal experience is the truest test of reality. Besides, we need for our faith to be life transforming and not simply a matter of building arguments. This emphasis is found in the New Testament, too.

Could there be grounds for some agreement between these two positions? Paul's comments in 1 Corinthians 9:19–22 could be applied to the issues before us. Perhaps there *are* different ways to present the claims of Christianity.

The content may be essentially the same, while the means of communicating it varies from person to person and from audience to audience. It might even be the case that what appear to some as quite different enterprises still share much common ground.[7]

It would appear, then, that there is room for more than one stance regarding this question of methodology. It should be acknowledged that fideistic stances can generate some beautiful attempts to communicate Christianity. Likewise, we could all gain from various evidenced connections between the resurrection of Jesus and other Christian doctrines and practices. As Paul suggested, our chief interest should be to communicate the Gospel, not to rule out other procedures. Methodological exclusivists who deny anyone's approach but their own may have a problem with this solution, but the majority should at least be open to the arguments presented here. It is in this spirit of methodological variety that I present more than one approach in this volume, treating historical, philosophical, counseling, and experiential issues. Granted, the overall flavor will be more evidential, but experiential pursuits are far from ignored.

So my approach might be used primarily in two ways. First, studying Christianity's strong foundation could strengthen the believer's faith. As when John the Baptist expressed his doubt in two questions directed to Jesus (Lk 7:18–23), sometimes evidence can play a role in strengthening one's faith. Jesus faced the challenges squarely and answered them with facts. But experiential studies on subjects like facing the fear of death, personal suffering, or the witness of the Holy Spirit can also strengthen a believer's faith, even if in a different way.

Second, I advance this approach to challenge unbelievers with the rationality of Christian theism. In particular, many of the arguments elaborated here do not rely on the inspiration or even the trustworthiness of the New Testament. For example, the first chapter on Jesus's resurrection builds only on data that are recognized by virtually every scholar who studies this material. Many of the other arguments utilize the same minimal basis. As Paul found out at Areopagus (Acts 17:22–34) and elsewhere, many unbelievers will at least listen and consider the arguments that are advanced. Good dialogue may occur, too. From a human perspective, we cannot ask for much more than that.

For any other result to follow, the Holy Spirit will have to be involved. Without the leading of the Spirit, one might be convinced but not finally changed. As philosopher Paul Moser asserts, "Argument can indeed remove some obstacles to God's self-revelation. God's *Spirit* is, however, the final source and seal of such revelation."[8]

Notes

1. More of these texts were published in the 1990s than in the other decades.

2. Hans Küng, *Eternal Life? Life after Death as a Medical, Philosophical, and Theological Problem*, trans. Edward Quinn (Garden City, N.Y.: Doubleday, 1984), 107.

3. Reginald H. Fuller, *The Formation of the Resurrection Narratives*, rev. ed. (Philadelphia: Fortress Press, 1980), 48.

4. See Acts 1:21–22; 2:29–36; 3:13–15, 26; 4:10; 5:30–32; 10:39–43; 13:30–37; 17:1–4, 24–31.

5. We will return in chapter 1 to a critical synopsis of whether several of the speeches in Acts (especially those embedded in 1–5, 10, 13, 17) reflect the early (and perhaps apostolic) kerygma.

6. A more detailed discussion of the work of the Holy Spirit is the subject of chapter 9.

7. A good indication of the kind of agreement that could exist between different methodologies is found in Steven B. Cowan, ed., *Five Views on Apologetics* (Grand Rapids, Mich.: Zondervan, 2000). In the conclusion, Cowan notes that, major differences in approach notwithstanding, the broad agreement among these contrasting methods is heartening (375–81).

8. Paul Moser, *Why Isn't God More Obvious? Finding the God Who Hides and Seeks* (Norcross, Ga.: RZIM, 2000), 23.

PART ONE

A RESURRECTION FAITH

CHAPTER ONE

The Resurrection of Jesus as History

The New Testament claims that the resurrection of Jesus is the center of Christian theology and practice. It is also recognized as such by almost all theologians today, even those who do not interpret this event literally. But whether the resurrection actually occurred has been questioned by critical scholars since the Enlightenment. This topic, then, continues to be important for Christians, especially since their faith is grounded on it.

By no means can a complete case for the historical fact of the resurrection be developed within the scope of this chapter. I outline some reasons for taking seriously the historicity of this event. Interested readers can consult a number of my other works on this subject, in which substantial background and various supportive arguments are provided, supplementing the concise apologetic presented here.[1]

The Resurrection and Historical Research

I do not inquire here as to the possibility of a supernatural realm. I look in the next chapter at some issues concerning the supernatural. At stake is whether Jesus's resurrection, if it occurred, could be considered a miraculous occurrence and what that might mean. In this chapter I am interested only in whether a man named Jesus of Nazareth died, and was then seen afterward; I am not interested in whether God was the author of that event.

In other words, I am only concerned in this chapter with whether any historically observable phenomena happened to Jesus after his death. My immediate questions are historical in nature, and history, like all inductive disciplines, is based on weighing the evidence derived from the sources before a decision is made. Historians must examine their data to ask whether an event actually occurred, in spite of the doubts that might be raised.[2]

A common objection to this approach is that history has no tools or abilities to investigate miracles. Besides, we are told, this subject is a matter of faith. So to employ history for a religious task is like trying to mix oil and water.

It must be repeated that this complaint misses the point. I have distinguished between a miracle-*claim* and a miracle. It is certainly possible to historically investigate the New Testament claim that Jesus died, as many scholars today, both conservative and liberal, have done. Similarly, it is possible to ask whether, in historical terms, Jesus was seen after his death.[3] The latter is the chief subject of this chapter. The further issue of whether the resurrection was a miracle performed by God in a theistic universe introduces an addition philosophical element and is not addressed until the next chapter. Here I am investigating only the historical portion of the claim that Jesus was raised: after dying by crucifixion, was Jesus afterward seen alive?

The concern that historical methodology alone cannot ascertain whether or not a miracle has occurred *is* justified. Clearly, more than historical tools are necessary. But this is still an entirely different claim from that which deprives historical inquiry of the right to do what it does best: look at the available data and make decisions in the areas that are open to its scholarly gaze. So we must clearly distinguish between the historical and the philosophical dimensions of the resurrection question. While knowledge is indeed integrated, research paths are multiple, and each discipline has its own strengths.

The original charge that miracles cannot be investigated in terms of normal research methods would obtain only if we knew that such events did not occur at all, or if they happened only in some nonobjective realm. In either case, it would constitute a proper assessment to deny investigation by historical methodology. However, since it is an open question whether miracles occur in normal history, it would seem to be at least possible to investigate *the historical portion* of these claims with regard to their accuracy.

While some still object to even a partial investigation of a miracle–claim, such dissatisfaction is often simply a form of a priori objection. But since I cannot rule out the possibility of miracles without an inquiry, and since it is claimed that miracles have happened in space–time history, this portion of the affirmation can be investigated.

Intriguingly, two former Oxford University scholars are very helpful here. Influential philosopher of history W. H. Walsh asserts that the only political or religious views that historians should bring to the subject of history are the ones that "they can justify on rational grounds." He thinks that "religious beliefs . . . may be held as a matter of rational conviction." When that is the case, "it is not only inevitable but perfectly proper that they should exert an influence on the historian's thinking."[4]

Historian William Wand proclaims that scholars ought not reject the possibility of an event before an investigation. Such a priori dismissals constitute improper historical methodology, even if we dislike the conclusion indicated by the data. Rather, the historian "must be as openminded as he can. If physical causation does not seem sufficient to explain the phenomena with which he has to deal, he will not regard a 'supernatural' cause as impossible."[5] Later he states that, while miracles cannot be proven, "there may well be occasions when such evidence as we have may seem to make a supernatural cause the most likely hypothesis."[6] Other historians have also applied their tools to the New Testament accounts about Jesus.[7]

Perhaps the best-known challenge to investigating claims like Jesus's resurrection is David Hume's (1711–1776) essay "On Miracles."[8] Hume's influential thoughts are perhaps still the major inspiration for scholarly rejections of the miraculous. He charges that such occurrences are contrary to our experience of nature's laws, which dictate that miracles do not interrupt the normal pattern of events. Further, we can never know that miracles have been caused by God.[9] Especially this latter idea will be addressed in the next chapter.

Hume also questions the historical evidence for miracle-claims. He thinks that it is always more likely that natural hypotheses can account for such reports. To support his critique, he argues from four supportive points. First, it is always possible that testimonies affirming miraculous events are somehow incorrect. Second, people enjoy gossiping about extraordinary events, and may even lie about their occurrence. Third, miracles are usually claimed among uneducated and unenlightened peoples. Finally, similar miracles are reported in different world religions.[10]

Hume's disputation of miracles fails noticeably and has often been critiqued. I have critiqued his essay in much detail elsewhere,[11] and will simply summarize some of my concerns here.

First, Hume commits several logical fallacies, especially regarding his definition of miracles and his assumption that human experience always favors the law of nature and opposes the miraculous. For instance, he defines these occurrences in such a way that, from the very outset, they cannot even be termed miracles unless all human experience opposes them! Additionally, he insists that no quantity of evidence could ever establish a miracle. This is anything but an unbiased look at the facts. In opposition to such an attitude, Wand asks "how a critical historian can do anything else than decide on the evidence before him—unless indeed he already holds some secret which will invalidate in advance any evidence that can be brought in favour of the phenomenon in question?"[12]

Philosopher George Mavrodes is more forceful in his objection to Hume's configuration of the case against miracles: "*These negative experiences, Hume's and yours and mine, are (for all practical purposes) completely irrelevant to the probabilities of R [some resurrections] and NR [no resurrections].* And the reason is simple and straightforward. Hume's sample is just too small. . . . And so is your sample and mine." But if a single resurrection did occur, then "the probability of his [Hume's] catching it is almost infinitesimally small. . . . So Hume's negative experience is irrelevant to their probability."[13]

Second, while extolling the strength of humankind's experience of nature's laws, Hume ignores a crucial distinction that could topple his entire project. If it is even possible both that God exists and that God may have temporarily set aside these laws in order to perform a miracle, then Hume may have an insurmountable problem. Granted, this is the chief issue for the next chapter, but there is a crucial application for the historical side, too. Here is the central issue: arguments regarding the strength of the laws of nature from the perspective of naturalistic premises cannot disprove the possibility that God performed an event in nature from outside of it. As with all such naturalistic theories, the more incisive question does not concern our experience of nature's order, but whether God has broken into history by superseding these laws by a superior power. If the resurrection occurred, for example, it just might indicate that God *did* temporarily suspend nature's laws in order to perform this event.

It is indispensable that we realize that we need *not* assume or even require God's existence here. This second rejoinder to Hume requires only the mere *possibility* that the resurrection *could* have been performed by an act of God. If it could have been, then this would indicate that, *at that very moment,* God's actions would actually *supersede* nature's laws. In other words, Hume's approach is backward. Our experience of nature is almost irrelevant at this point. The main issue is whether a supernatural event might possibly be caused by a greater power. And *we cannot make such a determination without first inspecting the evidence.* Thus an investigation of the proposed evidence for the resurrection is necessary. But Hume has chosen to deny such a path, hence some of his chief problems.

Third, Hume's writings appear to betray a rather Newtonian concept of natural laws as inviolable barriers that pronounce the final word on what may or may not occur. In contrast, many modern physicists hold that nature's laws are statistical, describing what *generally* occurs. If this is the case, these laws neither cause nor hinder events.[14] So we can only speak in terms of probability that certain events did or did not occur, and, again, this requires careful investigation.[15]

Given the configuration of modern physics, the laws of nature should not be considered obstacles that impede the occurrence of miracles. Philosopher Richard Swinburne argues that the notion of universal, fixed laws held sway between the eighteenth and the early twentieth centuries, but a statistical concept is more influential at present.[16] Swinburne adds: "it seems not unnatural to describe E as a non-repeatable counter-instance to a law of nature L. . . . To say that a certain such formula is a law is to say that in general its predictions are true. . . . It is clearly a coherent way of talking. . . . In such a case the conceptually impossible would occur."[17] Somewhat similarly, German physicist Werner Schaaffs asserts that "even the physicist must officially concede the possibility of intervention by God."[18]

The result of this critique is as follows: If the laws of nature are represented as inviolable, due to the strength of observation or something similar, then it begs the question to ignore alternative observational claims, such as the historical evidence for Jesus's resurrection. But if these laws are taken in the more modern sense as general and statistical, they present no unsolvable problems for the existence of miracles.

My fourth and fifth critiques concern Hume's four supportive arguments. Fourth, Hume briefly investigates a series of miracles supposedly performed by the eighteenth-century French Jansenists. He admits that there were excellent witnesses to these occurrences, including antagonists of the Jansenists, in a modern country and "in a learned age." Yet, he specifically rejects the occurrences, not because of insufficient testimony, but because of the "absolute impossibility or miraculous nature of the events," which he thinks "will alone be regarded as a sufficient refutation."[19]

Here we are reminded of C. S. Lewis's critique of Hume: "Unfortunately we know the experience against [miracles] to be uniform only if we know that all the reports of them are false. And we can know all the reports to be false only if we know already that miracles have never occurred. In fact, we are arguing in a circle."[20]

Fifth, all four of Hume's supportive points are almost impossible to apply fully to many historical studies, especially those of ancient times. For example, do we reject any historical accounts for which we do not have unquestioned evidence that argues against all possibility of error? What about historical treatments in which the author has a vested interest, like that of Julius Caesar's military exploits? Were these battles never fought? And what about ancient historical records taken from what some might term "barbarous nations"? A strict application of Hume's rules to history, then, would strip meaning from much of ancient history. Yet, even allowing for the error and self-interest of ancient authors, historians do not hesitate to write about what they think is probable. Strangely enough, Hume was well aware of this, as he did not apply these four criteria to his own multivolumed *History of England*.[21]

Other problems with Hume's argument might also be noted. Hume's strong empirical bias is problematical on more than one front.[22] Additionally, while Hume's argument depends on the uniformity of nature, he denies this principle in his other works.[23]

For reasons like these, among still others, it is not surprising that perhaps most scholars think that Hume was mistaken in several respects in his essay concerning miracles. Philosopher Stephen Davis asserts: "I believe it is now generally recognized that Hume overstates his case. We cannot a priori rule out the possibility of miracles or of rational belief in miracles. . . . It looks, then, as if Hume's argument against miracles . . . fails."[24] Raymond Brown refers to "the fairly obvious weaknesses of the Hume position."[25] Many other works, theological[26] as well as some technical philosophical essays,[27] have concluded similarly against Hume's position.

The theme of this section, including many of the Hume critiques, is that the resurrection of Jesus cannot be justifiably rejected without a careful study. The inductive method needs to be applied to the data, just as it is widely employed not only in history, but in science and other disciplines. To determine whether the resurrection actually occurred, we must sift through the sources in order to obtain the most probable conclusion. Such is the best means of arriving at valid historical data. As Wolfhart Pannenberg affirms: "The judgment about whether an event, however unfamiliar, has happened or not is in the final analysis a matter for the historians."[28]

The next step is to assemble some of the building blocks on which an investigation of Jesus's resurrection can be based. Using the historical method normally employed by historians,[29] I view below some of the primary and secondary sources, including eyewitness testimony, that claim that Jesus died and was later seen on several occasions. We will also entertain major critical responses in order to obtain a balanced conclusion.

The Historical Setting

At present, the topic of the historical Jesus could well be the most popular area of study in New Testament research. Scholars from across the liberal-conservative spectrum have honed their research talents on this subject. Their work presents us with a test case. One of the most popular approaches to historical Jesus studies is to begin with a list of historical facts that are admitted to by virtually all researchers. Frequently there is very little elaboration, justification, or argumentation for these facts. Of course, in order for these facts to be accepted as historical by the majority of researchers, the assumption is that such a basis could be provided if necessary.

Jesus Seminar cofounder Robert Funk, for instance, begins his study with a list of facts about Jesus that are agreed on by most scholars today. He declares: "These are data that a disinterested, neutral observer could have attested."[30] Jewish historian Geza Vermes builds his research from a similar starting point: "Let us begin then by selecting a few non-controversial facts concerning Jesus's life and activity, and endeavor to build on these foundations."[31] E. P. Sanders's approach is also to "rest the main themes of the study on unassailable data," providing lists of what is known about the historical Jesus.[32] Still other scholars utilize similar approaches.[33]

Theologians and historians of various persuasions and schools of thought still differ on the amount of historical content contained in the Gospels. But this does not keep them from a general consensus on certain events, including those of the last days of Jesus's life. Scholars usually agree that there are a number of known historical facts from this time period. I present below a list of some facts that are accepted as historical by virtually all scholars who research this area, regardless of the many differences in their thought.

1. Jesus died by Roman crucifixion.
2. He was buried, most likely in a private tomb.
3. Soon afterward, the disciples were discouraged, bereaved, and despondent, having lost hope.
4. Jesus's tomb was found empty very soon after his interment.[34]
5. The disciples had experiences that they believed were actual appearances of the risen Jesus.
6. Due to these experiences, the disciples' lives were thoroughly transformed, even being willing to die for this belief.
7. The proclamation of the resurrection took place very early, at the beginning of church history.
8. The disciples' public testimony and preaching of the resurrection took place in the city of Jerusalem, where Jesus had been crucified and buried shortly before.
9. The Gospel message centered on the death and resurrection of Jesus.
10. Sunday was the primary day for gathering and worshipping.
11. James, the brother of Jesus and a former skeptic, was converted when, he believed, he saw the risen Jesus.

12. Just a few years later, Saul of Tarsus (Paul) became a Christian believer due to an experience that he believed was an appearance of the risen Jesus.

These facts will form a vital part of my study of Jesus's resurrection. While scholars do not necessarily take the same approach to them, the near unanimity is simply amazing. With the exception of the empty tomb, which is still accepted by a majority of scholars, it is virtually unanimously thought that these are historical facts. The facts most widely held to be true, as well received as almost anything in the New Testament, probably are that Jesus died and that the disciples afterward were absolutely convinced that they had seen him again. We will return below to the historical basis for these and other particulars. It only makes sense that any conclusions should be the best explanations of data like these.

Naturalistic Theories

Building on a common historical foundation, my case for Jesus's resurrection, as summarized in this chapter, contains three major points. Initially, naturalistic theories attempting to explain the resurrection in natural terms have failed to viably account for all of the recognized facts. Alternative theories, such as those alleging various species of fraud, swooning, hallucination or other subjective psychological explanations, and legend have all failed to disprove this event. Even critical scholars seldom propose such theses, which is understandable for a number of reasons.

The primary reason for the failure of the naturalistic theories is that each hypothesis has multiple weaknesses, indicating a lack of viability. These problems largely come from the accepted historical data. While we cannot pursue here the details regarding the refutation of each alternative theory, I have shown these details elsewhere.[35] Perhaps an example will illustrate how these naturalistic views have fared.

The hallucination theory was chiefly popular in the nineteenth century. Various versions of the theory experienced a slight resurgence in the last twenty-five years of the twentieth century.[36] These attempts agree in suggesting that early believers' subjective experiences account for their belief that Jesus had risen. The advent of twentieth-century psychology and psychiatry, as well as a common body of historical facts, such as those already cited, has produced many substantial criticisms of these theories. As a result, few recent scholars have pursued these avenues.

Some of the problems with the hallucination theory might be very briefly mentioned. (1) Hallucinations are subjective experiences emanating from individual minds. As a result of their private nature, these occurrences are not collective or contagious. Since these private events cannot be shared, the same hallucination would not have been experienced by more than one disciple at the same time. Clinical psychologist and author Gary Collins summarizes this first problem: "Hallucinations are individual occurrences. By their very nature only one person can see a given hallucination at a time. They certainly are not something which can be seen by a group of people. . . . Since an hallucination exists only in this subjective, personal sense, it is obvious that others cannot witness it."[37]

(2) The psychological condition that typically produces hallucinations, characterized by belief, expectation, and even excitement,[38] was surely lacking. To charge the disciples with expecting Jesus's resurrection is to overlook the circumstance that they had just experienced: the recent and unexpected death of their best friend, in whom they had placed their hope. Their abandonment, along with Jesus's arrest, trials, beatings, crucifixion, and burial all occurred in rapid-fire succession. In psychological terms, the expected state of mind would be that of shock, disbelief, and despair. The stark realism of funerals bears out this conclusion.

(3) Perhaps the highest hurdle for hallucination theses to overcome is the variety of times, places, and personalities involved in these experiences. The emotional variety of the men and women involved, along with all the different times and places, exert great demands on this hypothesis. The requirement that each individual would be in precisely the right state of mind in order to experience hallucinations increases the odds exponentially against such explanations, so that they border on credulous.

(4) If Jesus's followers hallucinated, then his body would still have been located where he was buried. But an empty tomb is a troublesome piece of data for all subjective theses. If *any* body occupied that grave, the early Christians would have had a serious problem, since they preached an *empty* tomb. Another alternative theory is needed to account for this.

(5) Generally, hallucinations do not transform lives. When confronted by contrary data, such as others present not "seeing" the same thing, those who experience hallucinations usually abandon their thesis. That the disciples would have been willing to die for their faith in the resurrection without recanting is a powerful indication against this supposition.

(6) There is no data to indicate that the apostle Paul was in a frame of mind conducive to experiencing hallucinations. In fact, his religious devotion and zeal, his exemplary education, and his choice as the best candidate to lead the persecution against Christians, all militate against him being a candidate to produce subjective images of the risen Jesus.

(7) Although the circumstances were quite different, a similar problem exists for James, the brother of Jesus. His unbelief prior to Jesus's resurrection is a poor groundwork from which to postulate hallucinations.

Still other issues remain concerning the hallucination hypothesis. (8) Hallucinations usually result from mental illness or from physiological causes like bodily deprivation. But we are unaware of such circumstances being applicable to any of the disciples. (9) Further, the New Testament clearly differentiates Jesus's resurrection appearances from religious visions, implying a difference in quality. (10) And why did the appearances cease instead of increasing, as they had up until that moment? (11) Jewish theology taught a corporate resurrection at the end of time. What accounts for the very different claims involved in the case of Jesus?[39]

It is little wonder that hallucination hypotheses and similar subjective theses have generally been rejected by critical scholars. On several counts, these strategies have failed to explain the known data. In fact, the problems are so weighty that the few who prefer these theoretical options "would have to go against much of the current psychiatric and psychological data about the nature of hallucinations."[40] Intriguingly, hallucination approaches to the resurrection would seem to be at odds with current medical, psychological, and historical knowledge on hallucinations.

This provides an example of the fate of alternative theories.[41] As I noted, hallucination theses are not "straw man" scenarios, but have probably been the most popular alternative position over the last one hundred years. Yet, they have run aground in their attempt to explain the known facts. Critical scholars generally agree that these and other subjective hypotheses are refuted by the available data.[42] As Wolfhart Pannenberg asserts, concerning these psychological theses, "These explanations have failed, to date."[43] Other options are similarly confronted by many objections. Although we cannot provide the details here, none of the proposed naturalistic theories adequately explain all of the known historical facts.

The second reason for rejecting these alternative views is that, although more than one thesis is necessary in order to explain the entire critically recognized historical framework, *combining* these theories has also failed. Chiefly during the nineteenth century, various efforts were proposed that connected more than one of these scenarios. But it was generally conceded that, even as an individual attempt failed, linking another with it often confused matters significantly. Not only did the combination have to provide a plausible fit, but both theses had to be factually justifiable. Instead, the result seemed to be even more unwieldy, while still missing crucial historical elements.[44]

A third indication that the naturalistic theories have failed has already been discussed in the previous section. Over the last two centuries, that portion of critical scholarship that has more or less rejected the miraculous as being highly unlikely has frequently employed David Hume's essay against miracles as its chief inspiration.

For instance, many nineteenth-century liberal theologians identify Hume's essay as the impetus behind their rejection of miracles. Influential scholar David Strauss boldly asserts that Hume's critique conclusively disproves miracles. The issue has been completely settled.[45] Other liberal scholars also rely on Hume in dismissing miracles.[46] John Hermann Randall Jr. makes the incisive observation that, due to the influence of Hume's essay, nineteenth-century liberals as a whole reject the belief in miracles; they cite Hume's argument that such events interfere with the laws of nature.[47]

Despite the more recent lack of philosophical and theological homogeneity, especially in the last half of the twentieth century, some critical scholars continue to reject miracles, inspired by Hume's argument.[48] Even today, the influence of this philosopher's essay against miracles continues to be witnessed as evident by its many citations.[49] Mavrodes reports that Hume's infamous essay "is probably the most celebrated and most influential discussion of miracles in Western philosophical literature."[50]

But I have argued that there are strong reasons for rejecting Hume's argument against miracles, some of which were reported earlier in this chapter. Most contemporary scholars seem to agree that Hume oversteps his bounds. If this is the case, then critical scholars who have followed a general Humean argument, especially in places where this philosopher utilized weak or mistaken arguments, have perhaps rejected miracles on improper grounds. The antimiraculous arguments used by many since Hume may be flawed for similar reasons. Miracle-claims ought not be ruled out due to our experience of the laws of nature. Most crucially, we must ascertain whether there is a God who is more powerful than these laws and who may choose to transcend them on occasion. It would appear, then, that the Humean backdrop for rejecting miracles must be discarded.

It is intriguing that critical scholars during the last two centuries often concluded that the specific naturalistic theories fail to explain Jesus's resurrection. Even in the nineteenth century, when the naturalistic approaches were in their heyday, liberal theologians took turns exposing the many inadequacies in each. For example, Strauss administers the most devastating attack on the swoon theory—which was popularized by Karl Venturini, Heinrich Paulus, and others—exposing its weaknesses.[51] Seldom have more scholars, both liberal and conservative, agreed on the demise of a theory.[52]

Writing early in the twentieth century, both James Orr and Eduard Riggenbach remark that scholars no longer consider this theory to be viable.[53]

At the same time, Friedrich Schleiermacher and Paulus point out various blemishes in the hallucination thesis that Strauss, Ernest Renan, and others postulated.[54] Still another liberal scholar, Theodor Keim, argues the strongest case against the subjective–vision theory and is often credited with disarming this position.[55]

Alternative theories involving fraud had long since been laid to rest by the vast majority of nineteenth-century liberal scholars.[56] Later critical research, especially concerning Paul's report of an early Christian creedal statement in 1 Corinthians 15:3ff., devastatingly critiqued legendary views popularized by the *Religionsgeschichte* school of thought, which charged that the teaching of Jesus's resurrection was borrowed from other mythical beliefs.[57] These legendary views were also judged to fall short of the historical facts.

So the nineteenth-century liberals exposed many weaknesses in each other's theories. The result was that, shortly after the turn of the century, none of these theses was left standing. All of them failed to adequately account for the data surrounding Jesus's resurrection.

A final indication of the demise of these naturalistic theories is evident in the twentieth-century attitude. While the previous century witnessed the liberal scholars decimating one another's views individually, plank by plank, most critical scholars in the last century rejected these positions in a wholesale manner. Intriguingly, this more recent rejection is not confined to any one school of thought. Theologians holding a wide range of positions often agree in dismissing all of these naturalistic theories as untenable.

A major example from the middle of the century is Karl Barth, who lists the major naturalistic theories and states that these positions have fallen into scholarly disfavor for more than one reason. One issue is that they are inconsistent with the facts. Barth concludes that scholars no longer consider these theories to be tenable. Noting that "the older criticism took some strange paths," Barth took a final stab: "To-day we rightly turn up our nose at this." He concludes that "these explanations . . . have now gone out of currency."[58]

In a similar vein, Raymond Brown provides an even more detailed list of naturalistic theories. Then he asserts not only that these positions were not held in midcentury, but that they were no longer considered to even be respectable. Revivals of such views were ignored by serious scholars: "No longer respectable are the crude theories. . . . Occasionally some new mutation of the 'plot' approach will briefly capture the public fancy, but serious scholars pay little attention to these fictional reconstructions."[59]

As the twentieth century drew to a close, similar responses could be gleaned from the works of many critical theologians representing a wide variety of schools of thought, who agreed on the futility of these alternative theories. Just a sample of these scholars is impressive.[60] As James D. G. Dunn concludes: "alternative interpretations of the data fail to provide a more satisfactory explanation" than the New Testament proclamation that Jesus was raised from the dead by God.[61]

Some influential philosophers have agreed with this assessment. Stephen T. Davis provides some details regarding rejections of the resurrection: "All of the alternative hypotheses with which I am familiar are historically weak; some are so weak that they collapse of their own weight once spelled out. . . . [T]he alternative theories that have been proposed are not only weaker but far weaker at explaining the available historical evidence."[62] Oxford University scholar Richard Swinburne attests: "alternative hypotheses have always seemed to me to give far less satisfactory accounts of the historical evidence than does the traditional account."[63]

This recent trend in theological and philosophical circles is actually rather remarkable. That critical scholars across such a broad theoretical spectrum generally agree in rejecting naturalistic approaches as explanations for the resurrection of Jesus tends to indicate the many weaknesses of these alternative efforts. This trend serves as a final epitaph on the demise of naturalistic approaches.

It might fairly be said that, for a variety of reasons, alternative theories aimed at dismissing a historical resurrection have been unsuccessful. Each theory is opposed by several major objections, whether one or a combination of approaches is utilized. The failure of Hume's thesis and the general dismissal of alternative theses by both nineteenth- and twentieth-century scholarship are further indications of the inability of these naturalistic theories to gain much recent prominence. Alternative attempts have failed to account naturally for Jesus's resurrection, which remains unrefuted by such attempts.

Evidences for Jesus's Resurrection

The second major reason for postulating that Jesus's resurrection occurred in history is that it is supported by a number of corroborating evidences. We will be able to comment only briefly on each argument. But given the failure of naturalistic attempts to explain the resurrection, the existence of evidences that support the historicity of this event would increase its likelihood.

It should be mentioned that the evidences presented here are drawn from my list of generally recognized historical facts, as listed above. These events themselves are frequently supported by multiple strands of data, as I indicate below. This confirmation explains why these facts are so widely recognized by virtually all scholars, regardless of their approach and outlook. The most obvious advantage of using historically confirmed data is that there is little chance of it being rejected as unhistorical. The result of such a methodology is a potential case for the resurrection that is acceptable even by critical research procedures. There is no requirement that the New Testament be accepted as inspired. In fact, this groundwork is not even based on the New Testament being a reliable text.[64]

The Death of Jesus

Before I move to the resurrection, there is an important preliminary matter that needs to be briefly addressed. Why is the fact of Jesus's death due to the rigors of crucifixion so seldom questioned?

(1) A surprising number of ancient historical texts record the death of Jesus. These include: (a) 1 Corinthians 15:3 and several highly respected, primitive creedal reports that also predate the New Testament;[65] (b) the Gospel narratives;[66] (c) at least ten non-Christian texts;[67] plus (d) several noncanonical early Christian references to Jesus's death.[68]

(2) Many medical studies agree on the general cause of death by crucifixion. Victims died of asphyxiation plus other medical factors while hanging in the "low" position on the cross. Assuming that posture for more than a few minutes causes the individual to begin to asphyxiate from the pressure on the lungs caused by the intercostal, pectoral, and deltoid muscles.

(3) Ancient sources report that occasionally a final stroke to crucifixion victims guaranteed their deaths.[69] The spear wound to Jesus's side is an example, with medical opinion concluding that the weapon punctured his heart, ensuring his death. Also, if Jesus had been alive and the spear had pierced his pleural cavity, an obvious sucking sound would have alerted his executors.[70]

(4) The virulent critique by David Strauss, over a century ago, has been the chief reason persuading scholars that Jesus died by crucifixion. If Jesus had escaped death on the cross, he could not have accounted for the disciples' *belief* that he had been raised, a heavily evidenced belief that is acknowledged by virtually all scholars, as I argue below. A crucified but still-living Jesus would have been in horrible physical shape: bloodied, bruised, pale, limping, unwashed, and in obvious need of medical assistance. Such a condition would have hopelessly contradicted the disciples' belief that Jesus had appeared to them in a resurrected body. True, Jesus would have been alive, but not raised! Additionally, the frequently repeated New Testament teaching that believers would someday be gloriously raised just like Jesus would be groundless. Such a sickly body would hardly be an inspiration for theology.[71]

Accordingly, very few scholars today challenge the fact of Jesus's death by crucifixion. Even John Dominic Crossan announces: "That he was crucified is as sure as anything historical can ever be."[72] Borg thinks that Jesus's execution is "[t]he most certain fact about the historical Jesus."[73]

An Early Christian Testimony and Jesus's Appearances

Why does a generation of critical scholars usually take so seriously the New Testament claim that Jesus was raised from the dead? Here I survey a text from which may be drawn the most forceful arguments for the resurrection of Jesus.[74] Because of the immense volume of material here, and because there is a strong critical consensus on what can be known, I am more interested in listing conclusions than in providing detailed argumentation. I place a premium on the views of those who question an orthodox view of Jesus's resurrection.[75]

Virtually all scholars agree that 1 Corinthians 15:3ff. records an ancient oral tradition(s) that reports the Gospel data: Jesus Christ's atoning death, burial, resurrection, and appearances to many persons. Although the apostle Paul wrote the passage, it is not his material, but is actually much older than the book where it is recounted. As Fuller points out, "It is almost universally agreed today that Paul is here citing tradition."[76] Similarly, Jerome Murphy-O'Connor reports the "complete agreement" that "Paul introduces a quotation in v. 3b."[77]

That this material is traditional and pre-Pauline is evident for a number of reasons. Paul introduces the citation with the terms "delivered" and "received," which are the equivalent Greek terms for the technical rabbinic words that traditionally indicated the imparting of tradition, as in 1 Corinthians 11:23. Additional markers include verbal parallelism and stylized wording, non-Pauline terms, sentence structure, diction, the proper names of Cephas and James, and the possibility of an Aramaic original. This possibility is further indicated by Semitisms such as the Aramaic name Cephas (see Lk 24:34), the threefold usage of καὶ ὅτι (which is similar to words in the Aramaic and Mishnaic Hebrew narration), and the two references to the Scriptures being fulfilled.[78]

Critical scholars usually agree that this tradition introduced by Paul had a remarkably early origin. Joachim Jeremias calls it "the earliest tradition of all."[79] Ulrich Wilckens declares that the material "indubitably goes back to the oldest phase of all in the history of primitive Christianity."[80] Walter Kasper even states, "We have here therefore an ancient text, perhaps in use by the end of A.D. 30."[81] Most scholars who provide a date think that Paul received this creedal tradition between two and eight years after Jesus's death, or from approximately A.D. 32 to 38.[82]

Even skeptics frequently agree. Gerd Lüdemann thinks that "the elements in the tradition are to be dated to the first two years after the crucifixion of Jesus . . . not later than three years after the death of Jesus. . . . [T]he formation of the appearance traditions mentioned in 1 Cor.15.3–8 falls into the time between 30 and 33 CE."[83] Michael Goulder states that Paul's testimony about Jesus's resurrection appearances "goes back at least to what Paul was taught when he was converted, a couple of years after the crucifixion."[84] Thomas Sheehan agrees that Paul's formula "probably goes back to at least 32–34 C.E., that is, to within two to four years of the crucifixion."[85] Such skeptical agreement is not rare.[86]

Those who comment generally think that Paul received this very early testimony either in Damascus or Jerusalem. While placing the event in Damascus would make it even earlier, the majority prefer the scenario that Paul received this material in Jerusalem. The main reason for this preference is Paul's trip there, dated about three years after his conversion, when he went to visit Peter and James, the brother of Jesus (Gal 1:18–19). Both of these apostles appear in the list of Jesus's appearances (1 Cor 15:5, 7).[87] At a minimum, a number of scholars specify that wherever Paul received the material, the substance is Palestinian in origin.[88] In an intriguing comment, C. H. Dodd proclaims, "At that time he stayed with Peter for a fortnight, and we may presume they did not spend all the time talking about the weather."[89]

Also favoring the Jerusalem scenario, Paul uses the term ἱστορῆσαι in Galatians 1:18, indicating that his visit with Peter may have constituted an investigative inquiry. William Farmer argues that Paul's choice of this term signifies that he acted as an examiner or observer of Peter.[90] In an older but still very helpful study that reaches similar conclusions, G. D. Kilpatrick translates this term in Galatians 1:18 as Peter's attempt "to get information from Cephas."[91] Paul Barnett helpfully points out that the same word is used by ancient Greek writers like Herodotus, Polybius, and Plutarch, for whom it means "to enquire."[92]

What topic was Paul interested in examining? The immediate context both before and after this trip to Jerusalem indicates that Paul's subject was the nature of the Gospel message (Gal 1:11–17; 2:1–10). Of course, the resurrection was at the center of the Gospel proclamation (1 Cor 15:3–4). In concluding a detailed study, Hans Dieter Betz seems to agree that Paul's purpose on the initial trip was to glean reliable information about Jesus.[93] In Galatians 2:1–10, Paul explains that his later trip to Jerusalem was specifically for the purpose of checking the accuracy of his Gospel preaching with the apostles Peter, James, and John (cf. 2:2).[94] Thus, it seems most likely that Paul received the information regarding Jesus's resurrection appearances in Jerusalem just a very few years after the events themselves.

As Fuller states regarding the testimony in 1 Corinthians 15: "The importance of Paul's statement can hardly be overestimated." The pre-Pauline tradition in 15:3ff. presents the foundation for a discussion of Jesus's resurrection. This proclamation connects a clear presentation of the earliest Christian claims with those who were present and experienced these events.[95] Wedderburn says that the events here "are the foundations of the church."[96] The vast majority of critical scholars recognize this significance.

Jewish scholar Pinchas Lapide asserts that the tradition quoted by Paul "may be considered as a statement of eyewitnesses."[97] German historian Hans von Campenhausen surprisingly attests, regarding this early creed: "This account meets all the demands of historical reliability that could possibly be made of such a text."[98] A. M. Hunter declares that, because of the involvement of Paul, Peter, and James, this tradition is "*open to testing.*"[99] Howard Clark Kee goes even further: Paul's early traditions "can be critically examined and compared with other testimony from eyewitnesses of Jesus, just as one would evaluate evidence in a modern court or academic setting."[100] Dodd concludes that Paul's traditional material was obtained from witnesses so close to the original events that anyone who would charge that Paul was mistaken regarding the apostolic nature of the Gospel message must bear the burden of proof.[101]

Consequently, Paul's testimony in 1 Corinthians 15:3ff. is an invaluable report of the original witnesses' experiences: it helps to piece together what they actually perceived.[102] The data indicate this conclusion; interestingly, contemporary scholars agree.

Evidences for the Resurrection Appearances of Jesus

I turn now to additional indications that the resurrection appearances of Jesus occurred in history.[103] As before, I draw almost exclusively from the data that support my list of critically ascertained historical facts.

(1) I have shown that the tradition in 1 Corinthians 15:3ff. is critically agreed to be (a) both an exceptionally early account of Jesus's resurrection appearances and (b) traceable to excellent (probably eyewitness) sources, using the checks and balances that might fairly be exacted of an ancient text. Given on Paul's authority, and probably having been received from the chief apostles in the early to mid-30s A.D., this creedal confession provides some crucially important information, like the report of Jesus's appearances to several groups, including to five hundred persons at one time. Hengel calls this text "a highly compressed historical account."[104]

It is crucial to note, however, that this first argument does *not* depend on knowing the exact date on which Paul received this material, or precisely who gave it to him. Virtually no critical scholar disputes that, at the *very minimum*, this traditional material predates the writing of 1 Corinthians at approximately A.D. 55 Paul says that he preached the same message a few years earlier when he visited Corinth (15:1–2). Paul also clearly states that he received this Gospel content from someone else (15:3). It can hardly be denied, then, that Paul received the data at an early date. Further, being an apostle himself, it makes sense that he heard it from someone whom he deemed to be a trustworthy source. Even this minimal framework helps establish the historical scenario.

(2) Still, Paul did not need to rely on someone else's testimony in order to hear about the resurrection. He explains that the risen Jesus also appeared to him. (a) Paul provides this information more than once (1 Cor 9:1, 15:8; cf. Gal 1:16). (b) Non-Pauline confirmation of Paul's testimony appears three times in Acts (9:1–9; 22:1–11; 26:9–19).

That Paul was converted to the Christian faith is not denied. Yet such a drastic turnaround—from being an exceptional young scholar and chief persecutor of the church (1 Cor 15:9; Gal 1:13–14; Phil 3:4–7) to an apostle—certainly demands an adequate explanation. Paul was sure that he had met the risen Jesus.

One striking aspect of this argument is the unanimity even among skeptics, who acknowledge that Paul certainly had an experience that he thought was an appearance of the risen Jesus. Accordingly, they regard Paul as an eyewitness. Atheistic philosopher Michael Martin states: "However, we have only one contemporary eyewitness account of a postresurrection appearance of Jesus, namely Paul's."[105] Jesus Seminar member Roy Hoover explains why Paul's account is the proper place to begin: "The reason for starting here is simple and compelling: Paul's testimony is the earliest and the most historically reliable evidence about the resurrection of Jesus that we have."[106] More specifically, Hoover asserts: "The most important evidence about the resurrection with which Paul provides us is . . . a direct claim that he has seen the risen Jesus."[107] Other skeptics also agree on the crucial nature of Paul's witness.[108]

(3) Of course, it is critical that we know whether Paul's report regarding Jesus's resurrection appearances is accurate. (a) We have seen that Paul actually made at least two trips to Jerusalem to counsel with the apostolic leaders in order to ascertain the nature of the Gospel that he had been preaching (Gal 1:18–20; 2:1–10), which centered on Jesus's resurrection (1 Cor 15:3–4; Rom 10:8–10). The apostolic leadership, namely Peter, Jesus's brother James, and John, specifically approved Paul's message and accepted his ministry (Gal 2:6–10). (b) Substantiation of the apostolic recognition of Paul is also claimed in Acts 15:1–31. It is debated whether this account describes the same incident that Paul narrates in Galatians 2, or whether it describes an incredible *third* trip to Jerusalem by Paul for the same purpose of confirmation! Either way,

there are multiple sources verifying Paul's account that his Gospel preaching was confirmed by the leading apostles, the very witnesses who would know whether the resurrection appearances occurred. As Hengel attests, "Evidently the tradition of I Cor. 15.3 had been subjected to many tests" by Paul.[109]

Critical scholars agree that Paul's Gospel message had been approved by the other key apostles. Luke Timothy Johnson mentions the historical facts that even "the most critical historian can affirm without hesitation. Can anyone doubt, for example . . . a meeting between Paul and the Jerusalem leadership concerning the legitimacy of the gentile mission?"[110] As for the content of the meetings, "the disciples . . . accepted him [Paul] as being called to apostleship by the risen Christ, just as they had been."[111] Concluding his study of Paul's second trip to Jerusalem, Betz notes that "the positive result consists of the fact that his gospel and mission were officially acknowledged by the Jerusalem apostles. . . . [There was] a recognition of Paul and his gospel as theologically valid."[112]

(4) But confirmation does not flow only from the Jerusalem apostles to Paul. For his part, Paul knew, and approved, the resurrection message of the other apostles. (a) By citing the creed(s) in 1 Corinthians 15:3ff., Paul shows that he at least knew of the appearances to Peter, the twelve, the five hundred, James, and all of the apostles. (b) In his trips to Jerusalem, he met several of these apostles, including the individuals named in the list. His comment in 15:6 that most of the five hundred witnesses were still alive perhaps implies that he knew some of them, as well. (c) Most importantly for my purposes, after citing the early creed, Paul proclaimed that the other apostles were preaching the same message that he was regarding Jesus's resurrection appearances (1 Cor 15:11, 14–15). So we have Paul's direct statement that he knew of the appearances to the other apostles and agreed with their testimony. (d) The Gospels also report appearances to Jesus's disciples and to others (Mt 28; Lk 24; Jn 20–21; cf. Mk 16:6–7). Any confirmation provided by these separate Gospel narratives would further indicate Paul's point, but from other perspectives.[113]

Critical scholars readily agree that Paul knew of the resurrection appearances to other apostles and what they were reporting about their experiences. Johnson states: "Paul insists that he proclaimed to his communities what he also had received, and that his preaching was in agreement with the other apostles."[114] Witherington thinks that "Paul was in direct contact with various eyewitnesses of the life, death, and resurrection appearances of Jesus." This "shows where the common ground truly lay."[115] A wide range of scholars agree.[116]

(5) Critical scholars almost always acknowledge that James, the brother of Jesus, was also an unbeliever and perhaps even a skeptic during Jesus's public

ministry (Jn 7:5; Mk 3:21). Later we find James as the leader of the Jerusalem church (Gal 1:18–19; Acts 15:13–21). According to the early creedal state-ment (1 Cor 15:7), a major event that occurred between these times is that the resurrected Jesus appeared to James.

Critics draw their conclusion regarding James's prior unbelief not only from the multiple independent sources that attest this, but also based on the embarrassment that such unbelief would have caused. It is highly unlikely that the early church would include these comments about one of its chief leaders, and one of Jesus's own family members as well, unless they were true.[117] For it to be remembered over many decades, James's unbelief was probably rather staunch.

This critical conviction regarding James's conversion is so firm that Regi-nald Fuller concludes that, even if Paul had not included the early confession that records Jesus's appearance to James, "we should have to invent one" in or-der to account for both James's postresurrection conversion and the subsequent speed of his promotion to a weighty leadership position in the early church. With the majority of scholars, Fuller concludes that Jesus's appearance to James led to his conversion.[118]

Even more skeptical scholars generally accept this majority position. Lüde-mann proclaims: "Because of I Cor.15.7 it is certain *that* James 'saw' his brother."[119] Helmut Koester agrees: "that Jesus also appeared to . . . James . . . cannot very well be questioned."[120] In popular terms, John Shelby Spong sums up the matter nicely: "we can be certain of the fact that the brothers of Jesus were not impressed, were not followers of Jesus during his lifetime. They were scoffers, cynics, suspicious of Jesus' sanity. But something happened. . . . Look at James before Easter. Look at James after Easter. What caused a change that was this dramatic?"[121]

(6) Beyond the early tradition in 1 Corinthians 15:3ff., other creedal pas-sages in the New Testament also report the apostolic witness to Jesus's resur-rection appearances. A noteworthy number of these comments is drawn from early confessions embedded in sermons recorded in the book of Acts.[122] Most scholars think that at least some of these speeches reflect the earliest Christian preaching, since they contain snippets that are brief and theologically unde-veloped, and because they differ from the author's regular language patterns.[123] Jesus's resurrection appearances occupy the center of each tradition.

These creeds would potentially provide some of our very best insights into the early apostolic preaching after Pentecost. O'Collins thinks that this ma-terial "incorporates resurrection formulae which stem from the thirties."[124] John Drane states, "The earliest evidence we have for the resurrection almost certainly goes back to the time immediately after the resurrection event is alleged to have taken place. This is the evidence contained in the early sermons in the Acts of the Apostles." He adds: "But there can be no doubt that in the first few chapters of Acts its author has preserved material from very early sources."[125]

(7) That the tomb in which Jesus was buried was later discovered to be empty does not prove that Jesus's body had been raised, but it does strengthen the case for the resurrection. For one thing, it makes it much more difficult to formulate naturalistic theories. For another, it points in the direction of a physical event.

Many indications have been given that Jesus's tomb was unoccupied shortly after his death. Unfortunately, we will be able to list only a few. (a) The early tradition in 1 Corinthians 15:3–4 at least implies an empty tomb. The triple καὶ ὅτι clause, particularly when understood in a Jewish context, progresses from Jesus's death, to his burial, to his resurrection, to his appearances, thereby arguing that something happened to his body. In short, what went into the ground is what later emerged, however changed. (b) Another early traditional text in Acts 13:29–31, 36–37 announces more clearly that Jesus was placed in a tomb, then he was raised and appeared without experiencing any bodily decay.

(c) The Jewish leaders not only failed to disprove the proclamation that the tomb was empty, but their counterpolemic actually admitted the fact (Mt 28:11–15). This enemy attestation is another indication favoring the empty tomb, since the Jewish leadership could not eliminate this physical element of the early proclamation. (d) The empty tomb accounts are multiply attested, being found at least in Mark, M, John, and most likely in L. Attestation in just two or more independent traditions is a powerful indication of historicity. Historian Paul Maier attests: "Many facts from antiquity rest on just one ancient source, while two or three sources in agreement generally render the fact unimpeachable."[126]

According to researchers, two other arguments for the empty tomb are perhaps even stronger. (e) The Gospels are unanimous in their claim that women were the earliest witnesses to the empty sepulcher (Mt 28:1–10; Mk 16:1–8; Lk 24:1–9; Jn 20:1–2). This is a powerful indication of the authenticity of the report, since a women's testimony was generally disallowed in a law court, especially on crucial matters. To use women as the central witnesses in such a case would be intellectual suicide, unless they really were the first witnesses. (f) The city of Jerusalem is absolutely the last geographical location the disciples would preach the resurrection if Jesus's grave was still occupied. Anything other than an empty tomb would have made the resurrection message a moot point.

We have already acknowledged that the empty tomb is not as well accepted as the other historical facts enumerated in my list above, each of which is almost unanimously agreed on by scholars. But at present, it appears that a strong majority still accept the historicity of the empty tomb.[127] Historian Michael Grant concludes that "the historian . . . cannot justifiably deny the empty tomb," because the normal application of historical criteria to the texts indicates that "the evidence is firm and plausible enough to necessitate the conclusion that the tomb was indeed found empty."[128] James D. G. Dunn summarizes: "I have to say quite forcefully: the probability is that the tomb was empty. As a matter of historical reconstruction, the weight of evidence points firmly to the conclusion that Jesus's tomb was found empty." The chief alternatives are all worse.[129] Thomas Torrance speaks succinctly, listing the empty tomb as one of the "empirical correlates in space and time" that is "open to testing."[130]

(8) One gauge of the strength of the disciples' conviction that they had actually seen their risen Lord is their transformation, especially their willingness to die for their faith. Prior to the crucifixion the apostles abandoned and denied Jesus, fleeing in panic.[131] In contrast, Jesus's resurrection appearances radically altered the remainder of their lives, even to the point of martyrdom.[132] The remainder of the New Testament also witnesses to the disciples' metamorphosis as seen in their evangelism, ethics, and teaching. Extrabiblical sources, both Christian and non-Christian, also report these activities.[133]

The disciples' transformation, being willing to die, is disputed by virtually no one. True, transformations often occur even based on false causes, but there is a *qualitative* difference here. It is generally acknowledged that almost anyone who is willing to die for something genuinely believes in that cause. But the chief similarities stop here. Jesus's disciples suffered not only for their *belief* in a cause, but *precisely because they thought they had seen Jesus after his death*. In short, their transformation was not simply due to their *beliefs*, as is the case for those who live and die for other causes, but was expressly based on their experience with the risen Jesus. Without the resurrection experience, there would have been no transformation.

Critical scholars acknowledge, as Grant explains, that it was the disciples' belief that the resurrection happened that transformed their lives.[134] Wright asserts that "the first generation of Christians . . . announced and celebrated the victory of Jesus over evil. . . . That was the basis of their remarkable joy."[135] Meyer agrees: "That it was the Easter experiences which affected [the disciples'] transformation is beyond reasonable doubt."[136] Such acclamations could be multiplied: "Christianity was birthed by the resurrection faith."[137] "Only the appearances of Jesus brought about a new change of mood in them."[138]

(9) That the resurrection of Jesus was the *center* of early Christian belief also points to its reality. Its centrality means that it was investigated by believers and challenged by unbelievers. We have seen that Paul visited the

Jerusalem apostles on two or three occasions just to make sure that his preaching was truthful, since he knew that there was no Christian faith apart from the resurrection (1 Cor 15:14, 17). We are told that the resurrection was the pivotal proclamation in the early church (Acts 4:33) and that this bothered the Jewish leaders (Acts 4:1–2). Believers were counseled in their suffering since Jesus's resurrection secured heaven for them (1 Pt 1:3–5). The importance of the resurrection led to increased attention from believers and unbelievers alike. Yet, it repeatedly passed the test.

Once again, critical scholars readily admit the central role played by Jesus's resurrection. Elliott asserts, "Without this belief the sect of Nazarenes would have generally died out just as the other Messianic groups had disappeared."[139] Meyer comments: "The resurrection was their clarion-call, for it grounded their hopes."[140] According to Wright, the resurrection cast its light over the Gospels to such an extent that the main issue is attempting to delineate what pre-cross material did *not* get interpreted in light of the resurrection![141] With believers interpreting everything in light of the resurrection and enemies continually attempting to discount it, there were many occasions to investigate it. But it was repeatedly confirmed.

(10) A last consideration is the failure of the Jewish leaders in Jerusalem to disprove the resurrection, even though they lived precisely where Jesus had died and been buried just a brief time before. These ancient scholars were in the best position to expose any error, both because they strongly opposed his teaching and because their location allowed the most thorough inspection. In brief, these leaders had a motive, great location, and a method, but even as the resident skeptics, they did not refute the evidence.

As Dunn mentions, with the exception of the weak claim in Matthew 28:13–15, it is noteworthy that there is an "absence of any such counter claim in any available literature of the period."[142] Cranfield's response is more detailed: "There is also the highly significant fact that neither the Jewish nor the Roman authorities ever produced evidence to disprove the claim that Jesus had been raised. The Jewish authorities, in particular, had every reason to want to do so, and they must surely have been in a position to interrogate and search thoroughly."[143]

There are also some minor considerations having to do with the resurrection appearances that could be mentioned.[144] Since we are concerned with ancient documents, which are often uneven at best, it must be recognized that the evidences mentioned here certainly present a surprising array of data, all supporting the belief that Jesus appeared to many persons after his death.

In recent decades, critical scholars' appreciation of the quality and quantity of such data has typically grown. Fuller surprisingly proclaims, with respect to the state of research into the early Christian belief in the resurrection: "That within a few weeks after the crucifixion Jesus's disciples came to believe this is *one of the indisputable facts of history*." Regarding Jesus's appearances, the traditional cause of this belief, Fuller recognizes: "That the experiences did occur, even if they are explained in purely natural terms, is *a fact upon which both believer and unbeliever can agree*."[145] Dunn speaks similarly: "It is almost impossible to dispute" that the first believers had experiences that they thought were resurrection appearances of Jesus.[146] Even Jewish scholar Lapide concludes that Jesus rose from the dead and appeared to his followers.[147]

Clearly the key here is that Jesus's disciples had real experiences that caused them to conclude that they had witnessed appearances of the risen Jesus.[148] Granted, the initial response is to suppose that an alternative theory is applicable. But if no naturalistic theories, such as that of hallucinations, viably explain these appearances, the case looks a bit different. If there are a number of strong evidences in favor of the resurrection, as well, we need to be open to such an event, unless we know in advance that it could never occur.

It would appear that the skeptic needs to explain all ten evidences for Jesus's resurrection, as well as propose a probable naturalistic theory. In particular, when the multiple viewpoints favoring the eyewitness experiences of the disciples, Paul, and James are considered, along with the witnesses' corresponding transformations and the empty tomb, Jesus's resurrection becomes the best explanation for the facts. This is especially the case as long as a feasible naturalistic theory that accounts for all the historical facts remains so elusive.

The Minimal Facts

Throughout this chapter we have been working with a list of historical facts that is generally accepted by a large majority of the critical scholars who study this subject. But what if my list were challenged by some skeptical person? Or perhaps we are simply interested in discovering a reduced historical case that could still bear the weight of an investigation of Jesus's resurrection. What would such a case look like?

I limit this discussion to just six of my twelve minimal facts and the data that confirm each one:

1. Jesus died by Roman crucifixion.

2. The disciples had experiences that they thought were actual appearances of the risen Jesus.
3. The disciples were thoroughly transformed, even being willing to die for this belief.
4. The apostolic proclamation of the resurrection began very early, when the church was in its infancy.
5. James, the brother of Jesus and a former skeptic, became a Christian due to an experience that he believed was an appearance of the risen Jesus.
6. Saul (Paul), the church persecutor, became a Christian due to an experience that he believed was an appearance of the risen Jesus.

We have already considered above much of the evidence favoring each of these six facts. So we will summarize some of the data from a slightly different angle. Then we will view the case for the resurrection when the historical evidence is arbitrarily reduced to this bare-bones level.[149]

The *death of Jesus* due to Roman crucifixion is confirmed by medical insight into the process of asphyxiation, by the nature of the spear wound, and especially by Strauss's famous critique of the swoon theory. Historical sources for Jesus's death are provided in several early New Testament creeds, like 1 Corinthians 15:3; about a dozen non-Christian sources; and early noncanonical Christian writings.[150]

The *disciples' experiences* that they thought were actual appearances of the risen Jesus are best evidenced by the reports of crucial testimony, like the pre-Pauline creeds in 1 Corinthians 15:3ff. and Luke 24:34. Other Pauline texts, like 1 Corinthians 9:1, 15:8–11, and Galatians 1:13–2:10, provide more eyewitness confirmation. From these reports I gained many of the details in the ten evidences that I presented for Jesus's resurrection appearances. These experiences occurred to individuals as well as to groups. Other reliable texts in the New Testament, like portions of the Acts speeches and Mark's Gospel account, have also impressed scholars.[151] Such arguments account for the critical recognition of Jesus's death and the disciples' experiences as perhaps the two most widely accepted facts in the New Testament.

The entire New Testament testifies to the *transformation of the apostles* due to Jesus's resurrection appearances. Prior to Jesus's death, they abandoned him and went into hiding. But seeing Jesus again thoroughly modified the rest of their lives, making them willing to die for their message. Accordingly, many of them were killed. The earliest Christian writings testify that what the apostles taught and how they behaved were forever altered by Jesus's resurrection. Ancient non-Christian sources also reported these changes. Scholars today do not question the apostles' alteration.[152]

The resurrection was proclaimed at a *very early date*. It was not a message that took centuries or even decades to be developed and proclaimed. Hardly a commentator will dispute this fact.[153] We have already listed a large number of scholars who hold that the pre-Pauline creed(s) in 1 Corinthians 15:3ff. probably dates from the early to mid-30s A.D. But this is not the only early source for accounts of the resurrection. Probably a majority of scholars also think that the sermon summaries in Acts, each of which includes the deity, death, and resurrection of Jesus, also date from very early. Some would also place these traditions in the thirties. While having two sources even a century after an ancient report is often a luxury, we have independent sources from perhaps a mere five years after the crucifixion!

Further, Paul's epistles of 1 Corinthians and Galatians, which I have used heavily, are dated by scholarly consensus to approximately A.D. 55,[154] or just twenty-five years later, with some scholars accepting an even earlier time. Mark is usually placed at A.D. 65–75.[155] In sum, we have numerous early sources from five to forty years after Jesus's death, plus Matthew and Luke-Acts from approximately ten years later, John and Clement from perhaps fifteen years after that, and Ignatius another fifteen years later. In short, there are at least nine independent sources here, all attesting to the resurrection appearances of Jesus! Such richness of texts is almost unheard of in the ancient world.

The *conversion and transformation of James*, the brother of Jesus, need to be explained. As we have already detailed above, that James was an unbeliever during Jesus's public ministry is granted by almost all contemporary scholars, since this is attested both by multiple independent sources and by the principle of embarrassment. While we are not told that it was Jesus's appearance to James (1 Cor. 15:7) that caused his conversion, we have to provide the best explanation for the change and for James's promotion as one of the chief leaders in the early church. Given his previous skepticism, the appearance to James is significant.[156]

Finally, we have detailed above that *Paul's conversion and transformation* due to what he thought was an appearance of the risen Jesus also needs an explanation. Paul explains that he had been a zealous follower of Judaism, as well as a persecutor of Christians. Then he met the risen Jesus. Three secondary accounts in Acts provide more details. Paul's transformation is indicated by his evident commitment throughout his lifetime of ministry and writing, as well as his willingness to die for his faith. Additionally, naturalistic suppositions have failed to explain Jesus's appearance to Paul.[157]

It is difficult to overestimate the value of a brief case based even on such a severely reduced number of historical facts. By themselves, they can provide a powerful (though succinct) defense of Jesus's resurrection. These six historical facts are capable of dismissing each of the naturalistic hypotheses, as well as furnishing the most convincing evidences for Jesus's resurrection appearances. That these minimal historical facts, each of which is multiply evidenced, is capable of verifying the resurrection appearances of Jesus and refuting the alternative suggestions is simply amazing. A few examples of each might be helpful.

Earlier we provided almost a dozen criticisms of the hallucination theory. Even if we used the details pertaining only to these six minimal facts, essentially all of the criticisms would still follow, with the exception of the empty tomb. The swoon theory would fall just as we outlined above, due to the many historical and medical facts that support Jesus's death by crucifixion, the first of my six facts.

While there are various versions of the legend theory, they generally share the assumption that the resurrection story developed substantially away from the accounts of the original witnesses, usually over time, perhaps even borrowing from other ancient tales. But at every juncture, this thesis is substantially challenged by even the minimal facts. (1) We have seen the scholarly unanimity on the early proclamation of the resurrection message, as indicated by the creeds in 1 Corinthians 15:3ff. and Luke 24:34, along with the many early sermon summaries in Acts, all of which provide a very early date for this teaching, even in the 30s A.D.

(2) That we have an eyewitness report at least from Paul, and likely eyewitness testimony behind some of the early traditional sources just mentioned, indicates that the original core of the resurrection message was not derived from ancient myths and legends, but reflects the views of those who actually claimed to have had the primary experiences. Further, Paul's trips to Jerusalem to discuss the nature of the Gospel message with the key apostles (Gal 1:18–2:10; Acts 15:1–31), as well as Paul's knowledge that the other apostles were teaching the same message regarding Jesus's resurrection appearances (1 Cor 15:11–15), weaves a tight framework that preserves the earliest eyewitness testimony. Legends do not account for the origin of this original proclamation. In short, the earliest message concerning the resurrection appearances arose from actual, eyewitness experiences and not ancient legends.

Other problems concerning the legend thesis abound. (3) The disciples' transformation—to the point of being willing to die for their beliefs—makes the legend thesis look very tenuous, since their metamorphosis was specifically the result of their resurrection faith. (4) Paul's conversion from church persecutor to believer is left unexplained by this alternative theory, as is (5) James's transformation from skepticism.

(6) Even the popular charge that resurrection stories were rampant in the ancient world prior to Christianity has been seriously revised by scholars during the last few decades. Although details cannot be provided here, the pagan personages in these resurrection accounts were nonhistorical, their teachings differed significantly from those of Christianity, and, perhaps most importantly, there is no historical basis for the charge that these accounts predated Christianity.[158] Although additional critiques could be leveled at this thesis,[159] those already given are significant, even when drawn only from the minimal facts.

Besides refuting naturalistic theories, these minimal facts provide strong evidences for the resurrection. From my list of ten evidences, taken from the longer list of facts, the first six (along with numbers eight and nine) are also found in the minimal data. The combination of these evidences, seen in light of the failure of alternative theories, is sufficient to argue that the resurrection is the best explanation for the events described.

That virtually all recent commentators, even across a broad ideological and interdisciplinary spectrum, acknowledge the historicity of these six facts is significant. While this near unanimity does not guarantee the veracity of this material,[160] it does reflect the evidential force of the data that confirm each fact.

How might critics reply to this case? One response could be that the New Testament texts are tainted by discrepancies, or that they exhibit a widespread unreliability, legendary character, or even a general "cloudiness." These charges could certainly be addressed on grounds not discussed here, especially if individual issues were singled out. But, staying on track, the chief point in this chapter is that such challenges are all confronted by a major roadblock. The probability of the resurrection can be argued *even when only a minimum number of highly evidenced, critically admitted historical facts is employed.* In other words, to object that there may be various difficulties in *other* biblical areas is a moot point as far as my purposes are concerned, since it *does not affect the truth of these six facts.* This basis is what is needed to construct my case for the resurrection.

Another very common response might be to concede that "something," a real experience, happened *to the disciples.* Or, a bit more skeptically, some still contend that Jesus lives on through his teachings, but not in any literal manner. However, these responses are also inadequate, since they only address "something" *inside* the disciples, instead of also considering *what* the eyewitnesses really saw. Again, my central finding is very specific. *The minimal number of historically ascertainable, critically recognized facts is adequate* to argue what probably *did* happen: Jesus's followers actually saw him alive, somehow, after his death.

To let contemporary critical scholars make the point, E. P. Sanders lists as one of the "secure facts" that "are almost beyond dispute" that, after Jesus's death, "his followers saw him." But he does not know the exact sense in which this happened.[161] Reginald Fuller repeatedly asserts that "[e]ven the most skeptical historian" must "postulate some other event" that is *not* the disciples' faith, but "the cause of the Easter faith." The "irreducible historical minimum" is "a well-based claim of certain disciples to have had visions of Jesus after his death as raised from the dead."[162] So we need an event beyond the disciples' faith in order to explain what happened to them.

Elsewhere Fuller refers to the disciples' belief in the resurrection as "one of the indisputable facts of history" and the disciples' experiences as "a fact upon which both believer and unbeliever may agree."[163] James D. G. Dunn concurs: "It is almost impossible to dispute that at the historical roots of Christianity lie some visionary experiences of the first Christians, who understood them as appearances of Jesus, raised by God from the dead." Dunn cautions: "By 'resurrection' they clearly meant that something had happened to *Jesus* himself. God had raised *him*, not merely reassured *them*. He was alive again."[164]

There are certainly disagreements about the *exact* sense in which Jesus appeared. We cannot know *all* of the details, regardless of the depth of our research. But it does not follow that we should quit and simply say that the whole thing is inscrutable. Here is the crux of the matter: the known evidence to which virtually all scholars agree points strongly to the witnesses seeing Jesus. Since alternative theses such as that of hallucinations do not viably account for these experiences in natural terms, the best conclusion is that the witnesses actually saw the risen Jesus in some sense.

Put succinctly, rather than raising questions concerning other problem areas or what they think we *cannot* know about the New Testament texts, critics should focus on the facts that even they admit *can* be known.[165] The minimally known data are sufficient to indicate that Jesus's resurrection is by far the best historical explanation. We may still have many questions,[166] but the minimal historical facts are adequate to argue that, after Jesus was crucified and dead, he appeared later to his followers.

Conclusion

I have developed a threefold case for the resurrection of Jesus, drawn from a list of a dozen critically recognized historical facts. (1) Naturalistic hypotheses have failed to explain these data, as most critical scholars attest. (2) There are at least ten evidences that argue that Jesus was seen after his death. (3) An additional case was developed, based on half of the critically recognized facts, that was still capable of refuting the alternative theories, providing the best evidences for the resurrection, and doing all this with minimal data. It would appear to be easier to accept the resurrection, as incredible as such an event would be, than to cross this threefold barrier. To begin, one would have to offer a viable naturalistic theory, and probably more than one, in order to account for this case. Yet, the majority of critical scholars reject such attempts.

My brief investigation has led to the conclusion that Jesus's resurrection appearances are the most likely explanation for the historical facts. The claims of the earliest eyewitnesses appear to be vindicated. There are many reasons to think that they saw Jesus, while alternative scenarios have not fared well. Doubts based on other issues fail to change this conclusion, which has been built with critical concerns in mind.

But, as we have already remarked, this is only the historical side of the question. Even if Jesus's resurrection is a historical event, does it follow that God raised Jesus? Without God's involvement, we might be left with just a strange event, rather than a miracle. But how might the resurrection be connected with God?

Notes

1. Details may be found in some of my other publications on this topic, such as: *The Resurrection of Jesus: A Rational Inquiry* (Ann Arbor, Mich.: University Microfilms, 1976); *The Resurrection of Jesus: An Apologetic* (Grand Rapids, Mich.: Baker Books, 1980; Lanham, Md.: University Press of America, 1984); with Antony Flew, *Did Jesus Rise from the Dead? The Resurrection Debate* (San Francisco: Harper and Row, 1987); *The Historical Jesus: Ancient Evidence for the Life of Christ* (Joplin, Mo.: College Press, 1996); "Knowing that Jesus' Resurrection Occurred: A Response to Stephen Davis," *Faith and Philosophy* 2 (1985): 295–302; "Jesus's Resurrection and Contemporary Criticism: An Apologetic," *Criswell Theological Review*, 2 pts., vol. 4 (1989): 159–74; and vol. 4 (1990): 373–85.

2. For example, see: John Tosh, *The Pursuit of History*, 3rd ed. (Harlow, England: Longman, 1999), esp. chaps. 1–4, 6–7; Ernst Breisach, *Historiography: Ancient, Medieval, and Modern*, 2nd ed. (Chicago: University of Chicago Press, 1994), chap. 23.

3. For example, two influential agnostic scholars who argue forcefully that both Jesus's death and his appearances are historical claims are Gerd Lüdemann in collaboration with Alf Özen, *What Really Happened to Jesus: A Historical Approach to the Resurrection*, trans. John Bowden (Louisville, Ky.: Westminster John Knox Press, 1995), 4–6; and A. J. M. Wedderburn, *Beyond Resurrection* (Peabody, Mass.: Hendrickson, 1999), 12–23, 38. Neither Lüdemann nor Wedderburn accepts a historical resurrection.

4. W. H. Walsh, "Can History Be Objective?" in *The Philosophy of History in Our Time*, ed. Hans Meyerhoff (Garden City, N.Y.: Doubleday, 1959), 218.

5. See William Wand, *Christianity: A Historical Religion?* (Valley Forge, Pa.: Judson Press, 1972), 29–31.

6. Wand, *Christianity*, 51–52.

7. See Michael Grant, *Jesus: An Historian's Review of the Gospels* (New York: Scribner, 1977); Geza Vermes, *Jesus and the World of Judaism* (Philadelphia: Fortress Press, 1983); Paul Barnett, *Jesus and the Logic of History* (Grand Rapids, Mich.: Eerdmans, 1997); Paul L. Maier, *In the Fullness of Time: A Historian Looks at Christmas, Easter, and the Early Church* (San Francisco: Harper San Francisco, 1991); Edwin Yamauchi, "Jesus Outside the New Testament: What Is the Evidence?" in *Jesus under Fire: Modern Scholarship Reinvents the Historical Jesus*, ed. Michael J. Wilkins and J. P. Moreland (Grand Rapids, Mich.: Zondervan, 1995). C. Behan McCullagh, *Justifying Historical Descriptions* (Cambridge: Cambridge University Press, 1984), 17–33, briefly considers the subject of Jesus's resurrection in terms of historical theorizing.

8. Hume's essay "On Miracles" is found in section X of his work *An Enquiry Concerning Human Understanding*. The essay has been anthologized many times, including in Richard Wollheim, ed., *Hume on Religion*, Fontana Library of Theology and Philosophy (London: Collins, 1963).

9. Hume, "On Miracles," chiefly part I.

10. Hume, "On Miracles," chiefly part II.

11. For two of these treatments, see Gary R. Habermas, "Skepticism: Hume," in *Biblical Errancy: An Analysis of Its Philosophical Roots*, ed. Norman Geisler (Grand Rapids, Mich.: Zondervan, 1980), 23–49. Cf. also Habermas, *Resurrection of Jesus: A Rational Inquiry*, 82–113.

12. Wand, *Christianity*, 70–71.

13. George I. Mavrodes, "David Hume and the Probability of Miracles," *International Journal for Philosophy of Religion* 43 (1998): 176–77. We will turn in chapter 2 to some additional insights by Mavrodes that are also relevant to this chapter's discussion.

14. Werner Schaaffs, *Theology, Physics and Miracles*, trans. Richard Renfield (Washington, D.C.: Canon Press, 1974), for instance, 55, 65.

15. See Stephen Griffith, "Could It Have Been Reasonable for the Disciples to Have Believed That Jesus Had Risen from the Dead?" *Journal of Philosophical Research* 21 (1996): 317; Arthur Gibson, "Logic of the Resurrection," in *Resurrection*, ed. Stanley E. Porter, Michael A. Hayes, and David Tombs, *Journal for the Study of the New Testament* Supplement Series 186 (Sheffield, England: Sheffield Academic Press, 1999), 172–73.

16. Richard Swinburne, *The Concept of Miracle* (New York: St. Martin's Press, 1970), 2–3.

17. Swinburne, *The Concept of Miracle*, 27–28.

18. Schaaffs, *Theology, Physics and Miracles*, 66. For some similar critiques, see philosopher of science Stanley L. Jaki, *Miracles and Physics* (Front Royal, Va.: Christendom Press, 1989), 13–16, 59, 71.

19. Hume, "On Miracles," part II, 220, in the Wollheim anthology.

20. C. S. Lewis, *Miracles: A Preliminary Study* (New York: Macmillan, 1960), 102.

21. David Hume, *The History of England*, 6 vols. (London: Gilbert and Revington, 1848).

22. Jaki, *Miracles and Physics*, esp. 19–23.

23. For details, see Habermas, "Skepticism: Hume," 43. Cf. David Hume, *An Abstract of a Treatise of Human Nature* (Cambridge: Cambridge University Press, 1938, from the 1740 ed.), 14–16.

24. Stephen T. Davis, "Is It Possible to Know That Jesus Was Raised from the Dead?" *Faith and Philosophy* 1 (1984): 148, 150.

25. Raymond E. Brown, review of *Did Jesus Rise from the Dead? The Resurrection Debate*, by Gary R. Habermas and Antony Flew, *International Philosophical Quarterly* 27 (1987): 451.

26. See Wolfhart Pannenberg, "The Historicity of the Resurrection. The Identity of Christ," in *The Intellectuals Speak Out about God*, ed. Roy Abraham Varghese (Chicago: Regnery Gateway, 1984), 262–63; Gerald O'Collins, *Interpreting Jesus* (Mahweh, N.J.: Paulist Press, 1983), 57; Thomas C. Oden, *The Word of Life*, vol. 2 of *Systematic Theology* (Peabody, Mass.: Hendrickson, 1989), 499–500; Michael Goulder, "The Explanatory Power of Conversion-Visions," in *Jesus' Resurrection: Fact or Figment? A Debate between William Lane Craig and Gerd Lüdemann*, ed. Paul Copan and Ronald K. Tacelli (Downers Grove, Ill.: InterVarsity Press, 2000), 102.

27. For some examples, see Rodney D. Holder, "Hume on Miracles: Bayesian Interpretation, Multiple Testimony, and the Existence of God," *British Journal for the Philosophy of Science* 49 (1998): esp. 60–62; George N. Schlesinger, "Miracles and Probabilities," *Nous* 21 (1987): esp. 219, 230–32; George N. Schlesinger, "The Credibility of Extraordinary Events," *Analysis* 51 (1991): 125; Benjamin F. Armstrong Jr., "Hume on Miracles: Begging-the-Question against Believers," *History of Philosophy Quarterly* 9 (1992): 319, 327; John Earman, "Bayes, Hume, and Miracles," *Faith and Philosophy* 10 (1993): esp. 293, 305–6; John Earman, *Hume's Abject Failure: The Argument against Miracles* (New York: Oxford University Press, 2000); Roy A. Sorensen, "Hume's Scepticism Concerning Reports of Miracles," *Analysis* 43 (1983): 60; Jaki, *Miracles and Physics*, esp. 19–25, 32–33, 78–79, 92–93. For a rejoinder on behalf of a Humean skepticism, see Richard Otte, "Schlesinger and Miracles," *Faith and Philosophy* 10 (1993): esp. 93, 97.

28. Wolfhart Pannenberg, *Jesus: God and Man*, 2nd ed., trans. Lewis L. Wilkins and Duane A. Priebe (Philadelphia: Westminster Press, 1977), 98.

29. On historical methodology, see Tosh, *The Pursuit of History*; Breisach, *Historiography*; Meyerhoff, *Philosophy of History*; Wand, *Christianity*; and McCullagh, *Justifying Historical Descriptions*. For methodology in historical Jesus studies, see Grant, *Jesus*, appendix; and Barnett, *Jesus and the Logic of History*, chaps. 1–6. Probably the most noteworthy volumes in this second category are N. T. Wright, *The New Testament and the People of God* (Minneapolis: Fortress Press, 1992), esp. part II; Ben F.

Meyer, *The Aims of Jesus* (London: SCM Press, 1979), chap. 4; Ben F. Meyer, *Critical Realism and the New Testament*, vol. 17 in the Princeton Theological Monograph Series (Allison Park, Pa.: Pickwick Publications, 1989). My historical methodology cannot be outlined here, but the interested reader may consult the following sources: Habermas, "Historiography" in *The Historical Jesus*, appendix 1; Gary R. Habermas, "Philosophy of History, Historical Relativism and History as Evidence," in *Evangelical Apologetics*, ed. Michael Bauman, David W. Hall, and Robert C. Newman (Camp Hill, Pa.: Christian Publications, 1996), 91–118.

30. Robert Funk, *Honest to Jesus* (San Francisco: Harper San Francisco, 1996), 33; cf. also 32–34, 40, 237–39.

31. Vermes, *Jesus and the World of Judaism*, 3; cf. 3–6, 19–20.

32. E. P. Sanders, *Jesus and Judaism* (Philadelphia: Fortress Press, 1985), 321–22; also 10–11, 326–27. Sanders continues this approach in *The Historical Figure of Jesus* (London: Penguin Books, 1993), 10–14.

33. Other examples include Norman Perrin, *Rediscovering the Teaching of Jesus* (New York: Harper and Row, 1967), 37–47, for his criteria; Jürgen Moltmann, "The Resurrection of Christ: Hope for the World," in *Resurrection Reconsidered*, ed. Gavin D'Costa (Oxford: Oneworld Publications, 1996), 74–75; Luke Timothy Johnson, *Living Jesus: Learning the Heart of the Gospel* (San Francisco: Harper Collins, 1999), 10, 130–32; Thorwald Lorenzen, *Resurrection and Discipleship: Interpretive Models, Biblical Reflections, Theological Consequences* (Maryknoll, N.Y.: Orbis Books, 1995), 184–85.

34. The empty tomb is not as widely accepted as the other facts in this list. But it is still accepted by a majority of contemporary scholars. This is one of the conclusions from my study of resurrection sources published since 1975 in German, French, and English, as detailed in the introduction.

35. For example, Habermas, *Resurrection of Jesus: A Rational Inquiry*, 114–71, contains detailed refutations of the key naturalistic theories. Although it is usually not a naturalistic theory, for a critique of efforts to accept the resurrection as an occurrence beyond the realm of normal history, see 198–224. A major emphasis in this volume is that providing itemized, thorough refutations of each alternative hypothesis provides crucial indications of the historicity of the resurrection (323–26). For a very brief treatment of naturalistic theories, see Gary R. Habermas and J. P. Moreland, *Beyond Death: Exploring the Evidence for Immortality* (Wheaton, Ill.: Crossway Books, 1998), 113–26.

36. See Gary R. Habermas, "The Late Twentieth Century Resurgence of Naturalistic Responses to Jesus' Resurrection," *Trinity Journal*, n.s., 22 (2001): 179–96.

37. Gary Collins, letter to the author, 21 February 1977.

38. For example, cf. Leonard Zusne and Warren Jones, *Anomalistic Psychology: A Study of Extraordinary Phenomena of Behavior and Experience* (Hillsdale, N.J.: Lawrence Erlbaum, 1982), 135.

39. For recent scholarly sources, confirmation of these critiques, some new twists in the theory during the last few decades, as well as even more problem areas, see

Gary R. Habermas, "Explaining Away Jesus' Resurrection: The Recent Revival of Hallucination Theories," *Christian Research Journal* 23 (2001): 26–31, 47–49. For a more detailed refutation of the hallucination theory, see Habermas, *Resurrection of Jesus: A Rational Inquiry*, 127–45.

40. Collins, letter to author.

41. We will address briefly both the swoon and legend theories below. Since the nineteenth century, these and hallucination theories have been the most popular natural approaches.

42. For some examples of scholars who are critical of the hallucination theses, see Hans Grass, *Ostergeschehen und Osterberichte*, 2nd ed. (Göttingen, Germany: Vandenhoeck and Rupert, 1962), 96; Paul Tillich, *Systematic Theology* (Chicago: University of Chicago Press, 1957), vol. 2, esp. 156; Günther Bornkamm, *Jesus of Nazareth*, trans. Irene and Fraser McLuskey with James M. Robinson (New York: Harper and Row, 1960), 185; Joachim Jeremias, "Easter: The Earliest Tradition and the Earliest Interpretation," *New Testament Theology: The Proclamation of Jesus*, trans. John Bowden (New York: Charles Scribner's Sons, 1971), 302; Pannenberg, *Jesus: God and Man*, 95–97; Jürgen Moltmann, *Theology of Hope: On the Ground and the Implications of a Christian Eschatology*, trans. James W. Leitch (New York: Harper and Row, 1967), 172, 186, 198; John A. T. Robinson, *Can We Trust the New Testament?* (Grand Rapids, Mich.: Eerdmans, 1977), 123–25; Grant, *Jesus*, 93; J. K. Elliott, "The First Easter," *History Today* 29 (1979): 219; Raymond E. Brown, *The Virginal Conception and Bodily Resurrection of Jesus* (New York: Paulist Press, 1973), 90–92; Reginald H. Fuller, *The Formation of the Resurrection Narratives*, rev. ed. (Philadelphia: Fortress Press, 1980), 46–49, 94–96; Pinchas Lapide, *The Resurrection of Jesus: A Jewish Perspective* (Minneapolis: Augsburg, 1983), 125–26; A. M. Ramsey, *The Resurrection of Christ* (London: Collins, 1961), 41, 49–50; Helmut Thielicke, "The Resurrection Kerygma," in *The Easter Message Today*, trans. Salvator Attanasio and Darrell Likens Guder (London: Thomas Nelson, 1964), 84–91; Neville Clark, *Interpreting the Resurrection* (Philadelphia: Westminster Press, 1967), 100–101; George Eldon Ladd, *I Believe in the Resurrection of Jesus* (Grand Rapids, Mich.: Eerdmans, 1975), 136–38. For just a few of the more recent critical comments, some from scholars who are quite skeptical, see Ingo Broer, "'Seid stets bereit, jedem Rede und Antwort zu stehen, der nach der Hoffnung fragt, die euch erfüllt' (1 Petr 3,15): Das leere Grab und die Erscheinungen Jesu im Licte der historichen Kritik," in Broer and J. Werbick, eds., *"Der Herr ist wahrhaft auferstanden" (Lk 24,34): Biblische und systematische Beiträge zur Entstehung des Osterglaubens*, Stuttgarter Bibel-Studien 134 (Stuttgart, Germany: Katholisches Bibelwerk, 1988), cf. esp. 55–56; John Dominic Crossan, "Dialogue," in *Will the Real Jesus Please Stand Up? A Debate between William Lane Craig and John Dominic Crossan*, ed. Paul Copan (Grand Rapids, Mich.: Baker Books, 1998), 63; Marcus Borg, "The Truth of Easter," in *The Meaning of Jesus: Two Visions*, by Borg and N. T. Wright (San Francisco: Harper Collins, 1999), 132–33; Wedderburn, *Beyond Resurrection*, 96, cf. 116; John Drane, *Introducing the New Testament* (San Francisco: Harper and Row, 1986), 105; William Lane Craig, *Assessing the New Testament*

Evidence for the Historicity of the Resurrection of Jesus (Lewiston, N.Y.: Edwin Mellen Press, 1989), 392–400; John Shelby Spong, *The Easter Moment* (San Francisco: Harper and Row, 1987), 96; N. T. Wright, "Christian Origins and the Resurrection of Jesus: The Resurrection of Jesus as a Historical Problem," *Sewanee Theological Review* 41 (1998): 115–16, 120–21; Gerald O'Collins, *Jesus Risen: An Historical, Fundamental and Systematic Examination of Christ's Resurrection* (New York: Paulist Press, 1987), 107–9; Stephen T. Davis, *Risen Indeed* (Grand Rapids, Mich.: Eerdmans, 1993), 179, 183–84; James D. G. Dunn, *The Evidence for Jesus* (Louisville, Ky.: Westminster Press, 1985), 71–76; Barnett, *Jesus and the Logic of History*, 130–31; Lorenzen, *Resurrection and Discipleship*, 61, 124; Phillip H. Wiebe, *Visions of Jesus: Direct Encounters from the New Testament to Today* (New York: Oxford University Press, 1997), 210; Samuel Vollenweider, "Ostern—der denkwürdige Ausgang einer Krisenerfahrung," *Theologische Zeitschrift* 49 (1993): 41–43. Many other scholars could be added to this list.

43. Pannenberg, *Jesus: God and Man*, 96.

44. For some of these nineteenth-century efforts to both postulate and combine theories, see the classic work by Albert Schweitzer, *The Quest of the Historical Jesus: A Critical Study of its Progress from Reimarus to Wrede*, trans. W. Montgomery (1906; reprint, New York: Macmillan, 1968), 161, 166–72, 180–92. In addition to Schweitzer's jabs, including his pronouncement that the entire movement had failed (398–401), minutely detailed surveys and devastating critiques of these theories and their combinations are supplied by James Orr, *The Resurrection of Jesus* (1908; reprint, Grand Rapids, Mich.: Zondervan, 1965), whose entire work is aimed at providing critical interaction. Like Schweitzer, Orr concludes that the efforts of old liberalism failed (chap. 10). Another nineteenth-century example of detailed refutations is William Milligan, *The Resurrection of Our Lord* (New York: Macmillan, 1899), esp. 76–119.

45. David Friedrich Strauss, *A New Life of Jesus*, 2 vols., 2nd ed.; no translator provided (London: Williams and Norgate, 1879), 1:199.

46. For primary–source treatments of Strauss, Friedrich Schleiermacher, Heinrich Paulus, Bruno Baur, Ernest Renan, Otto Pfleiderer, and Adolf von Harnack, who owe their rejections of miracles to Hume's argument, see Habermas, *Resurrection of Jesus: A Rational Inquiry*, 114–17, 151–52, 286–88. A brief summary is provided in Habermas, "Skepticism: Hume," 32–35.

47. John Herman Randall Jr., *The Making of the Modern Mind*, rev. ed. (Boston: Houghton Mifflin, 1940), 553–54; cf. 293.

48. For primary–source treatments of Hume's influence on analytical philosophers in their rejection of the supernatural, including miracles, see Habermas, "Skepticism: Hume," 35–38. For the somewhat different path of Hume's influence on theologians like Paul Tillich, Rudolf Bultmann, and the early writings of John A. T. Robinson, see Habermas, *Resurrection of Jesus: A Rational Inquiry*, 117–18, 288–89. Harvey Cox affirms both his own reliance on Hume's rejection of miracles, as well as that of other contemporary scholars. See Harvey Cox, "A Dialogue on Christ's Resurrection," *Christianity Today* 12 (1968): 5–12.

49. Charles Hartshorne agrees with Hume that we must balance testimony regarding miracle claims (in Habermas and Flew, 137), even though he does not agree completely with Hume (142). Greg Cavin argues in favor of "the general Humean position" ("Miracles, Probability, and the Resurrection of Jesus: A Philosophical, Mathematical, and Historical Study" [Ph.D. diss., University of California, Irvine, 1993], abstract) as well as Otte, "Schlesinger and Miracles."

50. Mavrodes, "David Hume," 167.

51. Strauss, A New Life of Jesus, 1:408–12.

52. Schweitzer lists no proponents of the swoon theory after 1838, just three years after Strauss published his critique (Quest of the Historical Jesus, 56–57).

53. See Orr, The Resurrection of Jesus, 92; and Eduard Riggenbach, The Resurrection of Jesus (New York: Eaton and Mains, 1907), 48–49.

54. Friedrich Schleiermacher, The Christian Faith, 2 vols., ed. H. R. Mackintosh and J. S. Stewart (New York: Harper and Row, 1963), 2:420; Schweitzer, Quest of the Historical Jesus, 54–55.

55. Theodor Keim, Die Geschichte Jesu von Nazara, 3 vols. (Zurich, 1867, 1871, and 1872). On Keim's influence, see Orr, The Resurrection of Jesus, 219; Schweitzer, Quest of the Historical Jesus, 210–14.

56. Schweitzer lists no supporters of the fraud theory for over a century, since Reimarus's attempt in 1778 (Quest of the Historical Jesus, 21–22).

57. Fuller, Formation of the Resurrection Narratives, 9–14, 48; Pannenberg, Jesus: God and Man, 90–91. See below for a brief critique of legend theses.

58. Karl Barth, Church Dogmatics, 13 vols., ed. G. W. Bromiley and T. F. Torrance (Edinburgh: T. and T. Clark, 1961), 4:340.

59. Raymond E. Brown, "The Resurrection and Biblical Criticism," Commonweal, 24 November 1967, 233.

60. Tillich, Systematic Theology, vol. 2, esp. 155–56; Michael C. Perry, The Easter Enigma (London: Faber and Faber, 1959), 120–33; Bornkamm, Jesus of Nazareth, 181–85; Moltmann, Theology of Hope, 186, 198–200; Jeremias, "Easter," 302; Ulrich Wilckens, Resurrection: Biblical Testimony to the Resurrection: An Historical Examination and Explanation, trans. A. M. Stewart (Edinburgh: Saint Andrew Press, 1977), 117–19; Pannenberg, Jesus: God and Man, 88–97; Robinson, Can We Trust? 123–25; Lapide, Resurrection of Jesus, 120–26; John Macquarrie, "The Keystone of Christian Faith" in 'If Christ Be Not Risen. . .': Essays in Resurrection and Survival, ed. John Greenhalgh and Elizabeth Russell (San Francisco: Harper Collins, 1986), 18–22; Clark, Interpreting the Resurrection, 99–105; A. M. Hunter, Bible and Gospel (Philadelphia: Westminster Press, 1969), 111–12; Ramsey, The Resurrection of Christ, 48–53; Thielicke, "The Resurrection Kerygma," 87–91, 103–4.

61. Dunn, The Evidence for Jesus, 76. A more recent and similar testimony is that of Wright, "Christian Origins," 118–22.

62. Stephen T. Davis, "Is Belief in the Resurrection Rational?" Philo 2 (1999): 57–58.

63. Richard Swinburne, "Evidence for the Resurrection," in *The Resurrection: An Interdisciplinary Symposium on the Resurrection of Jesus*, ed. Stephen T. Davis, Daniel Kendall, and Gerald O'Collins (Oxford: Oxford University Press, 1997), 201.

64. Obviously, this is far from denying the authority of the New Testament. I am simply stating that these beliefs are unnecessary for the methodology being chosen here. For more details on such an approach, see Gary R. Habermas, "Evidential Apologetics," in *Five Views on Apologetics*, ed. Steven B. Cowan (Grand Rapids, Mich.: Zondervan, 2000), 99–100, 186–90.

65. In addition to 1 Cor 15:3, texts receiving scholarly attention are 1 Cor 11:26; the early speeches in Acts, esp. 2:22–36, 3:13–16, 4:8–10, 5:29–32, 10:39–43, 13:28–31, 17:1–3, 30–31; Rom 4:25; Phil 2:8; 1 Tm 2:6; 1 Pt 3:18. (Below I treat some of the scholarly reasons for supporting the historicity of these texts, esp. 1 Cor 15:3ff., which we address in detail in the next section.)

66. Mt 27:26–56; Mk 15:20–47; Lk 23:26–56; Jn 19:16–42.

67. There are at least ten non-Christian texts, of differing value, each reporting the death of Jesus. These include Tacitus (*Annals* 15:44), a disputed passage in Josephus (*Antiquities* 18:3), the *Talmud* (*Sanhedrin* 43a; cf. 106b), Lucian of Samosata (*The Death of Peregrine* 11–13), Mara Bar-Serapion (letter, British Museum, Syriac manuscript, additional 14,658), Thallus (from a Julius Africanus fragment), the so-called lost *Acts of Pilate* (Justin Martyr, *First Apology* 35). Gnostic works include *The Gospel of Truth* (20:11–14, 25–29), *The Gospel of Thomas* (45:1–16), and *The Treatise on Resurrection* (46:14–21). *The Toledoth Jesu* is a much later text. For details on these sources, see Habermas, *The Historical Jesus*, chap. 9.

68. Clement of Rome (*Corinthians* 7, 12, 21, 49), Ignatius (*Trallians* 9; *Smyrneans* 1; *Barnabas* 5), and Justin Martyr (*First Apology* 32, 35, 50; *Dialogue with Trypho* 47, 108). Reference notations for the apostolic fathers are taken from J. B. Lightfoot, ed., *The Apostolic Fathers* (1891; reprint, Grand Rapids, Mich.: Baker, 1971).

69. See the excellent study by Martin Hengel, *Crucifixion* (Philadelphia: Fortress Press, 1977), 70. Other relevent details are found in: Joseph Zias and Eliezer Sekeles, "The Crucified Man from Giv`at ha-Mivtar: A Reappraisal," *Israel Exploration Journal* 35 (1985): 22–27; Joseph Zias and James H. Charlesworth, "Crucifixion: Archaeology, Jesus, and the Dead Sea Scrolls," in *Jesus and the Dead Sea Scrolls*, ed. Charlesworth (New York: Doubleday, 1992).

70. For just a few of the many medical publications that provide details, see William D. Edwards, Wesley J. Gabel, and Floyd E. Hosmer, "On the Physical Death of Jesus Christ," *Journal of the American Medical Association* 255 (1986); J. E. Holoubek and A. B. Holoubek, "Execution by Crucifixion: History, Methods, and Cause of Death," *Journal of Medicine* 26 (1995): 1–16; Robert Bucklin, "The Legal and Medical Aspects of the Trial and Death of Christ," *Medicine, Science and the Law* (1970); John Wilkinson, "The Incident of the Blood and Water in John 19.34," *Scottish Journal of Theology* 28 (1975). For a detailed critique of the swoon theory, see Habermas, *The Historical Jesus*, 69–75.

71. Strauss, 1:408–12. For just a few scholars who think that Strauss's critique was decisive against the swoon theory, see Schweitzer, The *Quest of the Historical Jesus*, 56–57; Wright, "Christian Origins," 119; O'Collins, *Jesus Risen*, 100–101; A. E. Harvey, "A Short Life after Death," review of *The Anastasis: The Resurrection of Jesus as a Historical Event*, by J. Duncan M. Derrett, in *The Times Literary Supplement*, no. 4153 (1982); Pheme Perkins, review of *The Anastasis*, by Derrett, in *The Catholic Biblical Quarterly* 45 (1983): 684–85; T. S. M. Williams, review of *The Anastasis*, by Derrett, in *Journal of Theological Studies* 36 (1985): 445–47; cf. Otto Merk, review of *The Anastasis*, by Derrett, in *Gnomon-Kritische Zeitschrift für die Gesamte Klassische Altertumswissenschaft* 59 (1987): 761–63.

72. John Dominic Crossan, *Jesus: A Revolutionary Biography* (San Francisco: Harper Collins, 1994), 145; cf. 154, 196, 201.

73. Marcus J. Borg, *Jesus: A New Vision: Spirit, Culture, and the Life of Discipleship* (San Francisco: Harper Collins, 1987), 179; cf. 178–84.

74. The ensuing discussion follows closely several writings by the author. For some of the details, see Gary R. Habermas, "Jesus's Resurrection and Contemporary Criticism," part 2, 374–76; Habermas and Moreland, *Beyond Death*, 128–30; Habermas, *The Historical Jesus*, 152–57.

75. The sources below provide ample research materials for those who wish to pursue further details.

76. Fuller, *Formation of the Resurrection Narratives*, 10.

77. Jerome Murphy-O'Connor, "Tradition and Redaction in 1 Cor 15:3–7," *Catholic Biblical Quarterly* 43 (1981): 582.

78. See Lapide, *Resurrection of Jesus*, 97–99; Fuller, *Formation of the Resurrection Narratives*, 10–11; John Kloppenborg, "An Analysis of the Pre-Pauline Formula in 1 Cor 15:3b–5 in Light of Some Recent Literature," *Catholic Biblical Quarterly* 40 (1978): 351, 360; Murphy-O'Connor, "Tradition and Redaction," 582; Martin Hengel, *The Atonement: The Origins of the Doctrine in the New Testament*, trans. John Bowden (Philadelphia: Fortress Press, 1981), 36–39; Brown, *Virginal Conception*, 81, 92; Lüdemann, *What Really Happened to Jesus*, 12–13; Hans Conzelmann, *I Corinthians* (Philadelphia: Fortress Press, 1975), 251, 257; Norman Perrin, *The Resurrection according to Matthew, Mark, and Luke* (Philadelphia: Fortress, 1977), 79; Wedderburn, *Beyond Resurrection*, 113–14; Wilckens, *Resurrection*, 2, 15; John Meier, *A Marginal Jew: Rethinking the Historical Jesus*, 3 vols. (New York: Doubleday, 1987–2001), 2:139; Sanders, *The Historical Figure of Jesus*, 277; Joseph A. Fitzmyer, "The Resurrection of Jesus Christaccording to the New Testament," *The Month*, 2nd n.s., 20 (November 1987): 402–10; Hans-Ruedi Weber, *The Cross* (Grand Rapids, Mich.: Eerdmans, 1978), 59–60; O'Collins, *Interpreting Jesus*, 111; Robinson, *Can We Trust?* 125; Dunn, *The Evidence for Jesus*, 69–70; Rudolf Bultmann, *Theology of the New Testament*, 2 vols., trans. Kendrick Grobel (New York: Scribner's Sons, 1951, 1955), 1:296; cf. Willi Marxsen, *The Resurrection of Jesus of Nazareth*, trans. Margaret Kohl (Philadelphia: Fortress Press, 1970), 80; Bornkamm, *Jesus of Nazareth*, 182; Jeremias, "Easter," 306.

79. Jeremias, "Easter," 306.

80. Wilckens, *Resurrection*, 2.

81. Walter Kasper, *Jesus the Christ*, new ed., trans. V. Green (Mahweh, N.J.: Paulist Press, 1976), 125.

82. Durrwell states, "La formulation est, sans doute, antérieure à la conversion de Paul." See Francis X. Durrwell, *La Résurrection de Jésus: Mystère de Salut* (Paris: Les Éditions du Cerf, 1976), 22; Grass, *Ostergeschehen und Osterberichte*, 96; Reginald H. Fuller, *The Foundations of New Testament Christology* (New York: Scribner's Sons, 1965), 142, 161; Fuller, *Formation of the Resurrection Narratives*, 10, 14, 28, 48; Oscar Cullmann, *The Early Church: Studies in Early Christian History and Theology*, ed. A. J. B. Higgins (Philadelphia: Westminster Press, 1966), 65–66; Leonard Goppelt, "The Easter Kerygma in the New Testament," in *The Easter Message Today*, 36; Hunter, *Bible and Gospel*, 109; Ramsey, *The Resurrection of Christ*, 43; Pannenberg, *Jesus: God and Man*, 90; Brown, *Virginal Conception*, 81, 92; Ladd, *I Believe in the Resurrection*, 105; Geffrey B. Kelly, "'He Appeared to Me.' 1 Cor. 15:8 as Paul's Religious Experience of the End Time," in *Critical History and Biblical Faith: New Testament Perspectives*, ed. Thomas J. Ryan (Villanova, Pa.: Villanova University, 1979), 109; Fitzmyer, "The Resurrection of Jesus Christ," 409; C. H. Dodd, *The Apostolic Preaching and Its Developments*, 16; David Samuel, "Making Room in History for the Miraculous," *Churchman* 100 (1986): 107; Helmut Merklein, "Die Auferweckung Jesu und die Anfänge der Christologie (Messias bzw. Sohn Gottes und Menschensohn)," *Zeitschrift für die Neutestamentliche Wissenschaft und die Kunde der Älteren Kirche* 72 (1981): 2; Oden, *The Word of Life*, 497; Dunn, *The Evidence for Jesus*, 70; C. E. B. Cranfield, "The Resurrection of Jesus Christ," *Expository Times* 101 (1990): 169; Barnabas Lindars, "The Resurrection and the Empty Tomb," in *The Resurrection of Jesus Christ*, ed. Paul Avis (London: Darton, Longman and Todd, 1993), 124; John M. G. Barclay, "The Resurrection in Contemporary New Testament Scholarship," in *Resurrection Reconsidered*, 16, cf. 24; Peter Stuhlmacher, *Jesus of Nazareth—Christ of Faith*, trans. Siegfried S. Shatzmann (Peabody, Mass.: Hendrickson, 1993), 8; Leander E. Keck, *Who Is Jesus? History in Perfect Tense* (Columbia, S.C.: University of South Carolina Press, 2000), 139; Meier, *A Marginal Jew*, 3:139; O'Collins thinks that most scholars date this creed from the 30s A.D. and no one places it later than the 40s A.D. Even the latter still would not affect our major conclusions in this chapter. See Gerald O'Collins, *What Are They Saying about the Resurrection?* (New York: Paulist Press, 1978), 112.

83. Gerd Lüdemann, *The Resurrection of Jesus*, trans. John Bowden (Minneapolis: Fortress Press, 1994), 38.

84. Michael Goulder, "The Baseless Fabric of a Vision," in *Resurrection Reconsidered*, 48.

85. Thomas Sheehan, *The First Coming: How the Kingdom of God Became Christianity* (New York: Random House, 1986), 118; cf. 110–12, 135.

86. Robert Funk, Roy W. Hoover, and the Jesus Seminar, *The Five Gospels* (New York: Macmillan, 1993), 24; Jack Kent, *The Psychological Origins of the Resurrection Myth* (London: Open Gate Press, 1999), 16–17; Wedderburn, *Beyond Resurrection*,

111, 274 n. 265; Michael Grant, *Saint Paul* (Glasgow: William Collins Sons, 1976), 104; G. A. Wells, *Did Jesus Exist?* (London: Pemberton, 1986), 30; Conzelmann, *I Corinthians*, 254; Robinson, *Can We Trust*, 125.

87. Almost every scholar listed in endnote 82 who provides a location favors a Jerusalem scenario. Grass prefers Damascus as the locale, indicating an even earlier date (*Ostergeschehen und Osterberichte*, 96), and Fuller thinks most of the creed came from Damascus (*The Formation of the Resurrection Narratives*, 14, 28).

88. See Hengel (*The Atonement*, 38–39), John Alsup (*The Post-Resurrection Appearance Stories of the Gospel Tradition: A History-of-Tradition Analysis with Text-Synopsis*, Calwer Theologische Monographien 5 [Stuttgart, Germany: Calwer Verlag, 1975], 55), Joseph Fitzmyer ("The Ascension of Christ and Pentecost," *Theological Studies* 45 [1984]: 409–40), Goppelt ("Easter Kerygma," 36), and Grant Osborne (*The Resurrection Narratives*, 222). Even Lüdemann takes a similar stance (*What Really Happened to Jesus*, 12–13).

89. C. H. Dodd, *Apostolic Preaching*, 16.

90. For Farmer's study of the meaning of ἱστορῆσαι as employed in Gal 1:18 and the hint it provides in determining the nature of Paul's inquiry during his visit to the apostles in Jerusalem, see "Peter and Paul, and the Tradition Concerning 'The Lord's Supper' in I Corinthians 11:23–25," *Criswell Theological Review* 2 (1987): 122–30, in particular. See 135–38 regarding the apostolic, Petrine nature of this tradition.

91. G. D. Kilpatrick, "Galatians 1:18 ἱστορῆσει Κηφᾶν" in *New Testament Essays: Studies in Memory of Thomas Walter Manson*, ed. A. J. B. Higgins (Manchester, England: Manchester University Press, 1959), 144–49.

92. Barnett, *Jesus and the Logic of History*, 41. For some similar thoughts, see Joseph Doré, "La Résurrection de Jésus: A L'Épreuve du Discours Théologique," *Recherches de Science Religieuse* 65 (1977): 291, n. 11.

93. Hans Dieter Betz, *Galatians: A Commentary on Paul's Letter to the Churches in Galatia* (Philadelphia: Fortress Press, 1979), 76.

94. Some might question whether Paul's point in Gal 1:11–17 was to assert his independence from the other apostles. Paul received his commission to preach the Gospel message directly from Christ, not from any other apostles. But we must not press this language beyond Paul's obvious and overall intent. He is speaking here *specifically* about his direct call from the Lord, during which he was converted and called to preach the Gospel. We have no reason to think that he sought out an apostle at that time. But he is equally clear that, three years later, he *did* initiate a consultation with Peter and James (1:18–20). Then, fourteen years later, Paul is clear that he visited the apostles once again, in order to check out the Gospel that he was preaching, to ascertain if he was on the wrong path (2:2). So to say that he *never* consulted any other person is not only to miss his point, but it ignores Paul's two direct statements to the contrary.

95. Fuller, *Formation of the Resurrection Narratives*, 43–44; cf. 170.

96. Wedderburn, *Beyond Resurrection*, 116.

97. Lapide, *Resurrection of Jesus*, 99.

98. Hans von Campenhausen, "The Events of Easter and the Empty Tomb," in *Tradition and Life in the Church* (Philadelphia: Fortress Press, 1968), 44.

99. A. M. Hunter, *Jesus: Lord and Saviour* (Grand Rapids, Mich.: Eerdmans, 1976), 100.

100. Howard Clark Kee, *What Can We Know about Jesus?* (Cambridge: Cambridge University Press, 1990), 1–2.

101. Dodd, *Apostolic Preaching and Its Developments*, 16.

102. Strangely enough, even Perrin (*Resurrection according to Matthew, Mark, and Luke*, 80) affirms many of these same points.

103. The discussion here follows closely several writings by the author. For some of the details, see Gary R. Habermas, "The Evidential Method," in *Five Views on Apologetics*, 108–12; Gary R. Habermas, "The Resurrection Appearances of Jesus," in *In Defense of Miracles: A Comprehensive Case for God's Action in History*, ed. R. Douglas Geivett and Habermas (Downers Grove, Ill.: InterVarsity Press, 1997), esp. 265–68; Habermas and Moreland, *Beyond Death*, 130–33; Habermas, *The Historical Jesus*, 160–61.

104. Hengel, *The Atonement*, 37.

105. Michael Martin, *The Case against Christianity* (Philadelphia: Temple University Press, 1991), 81, 89.

106. Hoover, "A Contest between Orthodoxy and Veracity," in *Jesus's Resurrection: Fact or Figment?* 129.

107. Hoover, "A Contest," 130–31.

108. Lüdemann, *What Really Happened to Jesus*, 4; Funk, *Honest to Jesus*, 36, 40; Marcus Borg, "Thinking about Easter," *Bible Review* 10 (1994): 15; Perrin, *Resurrection according to Matthew, Mark, and Luke*, 80, 83; John Shelby Spong, *Resurrection: Myth or Reality?* (San Francisco: Harper San Francisco, 1994), 47; Grant, *Saint Paul*, 104.

109. Hengel, *The Atonement*, 38.

110. Luke Timothy Johnson, *The Real Jesus* (San Francisco: Harper San Francisco, 1996), 103.

111. Kee, *What Can We Know?* 1.

112. From Betz, *Galatians*, 96, 100. For some other critical scholars who agree, see Wolfhart Pannenberg, "Response to the Debate," in Habermas and Flew, *Did Jesus Rise from the Dead?* 132; Wolfhart Pannenberg, *Systematic Theology*, vol. 2, trans. Geoffrey W. Bromily (Grand Rapids, Mich.: Eerdmans, 1991), 355; Hengel, *The Atonement*, 36–38; Barnett, *Jesus and the Logic of History*, 126–27, 142; cf. Meier, *A Marginal Jew*, 2:219–20.

113. The issue of the resurrection narratives in the Gospels is a separate topic that takes us far beyond our emphasis on Paul's evidence. The interested reader could consult: Osborne, *The Resurrection Narratives*, part 2; Craig, *Assessing*, part 2; C. H. Dodd, "The Appearances of the Risen Christ: An Essay in Form-Criticism of the Gospels," in *More New Testament Essays* (Grand Rapids, Mich.: Eerdmans, 1968).

See also Stephen T. Davis, " 'Seeing' the Risen Jesus"; William P. Alston, "Biblical Criticism and the Resurrection"; and Richard Swinburne, "Evidence for the Resurrection," all in *The Resurrection*.

114. Johnson, *The Real Jesus*, 118.

115. Ben Witherington III, "Resurrection Redux," in *Will the Real Jesus?* 140.

116. Lüdemann, *What Really Happened to Jesus*, 13; Pannenberg, "Response to the Debate," in *Did Jesus Rise from the Dead?* 129; Hengel, *The Atonement*, 38, 69; Stuhlmacher, *Jesus of Nazareth*, 8; Meier, *A Marginal Jew*, 1:118; O'Collins, *Interpreting Jesus*, 110; Meyer, *The Aims of Jesus*, 15; Samuel, "Making Room," 107.

117. Meier, *A Marginal Jew*, 2:70.

118. Fuller, *Formation of the Resurrection Narratives*, 37. The majority of critical scholars agree here. For some examples, see Meier, *A Marginal Jew*, 2:70–71; Pannenberg, *Jesus: God and Man*, 97; Peter Stuhlmacher, "The Resurrection of Jesus and the Resurrection of the Dead," trans. Jonathan M. Whitlock, *Ex Auditu* 9 (1993): 49; E. P. Sanders, "But Did It Happen?" *The Spectator* 276 (1996): 17; Kee, *What Can We Know?* 61; Oden, *The Word of Life*, 490; Lorenzen, *Resurrection and Discipleship*, 143–44; Davis, "'Seeing' the Risen Jesus," 105–6, 138; William Lane Craig, "On Doubts about the Resurrection," *Modern Theology* 6 (1989): 63–64; Ladd, *I Believe in the Resurrection*, 91, 105–6, 138; Osborne, *The Resurrection Narratives*, 229–31. Two of the lone scholars who think that James was not an unbeliever before Jesus's appearance are Richard Bauckham and John Painter. See their essays in *The Brother of Jesus: James the Just and His Mission*, ed. Bruce Chilton and Jacob Neusner (Louisville, Ky.: Westminster John Knox Press, 2001). Even so, both Bauckham ("Jesus and James," 106–7) and Painter ("Who Was James? Footprints as a Means of Identification," 24) admit that the predominant view is that James was an unbeliever when Jesus appeared to him.

119. Lüdemann, *The Resurrection of Jesus*, 109; also *What Really Happened to Jesus*, 102, cf. 14.

120. Helmut Koester, *Introduction to the New Testament*, 2 vols. (Philadelphia: Fortress Press, 1982), 2:84.

121. Spong, *The Easter Moment*, 68. Other rather skeptical scholars who take the traditional view include Conzelmann, *Corinthians*, 258; Wedderburn, *Beyond Resurrection*, 116; Funk, *Honest to Jesus*, 33; Hoover, "A Contest," 135; Betz, *Galatians*, 78; Duncan M. Derrett, *The Anastasis: The Resurrection of Jesus as an Historical Event* (Shipston-on-Stour, England: P. Drinkwater, 1982), 98–99.

122. For the sermon segments in which this traditional material is found, see Acts 1:21–22; 2:22–36; 3:13–16; 4:8–10; 5:29–32; 10:39–43; 13:28–31; 17:1–3, 30–31.

123. For a list of some scholars who find early traditional statements in Acts, see Gerd Lüdemann, *Early Christianity According to the Traditions in Acts: A Commentary*, trans. John Bowden (Minneapolis: Fortress Press, 1989), 47–49, 112–15; Helmut Merklein, "Die Auferweckung Jesu und die Anfänge der Christologie (Messias bzw. Sohn Gottes und Menschensohn)," 2; Kloppenborg, "Analysis," 361; Hengel, *The Atonement*, 34; Elliott, "The First Easter," 215; Alsup, *Post-Resurrection Appearance Sto-*

ries, 64–65, 81–85; Raymond E. Brown, *An Introduction to New Testament Christology* (Mahweh, N.J.: Paulist Press, 1994), 112–13, 164; Fuller, *Formation of the Resurrection Narratives,* 44–45; Pheme Perkins, *Resurrection: New Testament Witness and Contemporary Reflection* (Garden City, N.Y.: Doubleday, 1984), 90, 228–31; J. Colin Hemer, *The Book of Acts in the Setting of Hellenistic History,* ed. Conrad H. Grempf (Winona Lake, Ind.: Eisenbrauns, 1990), 419–22, 427; Hugo Staudinger, "The Resurrection of Jesus Christ as Saving Event and as 'Object' of Historical Research," *Scottish Journal of Theology* 36 (1983): 322; Gerald O'Collins, *Interpreting the Resurrection* (Mahweh, N.J.: Paulist Press, 1988), 48–52; Fitzmyer, "The Ascension of Christ and Pentecost," 404, 412–13; Durrwell, *La Résurrection de Jésus: Mystère de Salut,* 22; Johnson, *Living Jesus,* 34; Meyer, *The Aims of Jesus,* 61, 64, 66; Lapide, *Resurrection of Jesus,* 91; Rowan Williams, *Resurrection: Interpreting the Easter Gospel* (London: Darton, Longman and Todd, 1982), 7–11; Barnabas Lindars, "The Apocalyptic Myth and the Death of Christ," *Bulletin of the John Rylands University Library of Manchester* 57 (1975): 367–68; Craig, *Assessing,* 36–38; Matthew Brook O'Donnell, "Some New Testament Words for Resurrection and the Company they Keep," in *The Resurrection,* 138; Francis Schüssler Fiorenza, "The Resurrection of Jesus and Roman Catholic Fundamental Theology," in *The Resurrection,* 225–26; Drane, *Introducing the New Testament,* 99; Joost Holleman, *Resurrection and Parousia: A Traditio-Historical Study of Paul's Eschatology in 1 Corinthians 15* (Leiden, Netherlands: E. J. Brill, 1996), 141; Barnett, *Jesus and the Logic of History,* 29; Donald Goergen, *The Death and Resurrection of Jesus: A Theology of Jesus* (Wilmington, Del.: Michael Glazier, 1988), 2:233; Lawrence S. Cunningham, book review in *Commonweal* 125 (1998): 27–28; M. Gourges, *À La Droite de Dieu: Résurrection de Jésus et Actualisation du Psaume 110:1 dans in Noveau Testament* (Paris: J. Gabalda et Cie Editeurs, 1978), esp. 169–78. Two older works with well-researched conclusions are Dodd, *Apostolic Preaching,* 17–31; and Max Wilcox, *The Semitisms of Acts* (Oxford: Clarendon Press, 1965), esp. 79–80, 164–65. Hemer's volume above has some similar research aims.

124. O'Collins, *Interpreting Jesus,* 109–10.

125. Drane, *Introducing the New Testament,* 99.

126. Maier, *In the Fullness of Time,* 197.

127. In my study of more than fourteen hundred recent scholarly sources on the resurrection, mentioned above, I have cataloged twenty-three arguments for the empty tomb, including some that overlap. More than one hundred contemporary scholars accept one or more of these arguments. About thirty-five scholars accept one or more of the arguments against the empty tomb. (Of course, many of the other sources do not even address this particular aspect.)

128. Grant, *Jesus,* 176.

129. Dunn, *The Evidence for Jesus,* 68.

130. Thomas Torrance, *Space, Time and Resurrection* (Grand Rapids, Mich.: Eerdmans, 1976), 189–90.

131. See Mt 26:56, 69–74; Mk 14:50, 66–72; Lk 22:55–72; Jn 18:25–27.

132. Examples of their transformation are found in Acts 2:41–47; 4:1–4, 8–21, 29–31; 5:17–32, 40–42. 1 Cor 15:9–11 is one Pauline report on the apostles' ministry.

1 Tm 3:16 records another early confession regarding the apostolic preaching. The apostles' willingness to die is seen in Jn 21:18–19; Acts 7:57–60, 12:1–3, 21:13, 25:11; Rom 14:8; 1 Cor 15:30–32; 2 Cor 4:7–14, 11:23–32; Phil 1:20–24; cf. 2 Pt 1:13–15. The martyrdom of Peter and Paul are mentioned in Clement of Rome (*Corinthians* 5), while somewhat differing accounts of Jesus's brother James's martyrdom are given by both Josephus (*Antiquities* 20:9:1) and Hegesippus (recorded in Eusebius, *Ecclesiastical History* 2:23). The martyrdom of John's brother James, Peter, and Paul are also included in Eusebius (*Ecclesiastical History* 2:9, 2:25).

133. See Christian testimonies in Clement of Rome (*Corinthians* 42) and Ignatius (*Smyrneans* 3 and *Barnabas* 5). Secular reports are found in Tacitus (*Annals* 15:44) and the disputed citation by Josephus (*Antiquities* 18:3); such a report is implied in Mara Bar-Serapion's letter (in the British Museum).

134. Michael Grant, *Saint Peter: A Biography* (New York: Scribner, 1994), 96.

135. N. T. Wright, *Jesus and the Victory of God*, vol. 2 of *Christian Origins and the Question of God* (Minneapolis: Fortress Press, 1996), 659.

136. Meyer, *The Aims of Jesus*, 60.

137. Johnson, *Living Jesus*, 6.

138. Staudinger, "Resurrection of Jesus Christ," 321.

139. Elliott, "The First Easter," 210.

140. Meyer, *The Aims of Jesus*, 68. See also Hans-Werner Bartsch, "Inhalt und Funktion des Urchristlichen Osterglaubens," *New Testament Studies* 26 (1980): 180.

141. N. T. Wright, *Who Was Jesus?* (Grand Rapids, Mich.: Eerdmans, 1992), 34.

142. Dunn, *The Evidence for Jesus*, 67; also in agreement are Robinson, *Can We Trust*, 123; Maier, *In the Fullness of Time*, 200; Paul Maier, "The Empty Tomb as History," *Christianity Today* 19 (1975): 4–6.

143. Cranfield, "The Resurrection of Jesus Christ," 170.

144. The institution of the Christian church was founded on the resurrection (Mt 28:18–20; Lk 24:45–49; Acts 1:4–8). Further, that Sunday has been the Christian day of worship ever since the early church (1 Cor 16:1–2; Acts 20:7) needs to be explained, especially considering that the first Christians were monotheistic Jews, accustomed to worshiping on Saturday. Sunday was a commemoration of the day of resurrection (Mk 16:1–2; 1 Cor 15:3–4).

145. Both quotations are from Fuller, *Foundations of New Testament Christology*, 142 (emphasis added).

146. Dunn, *The Evidence for Jesus*, 75.

147. Lapide, *Resurrection of Jesus*, esp. 125–28.

148. Even a sampling of the dozens of recent critical scholars who believe that Jesus's disciples had real experiences that led them to conclude that they saw appearances of the risen Jesus, whether or not the resurrection actually occurred, would be massive. Such a survey, including quite a number of highly skeptical scholars, might include: Koester, *Introduction to the New Testament*, 2:84; Goulder, "The Baseless Fabric," 48; Borg, "Thinking about Easter," 15; Crossan, *Jesus*, 190; Funk, *Honest to Jesus*, 40, 266; Hoover, "A Contest," 131, 92–97, 111, 141; Rudolf Pesch,

"Zur Entstehung des Glaubens an die Auferstehung Jesu: Ein neuer Versach," *Freiburger Zeitschrift für Philosophie und Theologie* 30 (1983): 87; Anton Vögtle in Vögtle and Rudolf Pesch, *Wie kam es zum Osterglauben?* (Düsseldorf, Germany: Patmos-Verlag, 1975), 85–98; John Galvin, "Resurrection as *Theologia Crucis Jesu*: The Foundational Christology of Rudolf Pesch," *Theological Studies* 38 (1977): 521–23; Conzelmann, *Corinthians*, 258–66; Perrin, *The Resurrection*, 80–83; Lüdemann, *The Resurrection of Jesus*, 37, 50, 66; Kent, *Psychological Origins*, 18–19; James Keller, "Response to Davis," *Faith and Philosophy* 7 (1990): 114; Hans Werner Bartsch, "Inhalt und Funktion des Urchristlichen Osterglaubens," *New Testament Studies* 26 (1980): 180, 194–95; James M. Robinson, "Jesus from Easter to Valentinus (or to the Apostles' Creed)," *Journal of Bibilical Literature* 101 (1982): 8, 20; Wells, *Did Jesus Exist?* 32, 207; Martin, *The Case against Christianity*, 83, 90; Spong, *Resurrection*, 51–53, 173; Sheehan, *The First Coming*, 91; Elliott, "The First Easter," 209–10, 220; Wedderburn, *Beyond Resurrection*, 47, 188; Karl Rahner, *Foundations of Christian Faith: An Introduction to the Idea of Christianity*, trans. William V. Dych (New York: Seabury Press, 1978), 265, 277; Wolfhart Pannenberg, "Die Auferstehung Jesu: Historie und Theologie," *Zeitschrift für Theologie und Kirche* 91 (1994): 320–23; Moltmann, *Theology of Hope*, 172–73; Brown, *Virginal Conception*, 125–29; Dunn, *The Evidence for Jesus*, 75; Johnson, *The Real Jesus*, 136; Kasper, *Jesus the Christ*, 124–25; Davis, *Risen Indeed*, 182; Staudinger, "Resurrection of Jesus Christ," 312, 318–20; Cranfield, "The Resurrection of Jesus Christ," 169; Williams, *Resurrection*, 97, 117–19; Alsup, *Post-Resurrection Appearance Stories*, 274; Fuller, *Formation of the Resurrection Narratives*, 47–49, 181; Jacob Kremer, *Die Osterevangelien—Geschichten um Geschichte*, 2nd ed. (Stuttgart, Germany: Verlag Katholisches Bibelwerk, 1981), esp. 153–55; Meyer, *The Aims of Jesus*, 60; Meier, *A Marginal Jew*, 3:70, 235, 252; Sanders, *The Historical Figure of Jesus*, 10–13, 278–80; Wright, "Christian Origins," 118; Joseph Doré, "Croire en la Résurrection de Jésus-Christ," *Études* 356 (1982), 532; Fiorenza, "Resurrection of Jesus," 238, 243–47; O'Collins, *Jesus Risen*, 118–19; Craig, *Assessing*, esp. part 3; Robinson, *Can We Trust?* 120–27; Philip Jenkins, *Hidden Gospels: How the Search for the Historical Jesus Lost its Way* (New York: Oxford University Press, 2001), 78; Grant, *Jesus*, 176; Drane, *Introducing the New Testament*, 101–4; Charles Austin Perry, *The Resurrection Promise* (Grand Rapids, Mich.: Eerdmans, 1986), 4; Lindars, "Resurrection and the Empty Tomb," in *The Resurrection of Jesus Christ*, 127; Lapide, *Resurrection of Jesus*, 125–28; Samuel, "Making Room," 108–10; Hansjürgen Verweyen, "Die Ostererscheinungen in fundamentaltheologischer Sicht," *Zeitschrift für Katholische Theologie* 103 (1981): 429; Lorenzen, *Resurrection and Discipleship*, 123, 130–32; Goergen, *Death and Resurrection*, 127–28, 261; William P. Loewe, "The Appearances of the Risen Lord: Faith, Fact, and Objectivity," *Horizons* 6 (1979): 190–91; Kee, *What Can We Know?* 1–2, 23, 86, 113; Witherington, "Resurrection Redux," 131–32; John Pilch, "Appearances of the Risen Jesus in Cultural Context," *Biblical Theology Bulletin* 28 (1998): 59; Adrian Thatcher, "Resurrection and Rationality," in *The Resurrection of Jesus Christ*, 180; Traugott Holtz, "Kenntnis von Jesus und Kenntnis Jesu: Eine Skizze zum Verhältnis zwischen historisch-philologisher Erkenntnis und historisch-theologischem Verständnis," *Theologische Literaturzeitung* 104 (1979): 10; Peter Stuhlmacher, *Was geschah auf Golgatha? Zur Heilsbedeutung von Kreuz, Tod und Auferweckung Jesu* (Stuttgart, Germany: Calwer Verlag, 1998), 58–64.

149. I say "arbitrarily" because, to my knowledge, no scholar grants *only* these facts. Thus, I am reducing the grounds without being asked or required by any scholar to do so.

150. For many details along with relevant sources, see the summarized discussion of Jesus's death above.

151. In our earlier discussion of evidences, we separated the various components of these experiences. The strongest arguments for the disciples' experiences are based on (a) the major pre-Pauline creed(s) in I Cor 15:3ff. and (b) the other Pauline passages just mentioned above, which contribute to many of the arguments that were presented earlier in this chapter. (c) Other crucial material supporting these experiences is found in the early traditions embedded in the preaching texts in Acts 1:1–11; 2:32; 3:15; 5:30–32; 10:39–43; 13:30–31; 17:2–3, 30–31. Two other creeds that report the resurrection appearances are Lk 24:34 and 2 Tm 2:8. (d) The Gospel narratives are found in Mk 16:1–8; Mt 28:9–20; Lk 24:13–51; and Jn 20:14–21:23. Several of these individual resurrection texts receive important critical attention. For example, most scholars think that Mark's is the earliest and most authoritative Gospel and hold that Mark ended his text at 16:8. Still, it is clear that Mark knew of Jesus's appearances, as is evident from the predictions of this event (8:31; 9:9, 31; 10:33–34; 14:27–28), the angelic report of Jesus's resurrection, the empty tomb, and the mention of Peter, along with the projected appearance in Galilee, which is tied back to 14:28 (16:4–7). (e) Much less evidential but still helpful material is found in the noncanonical Christian accounts of Clement of Rome (*Corinthians* 42), Ignatius (*Smyrneans* 3), and Justin Martyr (*First Apology* 50). (f) A much-debated non-Christian text that refers to Jesus's appearances is Josephus's *Antiquities* 18:3. An intriguing hint about the Christian teachings that emerged after Jesus's execution is found in Tacitus (*Annals* 15:44). Gnostic writings that theologize about the resurrection include *The Gospel of Truth* (25:25–34) and *The Treatise on Resurrection* (44:27–29; 45:14–23; 46:14–21; 48:10–19). Insinuations regarding Jesus's postdeath exaltation are located in *The Gospel of Thomas* (45:15–17) and *The Apocryphon of John* (1:5–12).

152. Details and sources are provided in the discussion of this point in the previous section.

153. John Meier states, "from the very beginning of Christian preaching about Jesus . . . [t]here was no period when" this teaching did not include Jesus's "life, death, and resurrection" (*A Marginal Jew*, 1:118). N. T. Wright asserts similarly: "there is no evidence for a form of early Christianity in which the resurrection was not a central belief" ("Christian Origins," 117). Fuller proclaims, "There was no period" when it was not the central proclamation (*Formation of the Resurrection Narratives*, 48).

154. For example, see Koester, *Introduction to the New Testament*, 2:103–4; Drane, *Introducing the New Testament*, 250–51, 288–89.

155. Koester, *Introduction to the New Testament*, 2:164–171; Drane, *Introducing the New Testament*, 181–84.

156. For details, see the discussion of James's conversion in the previous section above.

157. For example, it has been suggested that his persecution of Christians caused Paul overwhelming guilt, driving him to convert to Christianity. But the *evidence* for such remorse is severely lacking. (1) Paul's own testimony is that he performed this persecution with zeal (κατὰ ζῆλος), being faultless (γενόμενος ἄμεμπτος) regarding the Law (Phil 3:6; cf. Acts 22:3). In Gal 1:14, Paul described his persecution of believers as being exceptionally zealous (περισσοτέρως ζηλωτὴς). (2) Further, guilt would be a very weak explanation for Paul's unyielding Christian conviction, even to the death. In light of his former zeal and exceptionally potent training in Judaism, one would expect some sort of backlash against his recently developed Christian convictions, not an ongoing remorse lasting throughout his life. Yet, there is no sign that Paul doubted his conversion, considered reverting to Judaism, or ever questioned the reason for his initial remorse. (3) All the data we have points away from such a thesis. There is little need to respond to natural theses that fail to provide any evidence.

It has also been suggested that Paul suffered a hallucination, especially since his companions in the Acts accounts neither saw Jesus (9:7) nor understood the words of the voice (22:9). (1) But such an approach, which lists only subjective elements, ignores the objective references in the very same accounts. Paul's companions heard the voice, although apparently without comprehension (9:7), they clearly saw the light (22:9; cf. 26:13), and they responded by falling down, as did Paul (26:14). Moreover, the light blinded Paul for three days (9:8–9; 22:11). Why focus on the more subjective elements while disregarding the other factors found in the same texts? These latter factors cannot be dismissed without sacrificing the claim of subjective components. The more objective manifestations in the real world argue strongly against hallucinations, which are characterized by "perceptions" without corresponding objective or veridical referents. These accounts do not fit the definition.

There are other serious problems with such a hallucination thesis. (2) Since there is no textual basis for Paul's remorse, there is also a decided lack of any psychological preconditioning for a hallucination. In brief, it is very difficult to imagine why Paul would have either desired to forsake his deep and pious roots in Judaism or yearned to come face–to–face with the glorified Jesus, in whom he did not believe in the first place! (3) To the contrary, what we *do* know about Paul is that his conversion has indications of a direct act of God: an undeniably powerful commitment to Jesus Christ that apparently ended in martyrdom, no evidence of any reexamining his faith or recanting, along with a complete assurance that Jesus had appeared to him and many others, so that he based his faith on the resurrection (1 Cor 15:12–20, 30–32).

(4) Paul reports that Jesus was seen by five hundred people at once (1 Cor 15:6), so he plainly does not think Jesus appeared in a manner that was characterized by subjective elements. This challenge also fails to adequately address (5) the other

appearances to Jesus's disciples, complete with all of the varied details; (6) the empty tomb, where Jesus's body should still be located if hallucinations occurred; or (7) James's conversion. For other details regarding Paul's conversion, see the discussion in the previous section above.

158. Koester, *Introduction to the New Testament*, 1:176–91. Pannenberg concludes: "Under such circumstances it is an idle venture to make parallels in the history of religions responsible for the *emergence* of the primitive Christian message about Jesus's resurrection" (*Jesus: God and Man*, 91). A definitive work on the dating of the pagan stories is Günther Wagner, *Das religionsgeschichtliche Problem von Römer 6, 1–11* (Zürich: Zwingli Verlag, 1962), especially Wagner's excellent summary in part 3, sections A–B. For a scholarly bibliography on the entire subject, see Hildegard Temporini and Wolfgang Haase, comp., *Aufstieg und Niedergang der römischen Welt: Geschichte und Kultur Roms im Spiegel der neuren Forschung*, updated by Bruce M. Metzger (Berlin: Walter de Gruyter, 1984), esp. 1398–419.

159. Other critiques emerge from our longer list of critically acknowledged facts, especially the evidence for the empty tomb, which legends fail to explain. The centrality of the resurrection message and the lack of Jewish response are also relevant. For an explication of various versions, along with a host of problems for this naturalistic hypothesis, see Habermas, *Resurrection of Jesus: A Rational Inquiry*, 146–71.

160. John Riches correctly warns that agreeing to the historicity of facts does not guarantee the interpretations of those facts (*A Century of New Testament Study* [Valley Forge, Pa.: Trinity Press International, 1993], 115–24).

161. Sanders, *The Historical Figure of Jesus*, 10–13; cf. 280.

162. Fuller, *Formation of the Resurrection Narratives*, 2, 169, 181–82.

163. Fuller, *Foundations of New Testament Christology*, 143.

164. Dunn, *The Evidence for Jesus*, 75.

165. These six facts are so widely accepted by critical scholars that even a survey would involve an enormous undertaking. We will simply list here over fifty New Testament specialists, theologians, historians, and philosophers in recent decades who hold (or strongly imply) each of the facts: Bultmann, *Theology of the New Testament*, 1:44–46, 52, 60, 80–83; Tillich, *Systematic Theology*, 2:153–58; John Hick, *Death and Eternal Life* (Louisville, Ky.: Westminster John Knox Press, 1994), 171–77; Bornkamm, *Jesus of Nazareth*, 179–86; Koester, *Introduction to the New Testament*, 2:84–86, 100; Barth, *Church Dogmatics*, vol. 4, part 1, 334–36, 351–53; Emil Brunner, *Dogmatics*, 3 vols., trans. Olive Wyon (Philadelphia: Westminster Press, 1950–79), 2:363–78; Moltmann, *Theology of Hope*, 165–66, 172, 197–202; C. H. Dodd, "Appearances of the Risen Christ," 124–25, 131–33; Perrin, *Resurrection according to Matthew, Mark, and Luke*, 78–84; Robinson, *Can We Trust?* 113–29; Fuller, *Formation of the Resurrection Narratives*, 27–49; Grant, *Jesus*, 174–79; Pannenberg, *Jesus: God and Man*, 88–106; Wilckens, *Resurrection*, 6–16, 112–14; Jeremias, "Easter," 300–311; Werner Georg Kümmel, *The Theology of the New Testament: According to its Major Witnesses: Jesus—Paul—John* (Nashville: Abingdon Press, 1973), 102–5; Brown, *Virginal Conception*, 80–82, 128; Goppelt, "Easter Kerygma," 35–37, 43–53;

Elaine Pagels, *The Gnostic Gospels* (New York: Random House, 1979), 3–12; Marcus Barth and Verne H. Fletcher, *Acquittal by Resurrection* (New York: Holt, Rinehart and Winston, 1964), part 1 (Barth), 11–15, 37–39; Paul Van Buren, *The Secular Meaning of the Gospel: Based on an Analysis of its Language* (New York: Macmillan, 1963), 126–34; Wand, *Christianity*, 51, 59, 84, 93, 108; Hunter, *Jesus: Lord and Saviour*, 98–107; Ramsey, *The Resurrection of Christ*, 35–45; W. T. Jones, *A History of Western Philosophy*, 5 vols, 2nd ed., (New York: Harcourt Brace Jovanovich, 1969), 2:34–35, 39; Ladd, *I Believe in the Resurrection*, 36–43, 93, 109–11; Daniel Fuller, *Easter Faith and History* (Grand Rapids, Mich.: Eerdmans, 1965), 208–29; Thielicke, "The Resurrection Kerygma," 59–62, 86–91; Osborne, *The Resurrection Narratives*, 231–33, 276–77, 281–88; Perkins, *Resurrection*, 84–95, 196–210; Kee, *What Can We Know?* 1–2, 21–23, 60–61, 85–86, 90; Lapide, *Resurrection of Jesus*, 91–99, 125–31; Sheehan, *The First Coming*, 101–18; Barnett, *Jesus and the Logic of History*, 115–34, 159–61; Craig, *Assessing*, 36–38, 53–82, 163–96, 379–420; Sanders, *The Historical Figure of Jesus*, 10–13, 125–26, 133–36, 277–81; O'Collins, *Jesus Risen*, 99–147; Johnson, *The Real Jesus*, 110–22, 133–36; Spong, *Resurrection: Myth or Reality?* 47–56, 239–43, 255–60; Drane, *Introducing the New Testament*, 77–107; Funk, *Honest to Jesus*, 33–40, 260, 267–75; Murray Harris, *Raised Immortal: Resurrection and Immortality in the New Testament* (Grand Rapids, Mich.: Eerdmans, 1983), 5–11, 60; Lüdemann, *What Really Happened to Jesus*, 9–17, 102–5, 125–34; Lorenzen, *Resurrection and Discipleship*, 131–36, 141–44, 184–87; Clark, *Interpreting the Resurrection*, 89–101; Maier, *In the Fullness of Time*, 164–88, 204–5; John Dominic Crossan, *The Historical Jesus: The Life of a Mediterranean Jewish Peasant* (San Francisco: Harper Collins, 1991), 372–75, 397–98; Crossan, *Jesus*, 135, 145, 154, 165, 190; Davis, *Risen Indeed*, 15, 177–85; Bart D. Ehrman, *Jesus: Apocalyptic Prophet of the New Millennium* (New York: Oxford University Press, 1999), 227–31; Meier, *A Marginal Jew*, 3:67–71, 146–47, 234–35, 251–52, 625; Wedderburn, *Beyond Resurrection*, 4–15, 47, 113–17, 188; Wright, *The New Testament*, 111, 353–54, 400–401; Wright, *Jesus and the Victory of God*, 109–12, 480, 487, 551–52, 659.

166. We will address the nature of the resurrection body in chapter 6.

CHAPTER TWO

A Theistic Universe

I concluded in chapter 1 that Jesus died and that, afterward, he was seen by several of his followers. But this is only the historical portion of the question. I have not inquired as to whether this event was a miracle, actually performed by God. In this chapter I address the issue of whether God raised Jesus. Does God even exist? Can it be argued that God raised Jesus from the dead? How might God be connected with this event? I propose an answer here that involves two different paths.

A Theistic Context

If it can be successfully argued that naturalism is insufficient as an explanation of the universe and that an explanation like theism, which incorporates an external intelligent source, is plausible, then it may also be rational to believe that the resurrection of Jesus was an act performed in accordance with God's attributes and will. If this is a theistic universe, then we might require even less direct evidence to affirm God's intervention in this or other historical occurrences, since miracles might follow, due to what we would know concerning the nature of the universe. I also pursue a second approach to this question later in the chapter.

My initial point is stated well by atheist philosopher Antony Flew: "Certainly given some beliefs about God, the occurrence of the resurrection does become enormously more likely."[1] Philosopher Richard Swinburne similarly argues that, from a theistic worldview, "one rightly does not ask much in the way of detailed historical evidence for a miracle since miracles are the kind of events which one expects to occur in many or certain specific circumstances."[2]

It should be carefully noted that it is *not* my intention to attempt to *prove* the existence of God in this chapter. In order to accomplish the first task in positing the likelihood of a theistic universe, I simply list some fruitful paths presently being pursued in philosophical discussions. I also look briefly at some recent scientific findings. Theism is a rational option. Interestingly, the positive treatment of theism is currently enjoying a widespread resurgence.[3] Far from being assumed, such a conclusion is the result of multiple lines of argumentation, which indicate that the universe is much more complicated than naturalists envisage. I examine a few of these avenues.

Knowing Truth: An Epistemic Objection

In his work *Miracles*, C. S. Lewis proposes more than one argument against naturalism. The best known of these is detailed in his chapter 3, entitled "The Cardinal Difficulty of Naturalism."[4] Here Lewis points out that all knowledge depends on the legitimacy of our reasoning processes. Unless human reason is trustworthy, no scientific conclusion can be regarded as true and, even further, we can never know whether any proposition is true or false. Since all knowledge relies on our ability to think rationally, we may state a rule: *"no thought is valid if it can be fully explained as the result of irrational causes."*[5]

The result is that human reason is valueless if it can be accounted for irrationally. Likewise, any philosophical worldview that postulates that the human mind is a result of irrational causes is also unacceptable, for there would be no such thing as knowledge. Yet naturalism holds that the human mind developed by chance. From this scenario, it follows that our thinking may be simply a motion of atoms, and we have no reason to believe that we think rationally. Further, naturalistic arguments aimed at disputing this position must assume the very point it opposes, namely, the reality of rational thought.

Since the universe could be totally irrational, derived from irrational causes, even what appears to be rational could be exactly the opposite. How could we ever know the difference? In fact, we could not *know* anything if we exist and think by chance. Naturalists must simply *assume* that they can acquire knowledge. In Lewis's words, naturalism "would have destroyed its own credentials. It would be an argument which proved that no argument was sound—a proof that there was no such things as proofs—which is nonsense."[6] Or as Lewis states later, "If the value of our reasoning is in doubt, you cannot try to establish it by reasoning."[7]

The naturalist could take a pragmatic view, claiming to simply do what works. But Lewis argues that this answer is a retreat from the original thesis that naturalism is the correct worldview.[8]

If irrational beginnings cannot produce rational thought—at least thought we can *know* is rational—yet we still know certain things, then our thinking must have a rational origin. The chief alternative is to deny altogether the possibility of rational thought. But as Lewis said, even arguments aimed at disproving his position *assume* the rationality of truth.[9] Further, even a response to Lewis's argument that the universe must then be irrational would admit that something is knowable. Few would care to deny having the ability to reason to knowable conclusions, and Lewis's argument is a thoughtful challenge.

Other contemporary philosophers agree concerning the force of such an argument. Richard Purtill writes: "So a mindless nature could produce mind only by chance. But if mind is only a chance product of nature, how can we trust our reasoning powers, how can we expect our minds to give us the truth about anything?"[10] Purtill concludes: "Similarly, the chance that intelligence was produced by a random process is so small. . . . [I]t is overwhelmingly more probable that mind will be produced by a previously existing mind than by a process such as evolution."[11]

Peter Kreeft and Ronald Tacelli also note a major problem with naturalism here. Even if it is true, "then it seems to leave us with no reason for *believing* it to be true; for all judgments could equally and ultimately be the result of nonrational forces."[12]

Stephen Parrish is perhaps the most forceful in his version of the "transcendental argument": "to have any valid thought at all . . . one must presuppose the validity of the mind's operation. . . . For if one's thoughts are merely a disconnected series of brute facts, then no reason exists to think that one can know the truth about anything, including that one's senses are delusory."[13] Parrish concludes "that the Brute Fact Theory . . . falls to the transcendental argument because its falsity must be presupposed in order for there to be any justification or validity in thought."[14]

Perhaps the most influential recent version of this argument is that of Alvin Plantinga. In "Is Naturalism Irrational?" Plantinga acknowledges the similarities of his version of the argument to that of C. S. Lewis.[15]

Regarding the nature of truth, and, more crucially, our ability to know it, naturalism fails to offer a context in which we may obtain knowledge. If naturalism were true, we could not even know it. And what is more central to a worldview than the ability to know truth? That naturalism fails such a test is our initial indication that it is not the best explanation of the nature of reality.

The Source of the Universe

One argument that has become very popular in recent years concerns a theistic universe along with some reflections on cosmological issues. The Kalam argument can be stated very briefly:

1. Whatever begins to exist has a cause.
2. The universe began to exist.
3. Therefore, the universe has a cause.[16]

Regarding the first premise, Kreeft and Tacelli point out, tongue in cheek, that, "Most people—outside of asylums and graduate schools—would consider it not only true, but certainly and obviously true."[17] Nonetheless, William Lane Craig and other philosophers have argued for the truth of this premise.[18]

Craig supports the second premise by providing four subpoints, two philosophical and two scientific. The two philosophical arguments are as follows: First, an actual infinite cannot exist. A series of events in time, without a beginning, would be an actual infinite. Such a series of events without beginning cannot exist. If it could, and if the universe were an actual infinite, then an infinite number of historical events would already have occurred. But such a conclusion certainly appears to be mistaken.

To indicate the unreasonable repercussions involved in accepting the existence of an actual infinite, several antinomies are often presented. A favorite involves the example of a library that contains an actual infinite number of books, each of them colored either red or black. In such a scenario, there would be as many black books as black and red books combined! Or again, the red books could all be withdrawn without altering the total number of volumes present![19]

Second, even if an actual infinite is possible, we cannot get there by successively adding members. For example, it is impossible to count to infinity, cross an infinitely large distance, or climb an infinite number of stairs, since another number could always be added. By the same reasoning, neither would a past number of historical events qualify as an infinite. Thus, a collection formed in this manner would be finite, not infinite.[20]

Craig also supplies two scientific reasons to support the second premise. First, many recent discoveries have indicated that the universe is expanding and that all of its matter came into being at the time of the Big Bang, perhaps fifteen billion years ago. Adhering to this scenario, or assigning any other date to the beginning of the universe, means that it is still a limited number of years old. Accordingly, the universe is finite and the second premise is upheld on scientific grounds.

Further, the Second Law of Thermodynamics provides another scientific indication that the universe is finite. As Moreland describes it: "Applied to the universe as a whole, the second law tells us that the universe is wearing down irreversibly." He concludes that, "the universe did not always exist."[21]

Naturalists often agree that the universe has a cause. However, the Kalam argument demands more than this admission. The "source" of the universe could not be the universe itself or some phase of it, since it all came into existence at a point in time. Hence, the naturalistic assumption that nature is all there is appears to be highly problematic.

To be sure, much discussion has taken place regarding the Kalam argument.[22] But it has also gained a significant number of adherents. Parrish concludes, from an inductive angle: "That this complex, all encompassing structure arose for no reason at all . . . seems completely unbelievable to me. Thus, Craig's argument, although not as strong as he believes, is nonetheless a powerful claim as the alternative is extremely implausible."[23]

Scientific Arguments against Naturalism

Another species of argument against naturalism seems to be gaining the most momentum today. This is a series of scientific arguments that, especially together, are taken by a large number of scholars to indicate that there is an orderly pattern, purpose, or information structure in nature as a whole, but particularly in human and other life-forms.

Human life is exceptionally complex, and on a number of fronts. For instance, the production of amino acids, proteins, and enzymes is not only absolutely necessary for human life, but must occur in a very precise order. If every single marker is not in the exact spot it must occupy, the final result fails to obtain. This is a far more complex matter than is often imagined. For example, atheistic astronomer Sir Fred Hoyle and agnostic mathematician Chandra Wickramasinghe studied enzyme development. What they discovered shook the scientific establishment. They found that the likelihood of spontaneous processes accounting for the chance formation of the information content in life, such as the development of enzymes, is only one chance in $10^{40,000}$! Since it is highly unlikely that spontaneous generation could account for life, it is much more likely that "life was assembled by an intelligence." These scientists concluded that, "Indeed, such a theory is so obvious that one wonders why it is not widely accepted as being self-evident. The reasons are psychological rather then scientific."[24]

Later, in a symposium, Hoyle said that there was simply not enough time in the history of the universe for the evolution of life. He compared the chances of higher life-forms evolving to the chances that "a tornado sweeping through a junk-yard might assemble a Boeing 747 from the materials therein." Further, Hoyle stated that he could not understand why biologists would want to deny this.[25]

Likewise, Wickramasinghe reports: "All that I am sure about is that life could not have happened on earth spontaneously." He also confesses that, through his research, he accepted a theological answer, turning to theism.[26]

Even more incredible is the amount of information contained in DNA. Scientist Robert Gange explains that "270 million of these hemoglobin protein molecules of just the right combination reside in *each* of the 30 trillion red blood cells in your body. Did this just happen by chance? Some people have enough faith to believe that it did. . . . But where is the evidence that this system came into being by chance? There is none!"[27]

Gange adds that the amount of information found even in the DNA of an amoeba exceeds what is contained in great libraries! So we cannot be satisfied simply with the naturalist's contention that, contrary to all of the probabilities, we must have gotten here by chance. Simply "getting here" is insufficient. It is not a case of "poof" and we happened to have exactly the right conditions, resulting in the appearance of a one-celled organism. When life began, even for an amoeba, it was necessary that its DNA be encoded with more information than what is found in the library at Harvard University. Gange argues: "But the irrefutable fact is that information theory and the data from electron microscopy, when applied to living cells, force the conclusion that they have been *designed*. Why do they force the conclusion? Because they are jampacked with information that cannot be logically explained as the issue of natural processes within this universe." Combining this with other scientific data, Gange concludes that: "The logical answer is that [the universe] came from a Supreme Intelligence."[28]

Biochemist Michael Behe takes a different angle. Arguing in the area of cell design, he notes the presence of "irreducible complexity" whenever a cell has a number of interrelated portions, where subtracting any one portion would demolish the cell's function. The point here is that no gradual shift, growth, or adaptation of the cell is possible, since all elements must work together in order for the system to function. As Behe says, "it would have to arise as an integrated unit, in one fell swoop."[29]

Information-theory pioneer Hubert Yockey's research provides additional scientific evidence for these conclusions. In a landmark study of observed complexity in relation to naturalistic evolution of the earliest forms of life, Yockey concludes that the required amount of information is far too great and the time far too brief: "This is much too short to code a living system so evolution to higher forms could not get started. Geological evidence for the 'warm little pond' is missing. It is concluded that belief in currently accepted scenarios of spontaneous biogenesis is based on faith, contrary to conventional wisdom."[30] Further, he states that a naturalistic scenario "was invented *ad hoc* to serve as a materialistic reductionist explanation of the origin of life. It is unsupported by any other evidence and it will remain *ad hoc* until such evidence is found."[31]

Harvard University astronomer Owen Gingerich notes, "The amount of genetic information contained in the DNA in every cell of our bodies is so awesome that many distinguished scientists," like Francis Crick and Fred Hoyle, reject the notion that DNA could have evolved during Earth's five-billion-year history. Hoyle thinks that the only way to explain the data is by referring to "a super-intelligence." Gingerich concludes, "Compared to the human brain, stars are utterly trivial. So there are empirical reasons to suppose that the universe was designed and created for us."[32]

All of these discoveries have significantly changed the scientific landscape during the last few decades. But the research has been moving so quickly that scholars have seldom stopped to reflect systematically on these findings. Taking the next step, philosopher and mathematician William Dembski recently devised a means of testing whether intelligent design is present in a particular scientific process. He argues that "intelligent design provides the most effective challenge to naturalism to date." This is so, he asserts, because "God's design is also accessible to scientific inquiry."[33] On the other hand, Darwinian and other evolutionary theories are not well supported scientifically, and their empirical basis is "weak," "a metaphysical ideology with no empirical backing."[34]

Dembski proposes the application of two empirical tests in order to ascertain whether intelligent design is present in areas such as those that I have mentioned. These tests are complexity and specification, or "specified complexity."[35] Design can be detected when we have highly improbable, complex occurrences that also exhibit a highly identifiable, specified pattern. These tests are very similar to well-recognized methods that are used regularly in special sciences such as forensic science, artificial intelligence, cryptography, and archaeology. In these cases, testing is formulated to detect intelligent causes, which are identified by the presence of information, or more correctly, "informational pathways induced by intelligent causes." These tests are fully scientific, and can "demonstrate design rigorously" in terms of the information, unlike attempts to develop a natural theology.[36] Dembski applies his tests to Behe's instances of "irreducible complexity," and states that, according to "any formal complexity-theoretic analysis, they are complex in the sense required by the complexity-specification criterion."[37]

How do these findings apply to evolutionary models? Dembski charges that a number of "problems have proven utterly intractable not only for the mutation-selection mechanism but also for any other undirected natural process proposed to date." He lists the following examples: the origin of life, the genetic code, multicellular life, sexuality, the scarcity of fossil transition forms, the Cambrian explosion of life, complex organ systems, and "irreducibly complex molecular machines."[38]

Dembski's goal, then, is to establish theoretical, scientific guidelines by which to test alleged cases of teleology, using a criterion that is similar to that utilized in other information-seeking sciences. Behe comments: "before Dembski, rationally justifying a conclusion of intelligent design was an awkward, tentative affair. Elegant tools make us all feel smarter. Dembski invented the tools."[39]

Scientific teleological arguments aimed at both critiquing the shortcomings of naturalism and establishing theism are presently very popular. They vary widely in format as well as claims,[40] and might even be combined to provide more force.

Near-Death Experiences

The phenomena of near-death experiences (NDEs) may furnish another sort of substantial challenge to naturalism by demonstrating that some notion of life after death is probably a reality. Many thousands of persons have claimed that they remained conscious while their bodies hovered close to death. Some of these survivors later described some rather surrealistic scenes, frequently involving supernatural beings. But I am not interested here in the vast majority of these assertions.

My concern is with the many well-documented reports of individuals who have provided accurate descriptions of their surroundings while they were in a near-death state. In these cases, an extraordinary number of details were reported from the physical world, many of which were later verified. These reports include accurate descriptions of medical procedures (some of which were quite abnormal), the surroundings, and even clothing, jewelry, and minute details of conversations. Surprisingly, many accounts correctly report details from outside the immediate area, even miles away!

Some patients reported corroborated information that occurred while the individuals did not even have brain wave activity or a heartbeat. On certain rare occasions, the absence of EKG and EEG readings, as long as hours in duration, was measured during the time when corroborated details were reported. Still other instances involved persons who were blind, many from birth or immediately afterward, who mentioned visual details, even from beyond their immediate location, that were later confirmed. After the experiences, they continued to be sightless.[41]

One specific instance concerns a thirty-five-year-old woman who underwent surgery for a brain aneurysm. During the surgery, it was determined that an extraordinary secondary medical procedure nicknamed "standstill" was necessary. The blood was drained from her head, her body was cooled down to sixty degrees, her heart was purposely stopped, and her brain waves totally flattened. Cardiologist Michael Sabom attests that her brain was dead, as indicated by three different medical tests—a silent EEG, no brain-stem response, and an absence of blood in the brain. She was in this latter state for over an hour. After surgery, she reported an amazing array of details regarding about a half dozen points, including both occurrences and their timing, that were later corroborated from the medical records kept during the operation. Then she claimed to have visited a heavenly location where she had discussions with several deceased relatives. On an NDE Scale developed by University of Virginia psychiatrist Bruce Greyson, she scored what Sabom termed "an amazing depth" of NDE experience.[42]

Cardiologist Fred Schoonmaker made an eighteen-year study of twenty-three hundred cases of patients who had cardiac arrests. Of these, fourteen hundred persons reported rather typical NDEs. But this study also included seventy to seventy-five cases in which patients who were resuscitated from cardiac arrests later reported NDEs even though they had registered "flat" EEG readings, sometimes for exceptionally long periods of time, lasting from thirty minutes to three hours! Schoonmaker noted that many of these latter patients reported observable events that were corroborated by others.[43]

It is these evidenced NDE reports that are the most intriguing. Incredibly, some skeptics admit their inability to explain them in natural terms, and a few naturalists have even recognized the possibility of an afterlife due to this sort of evidence. Atheist philosopher A. J. Ayer is one of the many who himself experienced an NDE, but he could not explain it within his materialistic framework: "On the face of it, these experiences, on the assumption that the last one was veridical, are rather strong evidence that death does not put an end to consciousness."[44] Another prominent atheist philosopher, Antony Flew, not only confesses his inability to explain evidenced NDE reports, but admits some of their evidential value. He states: "For they certainly constitute impressive evidence of the possibility of the occurrence of human consciousness independent of any occurrences in the human brain. . . . [T]his evidence equally certainly weakens if it does not completely refute my argument against doctrines of a future life."[45]

NDEs are one of several types of evidence currently assaulting naturalistic thinking. If these experiences indicate some strong evidence for an after-life,[46] then this is another, rather specific, dilemma for a naturalistic world-view, which finds it difficult to fit such data into its belief system. Ayer and Flew seem to realize this.

Other arguments against naturalism or in favor of theism could be fruit-fully pursued, such as versions of the ontological argument by Alvin Plantinga and others,[47] or the much-cited anthropic principle.[48] If Richard Swinburne is right, perhaps a cumulative inductive approach that utilizes a number of arguments for theism can also be shown to be probable.[49]

Many scholars, by various means, have implied or even declared that we are on the verge of a new day in philosophy, theology, history, and even sci-ence. It has been asserted that naturalism is at least on the run, if not on the way out. One interdisciplinary volume dedicated to the growing failure of naturalism produced a series of interviews with twenty-five of the world's most influential scientists, philosophers, and theologians.[50] There is per-haps no better example than the revolution in philosophy occasioned by the full-orbed approaches of Alvin Plantinga, Richard Swinburne, and many other scholars.[51] Plantinga attests, "I think there is a definite shift towards theism" in recent philosophy.[52] In the last chapter we saw that the vast majority of critical scholars not only admit the minimal historical facts that lead to such a strong case for the resurrection of Jesus, but a startling number of them accept in some sense the reality of Jesus's appearances. In recent scientific research, Dembski even goes so far as to say, "Naturalism is the intellectual pathology of our age. It artificially constricts the life of the mind and shuts down inquiry into the transcendent. . . . Naturalism is the disease. Intelligent design is the cure. . . . [T]he tide has turned."[53] In particular, it might be said that "reality is in fact a much richer place than naturalism allows."[54]

The arguments mentioned in this chapter present a formidable case, at the very least, for the failure of naturalism. Some scholars have provided far more details than we could here, employing these or other arguments in order to additionally postulate the likelihood of theism. Together, these points argue for the ability to know truth, a creative source external to the universe, an intelligent designer for the sort of life we find, and an afterlife. These various steps move in the direction of theism. Further, if the resurrection of Jesus oc-curred, a theistic universe *might* be the most probable explanation: God at least *could have* raised Jesus from the dead. I return to this subject below and in the next chapter.

Two Contrasting Paradigms

I concluded in the first chapter that the resurrection of Jesus was a historical event. In this chapter I have argued that human knowledge, the existence of the universe itself, the complexity of life, and the reality indicated by near-death experiences all indicate the presence of intelligent design. From a variety of these and other arguments, then, it appears that we live in a theistic universe. Of course, many still argue that this same reality can best be explained by naturalism. Which of these two general options best explains the data?

One paradigm option dictates that Jesus's resurrection, human knowledge, the existence of the universe, the presence of life, evidenced NDEs, along with everything else in the universe, are all compatible with naturalism.[55] As such, God would not exist and all of these phenomena would have natural explanations. For example, the resurrection might be seen as a "freak event" of nature, a random occurrence.

Conversely, the other paradigm option dictates that the resurrection of Jesus occurred in a theistic universe that is further characterized by the possibility of knowledge, an ordered beginning, complex life, and life after death. As such, the resurrection most likely would be an orderly act of God, performed for the purpose of bringing about a specific goal. It would not be a random event, but would also be characterized by order, design, and purpose.

Admittedly, one or the other of these paradigm options is often *assumed* to be the correct scenario. Thus, instead of requiring that the question be solved by the known data, people often base their decision on assumptions.

For example, the naturalistic paradigm often assumes that God does not exist, that the universe and life within it are ultimately due to chance, and that miracles cannot occur. So, obviously, Jesus's resurrection does not provide any real significance. But this position is often presupposed in spite of any information that we may possess. Certain facts are ruled out in advance, apart from any investigation. As I have argued, such an approach is neither scientific nor historical.

Likewise, the theistic paradigm is also assumed by many. Some apparently think that Jesus's resurrection automatically indicates the truth of certain theological interpretations. Just because it is inexplicable, the event is quickly proclaimed a miracle, thereby involving supernatural activity. It is presupposed that God performed the event, simply because of its oddity. In short, God must have raised Jesus, since no one else could have done so.

The problem with such stances is that those who hold either paradigm often seem to *assume* their view. Perhaps we too seldom examine our own beliefs. Regarding the resurrection, for instance, many naturalists seem to think that its very "oddness" indicates that it is simply a freak, chance occurrence, or that it never happened at all. Conversely, theists often declare that this very same "oddness" demands God's intervention!

The major question in this entire impasse, of course, concerns the truth of the respective positions. Which one makes the most sense of the available data? Not surprisingly, I propose that the theistic paradigm is superior to the naturalistic paradigm. Rather than taking this as an assumed position, I argue that an investigation reveals that it makes the most sense by far of what we know. Two major, independent lines of argument will be presented to buttress this claim.

First, I have already made the point that material such as that presented earlier in this chapter argues that naturalism is probably incorrect. This worldview does not do the best job of explaining our most recent research. Additionally, this is most likely a theistic universe, as shown by many scholars beyond our survey in this chapter. The arguments mentioned earlier provide many indications that confirm these claims.

If this is an accurate assessment, indicating a created, orderly, and purposeful universe, then we may proceed to a further, *prospective* point. In a theistic universe, Jesus's resurrection was probably also a purposeful event, performed by a being with attributes (as indicated by research such as that mentioned above) that would most likely be required in order to perform such an event. For example, the resurrection would seem to require an enormous amount of both knowledge (omniscience?) and power (omnipotence?). The arguments that I pursued in this chapter indicate an ample supply of both. I maintain below that the resurrection was also an orderly event, occurring to a certain individual for a particular purpose. I have already made some observations regarding certain indicators that this is an orderly world. It seems that the resurrection, if it occurred, also would have proceeded from a supernatural being.

Given this scenario, Jesus's resurrection would provide some insightful direction in addressing another vexing question regarding the world religions. Not only could it be argued that theism would follow most directly from the resurrection, but there are perhaps some hints here in deciding which version of theism is best indicated by my data.

So my initial, prospective path begins with indications that naturalism is probably mistaken and that theism is most likely true. These indications include the ability to know truth, the existence of the universe, the exceptional complexity of life, and at least a minimal concept of an afterlife, as well as many additional arguments presented by other scholars, some of which we have mentioned briefly. The case for theism far exceeds anything that we could develop in this chapter. The next move progresses from this realization to the resurrection of Jesus, as an event that seems to require God's actions. These data are far more in accordance with the theistic paradigm option mentioned above. Therefore, arguing prospectively from the nature of the universe to God performing the resurrection of Jesus according to his attributes and for his purposes seems to provide the best context for this historical event.

A second, *retrospective* path will be pursued in detail in the next chapter; briefly, its direction is as follows. The brute fact of Jesus's resurrection alone *cannot* establish a worldview by itself, since it lacks any special, internal meaning. Historical facts are not self-interpreting. They require a context in order to achieve special significance. However, when events are coupled with other factors, meaning may ensue. For example, that a Roman military commander crossed a small river in northern Italy in 49 B.C. might seem rather insignificant, at least when taken in isolation. But new insight develops when it is understood in its context: Julius Caesar lead an army across the Rubicon River, which, against the background of Roman law, constituted an act of civil war.

Jesus's resurrection must also be placed in its own context. The context of the event, and especially details regarding the person who was raised, may provide additional, compelling reasons to accept the likelihood that this is a theistic universe. Some worldview implications might follow. Thus, the historical event of the resurrection in the context of the surrounding facts, especially regarding the person and message of Jesus, might just combine to indicate, from another angle, that the theistic paradigm option provides the most probable answer concerning the cause and purpose of this occurrence.

So what sort of context for the resurrection do we find? Again, this is the subject of the next chapter, but I can provide a few initial comments. According to the Gospels, Jesus claimed to be deity. He also taught a unique religious message, and claimed that he was obeying his Father in a very special sense. He even declared that eternal life awaited those who specifically believed and followed him.

But were these claims true? To verify them, the Gospels assert that Jesus performed miracles as signs of his credibility. We are even told that he identified his resurrection and predicted in advance that this event would be the ultimate vindication of his message and his own claim to deity. The sum of these teachings comprised Jesus's personal belief in Christian theism. It makes sense that Jesus was in the best position to interpret the meaning of this event. And he claimed that God's action in his resurrection would verify his teachings. We need to entertain at least the possibility that Jesus was correct: that this unique historical event combined with Jesus's unique claims might indicate that his theistic worldview was corroborated. But we will have to examine these details in greater depth in the next chapter.

While this second path does not begin with arguments against naturalism or in favor of a theistic universe, neither is the existence of God simply being assumed. Rather, beginning with Jesus's resurrection and viewing this event in the context of Jesus's person and message, it argues retrospectively that God's action in this event is the most likely explanation. Thus, while theism must be true as a prior condition, it is not being presupposed.

A quick overview will provide further details showing that the retrospective approach does not argue circularly to invoke God's existence. I place this entire discussion in the framework of a scenario in which two paradigms are set forth, each attempting to explain all of this data. I propose that we view what both naturalism and Christian theism teach concerning the universe, God, the resurrection of Jesus, Jesus's person and claims, life after death, and so on. Which paradigm is supported better by the data? My strategy does not assume either paradigm, but attempts to decide which one is better evidenced.

Further, the retrospective argument is somewhat similar to particular forms of the classical theistic arguments. It is perhaps closest to the inductive teleological argument, in that it concentrates on an overall, purposeful pattern of interworking events that converge in the person of Jesus. And just as teleological arguments need not assume or invoke God's existence in a circular fashion, neither does my approach here.[56]

Lastly, I hope to show in the next chapter that additional background data exist in order to provide a more expanded context for interpreting the resurrection. Such a result would make an even tighter case for Jesus's theistic worldview, also avoiding any prior assumption of theism. After all, if Jesus's resurrection confirmed his claims to be deity, then we have to look no further than this to discover a theistic universe.[57]

I began by arguing against naturalism and in favor of a theistic universe. I proceeded prospectively from God's existence to the resurrection, as an event that required God's attributes.

My second move is to retrospectively couple Jesus's resurrection with the context of his person and message, to see if it can be determined from another direction that God raised him. I only hinted at this latter approach, which awaits a detailed treatment in the next chapter. It is sufficient at this point to mention the possibility that there is enough data here that an interpretation could be advanced that establishes Jesus's theistic worldview.

The Resurrection and the Laws of Nature

A miracle is generally thought to have some relation to the laws of nature. A harsh way to describe this relationship is to define a miracle as a violation of these laws, brought about by the action of God or another supernatural agent.[58] But many prefer to say that miracles interfere with, or supercede, the laws of nature through a greater power.[59] How can it be ascertained that such an occurrence has actually interfered with the normal course of nature? Do we have some hints?

According to atheistic philosophers J. L. Mackie and Antony Flew, two conditions must obtain in order to show that a miracle has occurred. A particular event must have occurred, and it must be opposed to a known law of nature.[60] Obviously, these philosophers think that such a case would be difficult to demonstrate. I have already researched in some depth the first condition regarding the resurrection of Jesus. Here, I take the lead of these philosophers and ask whether such an event would be contrary to a known law of nature.[61]

Perhaps the clearest case of an event superseding the laws of nature would be a nonrepeatable occurrence that clearly counters an established law.[62] This is not to disparage examples that may happen more than once, for they could still constitute acts of God. The point here is that nonrepeatable phenomena are easier to evaluate.

In contrast, if events appear to violate a natural law but still happen regularly under similar circumstances, this probably indicates that a supposed law is not really a law of nature. Rather, if an occurrence can regularly be induced, this is a strong clue that the "law" needs either an adjustment or a wholesale change in order to account for the phenomena.

Returning to the possibility of a true miracle, the presence of a few criteria might be very indicative. It should be determined whether or not an occurrence truly counters a law of nature. Would an adjustment in the law provide an equitable solution? Does the event reoccur under similar circumstances?

Conversely, there may be some key indications that the original law correctly expresses the nature of reality. If the law clearly applies to all situations except one, this would argue that we might be on the right track. Or formulating a new or different law could be unworkable, due to the necessary qualifications and adjustments. In fact, in a case where the event strongly contradicts what is known about nature, revising or expanding the law in order to account for the particular occurrence may be virtually impossible.[63]

As criteria like these are satisfied, it becomes increasingly possible that an event could actually be a miracle. It might really constitute an interference with nature's laws. In short, the best case could be made for an event that is nonrepeatable, that definitely counters a law of nature, and that is the only known exception to the law. If no viable adjustments to the law could be formulated in order to allow for this deviation, then the case for the law having been superseded would grow even stronger.

After examining this issue regarding the laws of nature, Swinburne concludes by listing certain events as examples of occurrences that, if historical, could be called violations of the laws of nature. These would include the resurrection of someone who had been dead for a full day, water changing to wine without the addition of any chemicals or catalysts, or a person recovering from polio in one minute. "We know quite enough about how things behave to be reasonably certain that" such events do not happen in the physical world.[64] Similarly, R. F. Holland provides examples that he thinks answer the naturalists' concerns about miracles.[65] Even Mackie agrees that a resurrection from actual death would be a miracle.[66]

In this chapter I have taken a twofold look at Jesus's resurrection as a specific example of a miracle. I have argued prospectively from theism to this event, as well as hinting at the approach taken in the next chapter, which retrospectively combines this event with the person and teachings of Jesus in order to corroborate Jesus's theistic worldview.

In this section, I have added an additional point. The resurrection of Jesus also fares exceptionally well as an example of an actual interference with the laws of nature. In fact, it may even be the best historical example of such an event. Specifically, it fulfills the criteria set forth by Mackie and Flew. As far as we know, it was a nonrepeatable event.[67] Few would argue that such an event could occur without violating one of our most secure natural laws: An irreversible state of death cannot be reversed in order to allow a fully dead person to return to life by any natural means. And, as far as we know, Jesus's resurrection is the only well-evidenced exception to this law (especially if it occurred in a glorified body), which has otherwise claimed countless lives.

There does not appear to be any way to modify, adjust, or expand this law of death. That is why it is our greatest enemy. Neither can we substitute a new law in its place. But at the same time, we have seen that some events cannot be subsumed under any law. Jesus's resurrection seems to be just such an event. The dead simply do not rise by any natural means. Few natural laws are more universally recognized.

As I just hinted, the body in which Jesus rose from the dead may be a further indication that no natural law can be made to account for this event. Paul and others reported that Jesus returned in a supernatural body with powers that also transcended natural laws, including that of never having to die again. This was recorded in the same testimony that I examined in chapter 1. This separates Jesus's resurrection from resuscitations.[68]

To sum up briefly, the resurrection of Jesus would definitely be contrary to nature's laws. As far as we can tell, it was a nonrepeatable event, and appears to be the only well-evidenced, historical exception to these laws. Adjusting the laws or formulating new ones still would not make room for the resurrection. Further, we are told not only that Jesus rose again after his death, but that he also returned in an immortal body with new powers. Such a transformation would provide another strong indication that this was not a freak occurrence of nature, but an event performed by God. Intriguingly, although Hume refuses to believe that any resurrection has taken place, he admits that such an event would be a miracle, involving supernatural intervention.[69]

Some Objections

Some critics have addressed miracle-claims by proposing a variety of challenges. But they take a different approach from the naturalistic theories against the evidence for the resurrection, which are a posteriori in nature. In contrast, these more general objections to miracles are usually of an a priori nature, challenging miracles *before* the evidence is set forth. In other words, these critics raise objections to the very concept of miracles, almost ignoring any evidence that might be raised in their favor. In so doing they walk a narrow line between providing a priori *objections* and ongoing a priori *rejections* of such events. While the former are appropriate challenges, even Mackie and Flew reject the latter.[70]

Empirical Concerns

In the past, many of these objections took a variety of paths to support a strongly empirical stance that pitted what was perceived to be the scientific method against the historical or other alleged ways of evidencing miracle-claims. Usually arising from the older post-positivistic, analytic philosophical tradition, they shared the contention that we do not have scientific evidence for miracles.[71] For instance, it was claimed that scientific, lawful events are predictable, while miracles are not.[72] Similarly, while the laws of nature are repeatable, historical claims made in favor of miraculous events are not.[73] Or it was claimed that there was a conflict between the laws of nature and real exceptions to these laws.[74]

Such objections to miracles, based generally on the advantages of the scientific method, are misplaced. There are a variety of reasons why this is the case.

First, while the scientific method is an excellent means of learning, it suffers from serious limitations regarding its own inabilities.[75] For example, there are many areas of science that are both unpredictable as well as unrepeatable. Geology and paleontogy, like historical archaeology, chiefly rely on physical traces from events that cannot be reenacted in the laboratory. Biology studies living creatures, presenting very different problems for both prediction and repeatability. Contemporary physics involves all sorts of experimental conclusions that must rely on indeterminate probabilities rather than any knowledge of exact outcomes. Human error and even deception cannot be eliminated by the scientific method, either. Further, science must rely on the discipline of historical research, and could not survive without it, since scientific research is regularly built on the work of past scientists. So science makes many historical judgments. In short, while the scientific method is extremely useful in the pursuit of knowledge, it has many of the same limitations that history does. This is simply the nature of certain types of inductive research. But science per se presents no absolute barriers against supernatural events.

Second, arguably the chief reason for the fall of positivistic methodology is that the claim that truth is derived only from scientific methodology is self-refuting. The exclusive use of the scientific method cannot test the assertion that only science yields truth. Science can indicate the truth of many modern claims, but it cannot show that there is no knowledge apart from science. Actually, such a strict empirical claim is itself unscientific, since it cannot be tested. Similarly, to require predictability or repeatability of historical events makes the same error, since this assumes that these scientific standards not only obtain for science (which is highly problematic in itself), but are also a necessity for other disciplines. Once again, we find ourselves in the same predicament. The charge that levels these requirements cannot be demonstrated scientifically and therefore cannot be extended to other disciplines. Skewed scientific preferences cannot annul Napoléon's defeat at Waterloo! This species of empiricism cannot rule out miracle-claims, since it flunks its own test. If there are other paths to knowledge, it may just be that miracles are one of the items that might be known.

Third, there is little dispute regarding the necessity of historical investigation, and even strong philosophical empiricists readily embrace it as a means of obtaining knowledge. Prominent scholars like David Hume, Bertrand Russell, A. J. Ayer, and Antony Flew do not hesitate to acknowledge the value of historical inquiry.[76] Obviously, they do not accept the historicity of miraculous events. But we have seen that the evidence for the resurrection of Jesus is truly exceptional, even using only the minimal historical facts as accepted by skeptical scholars.[77] Therefore, this event should not be rejected without an investigation.

Fourth, I argued in chapter 1 that at least the *nonsupernatural* portion of a miracle-claim definitely *can* be investigated. It can be historically ascertained that Jesus died. It is also admitted by virtually all scholars that Jesus's followers thought that they saw him alive a brief time later. Scholars can readily examine these two historical facts, and then entertain the question of which hypothesis best fits the data that we know. Many argue that neither the scientist nor the historian has the proper tools for evaluating whether or not God was involved in this process. However, on the one hand, this would not prevent them from *believing* that God raised Jesus. On the other hand, philosophers and theologians are better equipped to evaluate the next step regarding God's involvement, based on other highly evidenced data that I address in chapter 3.

Fifth, in light of the excellent historical data supporting the historicity of Jesus's death and resurrection appearances, continued attempts to ignore this data without an investigation would appear to constitute an ongoing a priori rejection of the possibility that this may be the very information we need to answer the question. Scholars must not reject well-evidenced events simply because they do not fit their worldview. As I have already noted above, both Mackie and Flew object to such dismissals of the evidence, and Flew, for one, has discussed the material on more than one occasion.

Sixth, I should simply mention the possibility that if there are verifiable miracle-like occurrences *today*, this could increase the likelihood that past miracles may have occurred. While definitely not attempting to build a case here, I note that such might be a worthwhile pursuit. One example might be the recent double-blind medical experiment on answered prayer.[78] Like studies of near-death experiences, this would further help to address the nature of reality, for if there is life after death, then the resurrection becomes more likely as a specific example. Mackie amazingly points out that "anyone who is fortunate enough to have carefully observed and carefully recorded, for himself, an apparently miraculous occurrence is no doubt rationally justified in taking it very seriously."[79]

So for a wide variety of reasons, then, miracles do not lack strong evidence. This is especially the case regarding the resurrection of Jesus. Appeals to the scientific method do not change this situation.

Adjusting the Laws of Nature
Another common response in protesting the reality of miracles is to contrast miracle-claims with the laws of nature. Some scholars have argued that these

laws should be expanded or reworked in order to allow for the occurrence of inexplicable events.[80] After all, odd happenings, even singular events, are not rare. Others have declared that any events that have occurred in nature should be considered natural.[81] Admittedly, these responses are more creative than the previous ones. However, they still exhibit a number of serious shortcomings.

First, it is true that most events are not miracles, including most of those that have been labeled as such. As a result, we should begin by making a determination as to whether natural causes might be the best explanation for odd happenings. However, we need to realize that this solution might simply be inadequate. If a careful investigation fails to provide a satisfactory explanation, and the conditions warrant the possibility of the miraculous, then we should be willing to check the feasibility of supernatural causation, as well. While supernatural causation is not the initial option, it may still become the most likely scenario. But to continually refuse to consider miracles as real possibilities, or to assert that nature only allows natural events, constitutes an a priori rejection. This is question begging in that it *assumes* a position from which it then rules out certain events. *Of course* any events that really happen must do so in the natural realm. But automatically assuming that this requires that they arise only from natural causes simply bypasses the question regarding their origin. It even appears that the purpose for these maneuvers is to make the statement that *nothing* ever really qualifies as a miracle. But if a miracle actually occurred in history, how could we know it without checking?

Second, we should consider the possibility of the miraculous when certain well-defined conditions obtain: (1) when it has been determined that all natural explanations are improbable, (2) when the event in question actually occurred, and (3) when the data seem clearly to contravene a natural law. On such occasions, a supernatural explanation should be strongly entertained.[82] In the case of Jesus's resurrection, I have already provided a detailed discussion of the first two of these issues in chapter 1.

I considered the third issue, which most clearly addresses the current objection, earlier in this chapter. To summarize that discussion, the best determination of the miraculous can be made when certain events exhibit characteristics of true interferences with nature's laws. The strongest case obtains when an event has not been repeated, when an event clearly transgresses a well-established law of nature, and when proposed extensions of the law fail to explain the occurrence. Swinburne concludes that the resurrection of a truly dead man would clearly fulfill all three conditions.[83]

So in chapter 1 and this chapter I have concluded that naturalistic hypotheses do not explain Jesus's resurrection, that the event actually occurred in history, and that it definitely counters one of the best-established laws of nature. Furthermore, no reformulation or expansion of these laws could better explain the data, especially when the early sources confirm that Jesus's resurrected body possessed supernatural qualities which nature could not duplicate. The chief issue for the naturalist is that we obviously cannot amend the law so that it applies to everyone but Jesus alone! In brief, this objection simply cannot account for the case of the resurrection.

Third, the entire mind-set that places the laws of nature in opposition to miracle-claims may simply be inadequate. As pointed out in the last chapter, among the most difficult problems for such a nonmiraculous mind-set is that it may simply be misplaced—an attempt to answer the wrong question. The central issue, however, is not whether an event can be ruled out by a particular law of nature. More crucially, could God have superseded nature by a *superior power*? Simply assuming that science can explain everything naturally fails to answer whether God may have intervened in order to act briefly, even inexplicably. This distinction is crucial because, if a miracle *did* occur, evidence for that event would actually be *superior* to the scientific data detailing nature's laws, since this would mean that, *at that particular moment*, God had acted in a manner that nature cannot totally explain. Incredibly, the tables would be turned here, for this would indicate that certain historical evidence signaled a brief instant when nature was actually superseded by a superior power. At that moment, nature's laws would have been trumped by divine intervention! This response applies to other objections, as well.

Fourth, I have said that miracles are not self-interpreting; a larger context is necessary for their interpretation. In this chapter I have given some philosophical parameters for these events. The purpose of the next chapter will be to provide a theological context in which to interpret the resurrection data. So we are not studying the resurrection in a vacuum, but as it fits into an entire philosophical and theological context. But we must not miss the point that if such a broader context exists, then this is an additional indication that the Christian theistic worldview is far more than an occasional lapse in nature's laws. There are many indications that miracles are purposeful, and that they fit into a larger, coherent context.

I conclude that questions concerning the laws of nature are helpful in ascertaining the existence of miracles. At least in the case of Jesus's resurrection, we have a number of indications that adjustments in these laws still cannot explain the evidence.

The Possibility of Future Explanations

Critics have also countered that, at some future time, any given event might be explained by natural processes. After all, science has done precisely this on many occasions, particularly concerning natural phenomena, such as eclipses, that were once thought to have supernatural causes. As a result, we can never conclude that an event is permanently inexplicable. Perhaps the natural law it seems to violate will even be adjusted in the future.[84] Several considerations militate against these suggestions.

First, this objection cuts both ways. This sort of challenge could be leveled at virtually any bit of knowledge regarding the physical world, from the future possibility of discovering the Earth is flat to a reversal of key elements of astrophysics. Then what if, after merely stating the *possibility* that such scientific truths *might* be overturned, we began to teach that current science could therefore not be trusted? Or perhaps, in the future, the realization of a supernatural dimension may return in full force. After all, the absence of a viable naturalistic theory and the presence of many strong evidences may someday be the chief reasons why the resurrection becomes recognized by all as a historical event!

Second, as Swinburne states, "all claims to knowledge about the physical world are corrigible." Most of what we currently consider to be knowledge is inductive in nature, and is therefore subject to the possibility of future change anyway. Permanent inexplicability is certainly a strange bedfellow to assign to any inductive research, which carries no future guarantees, so why should this notion be applied to miracles? Even in everyday life, "we must reach provisional conclusions . . . on the evidence available to us."[85] Accordingly, if a philosophical or theological claim needs to be reexamined later, so be it. For instance, if belief in Jesus's resurrection is questioned, Christians will still research and respond accordingly. Since miracle-claims are subject to future discussion anyway, what difference does it make? What is the issue here? We must still continue to draw conclusions at present, since this is the nature of life. Of course some knowledge will change in the future, but it is also plain that our present knowledge cannot be held hostage by future considerations. Suspending present conclusions is not the way to handle the issue. We *must* make our decisions based on the best of our knowledge. In the meantime, we should not overrule the data without a viable reason for doing so, based on the mere hope that things may be different in the future.

Third, most of our better-established beliefs will probably never change. We have acquired extensive information regarding our world and it is unlikely that there would be such major adjustments that "miracles" would suddenly become only common events. As Swinburne concludes, we know enough to conclude that the resurrection of a fully dead man is a violation of nature's laws. This is not likely to change in the future. Such an event is "physically impossible."[86] After all, the resurrection has been systematically questioned by skeptics for almost two millennia without a reworked concept of nature's laws.

Fourth, this criticism appears to commit the genetic fallacy of informal logic. Discovering how some religious beliefs originated is an insufficient response because it questions the origin of a position instead of the view itself. Just because our ancestors were not scientists, and held some beliefs that we now know to be false, it does not follow that Julius Caesar never died by assassination. That Christians have erroneously attributed some natural phenomena to God likewise proves nothing concerning theism, even as false scientific views of the past prove nothing against modern science.

Fifth, questions are definitely helpful in honing one's position. But to continue rejecting miracle-claims by proposing almost any other explanation in their place, in spite of the available evidence, is yet another example of an a priori rejection of these events. This is in contrast to the inductive method of basing our decisions on the best evidence.

In conclusion, inductively derived data are always open to the possibility of future review. However, this is no challenge to evidence that may exist presently for miracle-claims. As in almost every area of life, we need to make decisions based on our current information.

Antecedent Probability

One of the more popular challenges to miracles is to assert, even prior to an examination of the claims, that miracles are so improbable as to be considered highly unlikely, if not practically impossible. The chief reason for this contention is that the universe as we know it, with its natural laws and in light of modern scientific study, does not seem to be the sort of place that allows miraculous events.[87] Therefore, whatever happened to Jesus after his death, he simply was not raised from the dead. This is a thoughtful objection, although it is confronted by many very serious problems.

First, as I have noted before, this stance easily becomes an a priori rejection of all miraculous events, if it is taken too far. Since those who hold this position sometimes claim that virtually *no* amount of evidence could ever identify an event as a miracle, the caution of a priori rejection is especially applicable here.[88]

But a more forceful a priori argument could also be leveled at a critique of miracles based on prior conditions. Parrish notes that a major problem with antecedent probability is, "If one knew atheism were true, then one would be completely justified in assigning miracles a very low order of antecedent probability. However, the possibility of miracles cannot be summarily rejected when using them as evidence to decide between some variety of theism and atheism, as that would be begging the question." He continues: "many philosophers . . . not only accept a naturalistic or atheistic world-view with its corresponding probability structure, but also take such a viewpoint for granted. Atheism, with its corresponding probability structure, is held to be the neutral and objective viewpoint, rather than one viewpoint among many."[89] Parrish summarizes later that "one cannot properly speak of the 'antecedent improbability' of miracles. . . . In debating between two or more rival views, the truth of one probability structure should not be assumed nor should the a priori antecedent probability of the specific alleged miracle."[90] If Parrish is correct, the entire program of establishing the antecedent likelihood of miracles begs the question by assuming from the outset a prior philosophical position that they are unlikely.

Second, I have already addressed briefly in this chapter several reasons why this may be a theistic universe. If the universe were theistic, this alone would *significantly* alter the nature of criticism based on a naturalistic starting point. For example, although David Owen favors this objection, he still concedes that the existence of God could make belief in miracles a rational position.[91] In fact, a number of scholars have argued that God's existence significantly changes the entire scenario, opening the door quite significantly to miracles.[92] When the probability of this crucial background information is considered, Bayes Theorem can be turned *in favor* of evidence for miracles. Incredibly, in a recent argument of this sort, Richard Swinburne stated that, using a Bayesian approach, the probability that the resurrection of Jesus actually occurred can be computed at 97 percent![93]

Third, the entire underpinning offered in support of antecedent probability has been severely questioned, and on more than one front. We simply lack the necessary data to know that miracles do not occur. Mavrodes asks, "On what basis should we assign the miracle probability?"[94] Mavrodes argues that our experience of whether or not miracles have occurred is "*completely irrelevant to the probabilities of R* ["some resurrections"] *and NR* ["no resurrections"]. And the reason is simple and straightforward. Hume's sample is just too small. . . . And so is your sample and mine." Granted, a resurrection would be rare, and if one did occur, then the probability that Hume experienced it "is almost infinitesimally small. . . . So Hume's own negative experience is irrelevant to [a resurrection's] probability."[95]

The obvious critical suggestion here would be to expand our testimony to include that of many others, but Mavrodes charges that there are at least two serious problems with such a move. Initially, this militates against the very nature of the objection that this is an *antecedent* conclusion of probabilities drawn *before* such experience gathering. But much more seriously, once we expand our inquiry to include the experience of many others, we receive miraculous reports. We cannot ignore these simply because they do not fit our purposes or even because we think they are false. Such conclusions now drag us into the evidence itself, and Jesus's resurrection is staring us in the face! Mavrodes thinks that we must choose between utilizing a small, even personal, statistical example, which is much too minute for our purposes, or expanding our sample and thereby encountering miracle-claims. But where does this leave us? "In any case, however, the project . . . provides no basis for assigning a low antecedent probability to singular miracle claims, such as that of Jesus's resurrection."[96]

Fourth, an equally crucial issue concerns the nature of our world. If miracle-like events are observed *at present*, then this entire objection comes crashing to the ground. Many think that this is clearly a naturalistic universe, based on what we observe around us. But how many clear, well-evidenced examples would it take to show that there is more than this physical world? How do we know whether God has superseded the laws of nature unless we check the possibilities? In this chapter alone, I have produced some considerations in favor of the existence of intelligent life and some intriguing evidence favoring near-death experiences. I have also mentioned the statistically significant, double-blind medical experiment involving the possibility of answered prayer and healing. Other potential avenues could have been included, as well, although I cannot defend them within the parameters of this chapter. Examples like these, and others, could significantly change our thoughts concerning the nature of this world. If life after death *alone* is likely, as indicated by the evidence for near-death experiences, we would have to be more open to the specific example provided by Jesus's resurrection. Subsequently, not only might the entire backdrop for the claimed naturalistic objection disappear, but it might turn the subject in the opposite direction. If there are reasons to believe that this world includes supernatural events, then the evidence favoring Jesus's resurrection would be another major example that this universe is much more complicated than naturalists think!

So it is very difficult to even establish the challenge of antecedent probability. Besides the seeming a priori nature of some of these claims, including the question-begging nature of the objection itself, the existence of God, the evidential inability to establish a low probability against miracles, and indications even in our modern world that naturalism is too narrow all militate heavily against this challenge.

Critical Scholars, Jesus's Resurrection, and a Theistic Universe

Some scholars oppose rational arguments based on Jesus's resurrection, as I noted in the introduction, often due to their belief that we ought not argue for the truth of any doctrine, since theology is based on faith. But other scholars disagree. Even critical scholars frequently argue from Jesus's resurrection to the likelihood of a theistic universe. They think that the resurrection, either explicitly or implicitly, indicates a theistic universe, at least for believers.

For example, historian Michael Grant notes that, for Christians, the resurrection "conferred utterly satisfying evidence of the divine power's sovereign penetration and destruction of the whole man-made fabric of the history of the world."[97] Donald Goergen provides some details: "What can be stated with assurance about Jesus's resurrection is . . . its reality as an act of God. It is God who raises the dead to life. It is God who likewise raised Jesus from the dead."[98] Adrian Thatcher adds: "When God raised Jesus, a divine agent was acting. . . . When God raised Jesus, he had good reasons for doing so."[99] The result, as N. T. Wright points out, is that the resurrection "did indeed demonstrate that the God of Israel was the one true God. . . . [I]t was time to bow the knee before the true God."[100]

Why does this follow? Stephen Davis asserts that the resurrection is "very difficult for religious skeptics to explain naturalistically," so they have to deny it. More explicitly: "The resurrection of Jesus appears to be a hard miracle—skeptics apparently cannot agree that it occurred . . . without abandoning religious skepticism."[101] William Lane Craig thinks that the unnatural characteristics of the resurrection event, along with its "religio-historical context," indicate that it was God who performed this event. He comments: "But I know of no critic who argues that the historical evidence shows that Jesus did rise from the dead, but that this was a purely natural occurrence."[102] It would appear that the critic is faced with explaining both the historicity of the resurrection as well as its claimed unique context.[103]

Some recent scholars have raised questions here.[104] But far more have supported the contention that Jesus's resurrection either requires, or at least is most consistent with, a theistic universe. The best conclusion is that the resurrection, in its context, indicates the reality of a theistic universe.[105]

Conclusion

Mackie and Flew have argued that, in order for a miracle to have occurred, two prerequisites are necessary. First, the event in question must actually have happened, and second, it would have to contravene or override a natural law.[106] To the first point, I append a subcondition: it needs to be determined that natural explanations of the event in question are improbable. If these three qualifications obtain, a supernatural explanation should be strongly considered. In chapter 1, after a detailed discussion, I argued that the case of Jesus's resurrection fulfills both the first condition and my subcondition. In this chapter, I have considered the second condition (along with other relevant philosophical issues) from various perspectives, concluding that the resurrection of Jesus also fulfills this prerequisite.

I began by briefly viewing naturalism's failure and a few issues that have led some scholars to conclude that this is a theistic universe. I surveyed four sorts of arguments: our knowledge of truth, the Kalam cosmological argument, several challenges from scientific teleology, and near-death experiences. Then I mentioned some hints provided by other scholars, as well. Although I by no means claimed any "proofs" for God's existence, it does appear that a strong case might be made both against naturalism and in favor of theism.

After viewing the naturalistic and supernaturalistic paradigms as two possible and competing options for the nature of the world in which Jesus's resurrection occurred, I concluded that the supernatural paradigm is superior. In such a universe, the resurrection was most likely performed by God. This was argued on two grounds.

Prospectively, if this is a theistic universe, it is very likely that God performed a miracle in raising Jesus from the dead in an orderly, purposeful manner, since this event would require the exercise of God's attributes. Here we are reminded of the testimony provided by atheistic philosopher Flew, stated earlier in this chapter: "Certainly given some beliefs about God, the occurrence of the resurrection does become enormously more likely."[107] The stronger the arguments become for a theistic universe, the clearer becomes the path that leads to Jesus's resurrection.

Additionally, I hinted at a second, retrospective approach that combines Jesus's resurrection with his unique teachings, claims concerning himself, and actions in order to vindicate his supernatural view of the world. If we find that the unique event of the resurrection occurred to the only person who taught what we are told that he did, especially regarding miraculous occurrences, then we have another very probable indicator that God raised Jesus from the dead and thereby confirmed his theistic message and worldview. It seems that this conclusion would provide two potential paths for arguing from the resurrection of Jesus to a theistic universe. I pursue this option in the next chapter.

Then I viewed Jesus's resurrection from another angle: as an event that God miraculously performed by temporarily suspending or superseding nature's laws. This conclusion is indicated because the resurrection of Jesus certainly opposed the laws of life and death, and was nonrepeatable, the only evidenced event of this kind in history. And if Jesus was raised in an immortal body that exhibited special powers beyond the capabilities of nature, this additionally complicates any attempt to explain this event in natural terms. Once again, it looks as if God miraculously performed Jesus's resurrection.

Philosophical, a priori objections do not seem to be able to sidetrack our developing case for understanding Jesus's resurrection as a miracle. The historical data pass the evidential tests. The relevant laws of nature cannot viably be expanded or changed in order to naturally accommodate the occurrence of this event. Appeals to future reassessment are acceptable, since this is the nature of inductive studies, but we cannot decide at present what those future studies may reveal. And attempts to reject miracle-claims due to prior improbabilities fall to a host of critical issues.

While contemporary theological scholars sometimes dislike approaches that "rationalize" or provide evidence for faith, perhaps even a majority conclude that theism follows from Jesus's resurrection, either explicitly or implicitly. But as I remarked in the introduction, even if one disagrees with the need for or importance of such arguments, other theological and practical paths still emerge from the truth of the resurrection. I will consider some of these avenues in the remainder of the book.

I have said repeatedly that miracles (like historical events in general) are not self-interpreting. This chapter provided a few *philosophical* parameters for miracles, placing these events in a theistic universe, unexplained by nature's laws. The next chapter will argue for a *theological* context in which to interpret the data regarding the resurrection of Jesus. Far from treating the resurrection in a vacuum, attempting to make it speak for itself, I am placing it within a philosophical and theological context.

The major arguments presented or mentioned in this chapter have the potential to independently assert that naturalism is most likely mistaken, and that this is probably a theistic universe. From different angles, they converge in connecting the God of the universe to his raising Jesus from the dead. Together they present a much stronger, unified case. It is likely not only that the resurrection of Jesus occurred in history, as I argued in chapter 1, but that God performed this event, thus requiring his existence and action in a theistic universe. It appears that God did temporarily set aside the laws of nature in order to perform this miracle. But if this event was miraculous, we would expect that it was performed for a specific purpose. Why was Jesus raised from the dead? I turn to this issue next.

Notes

1. In Habermas and Flew, *Did Jesus Rise from the Dead? The Resurrection Debate*, ed. Terry L. Miethe (San Francisco: Harper and Row, 1987), 39; cf. also 3, 49–50.

2. Richard Swinburne, *The Concept of Miracle* (New York: St. Martin's Press, 1970), 71; cf. 65–71.

3. Some volumes that attempt to argue the rationality or probability of theism from a variety of perspectives are: Alvin Plantinga and Nicholas Wolterstorff, eds., *Faith and Rationality: Reason and Belief in God* (Notre Dame: University of Notre Dame Press, 1983); Richard Swinburne, *The Existence of God*, rev. ed. (Oxford: Clarendon Press, 1991); Richard Swinburne, *The Coherence of Theism* (London: Oxford University Press, 1977); Alvin Plantinga, *God, Freedom, and Evil* (Grand Rapids, Mich.: Eerdmans, 1977); Alvin Plantinga, *Warranted Christian Belief* (New York: Oxford University Press, 2000); George I. Mavrodes, *Belief in God: A Study in the Epistemology of Religion* (New York: Random House, 1970); C. F. Delaney, ed., *Rationality and Religious Belief* (Notre Dame: University of Notre Dame Press, 1979); C. Stephen Evans and Merold Westphal, eds., *Christian Perspectives on Religious Knowledge* (Grand Rapids, Mich.: Eerdmans, 1993); Stephen T. Davis, *God, Reason, and Theistic Proofs* (Grand Rapids, Mich.: Eerdmans, 1997); John Donnelly, ed., *Logical Analysis and Contemporary Theism* (New York: Fordham University Press, 1972); J. Budziszewski, *Written on the Heart: The Case for Natural Law* (Downers Grove, Ill.: InterVarsity Press, 1997). For a summary of many theistic arguments, see Norman L. Geisler and Winfried Corduan, *Philosophy of Religion*, 2nd ed. (Grand Rapids, Mich.: Baker Book House, 1988), part 2.

4. C. S. Lewis, *Miracles: A Preliminary Study* (New York: Macmillan, 1960). An earlier edition of the chapter (published in 1947) was entitled "The Self-Contradiction of the Naturalist," and took a less-nuanced angle. Lewis revised the chapter in the 1960 edition after a celebrated 1948 debate with Cambridge University philosopher G. E. Anscombe. For a brief description and assessment of the debate, see Katherine Harper's article on Anscombe in *The C. S. Lewis Readers' Encyclopedia*, ed. Jeffrey D. Schultz and John G. West Jr. (Grand Rapids, Mich.: Zondervan, 1998), 81.

5. Lewis, *Miracles* (1947 ed.), 19–21. Very similar comments are also made in the 1960 edition (14–15, and esp. 26).

6. Lewis, *Miracles* (1960 ed.), 15.

7. Lewis, *Miracles* (1960 ed.), 21.

8. Lewis, *Miracles* (1947 ed.), 21–24. Lewis expands the edited (1960) argument (15–24).

9. In both editions, Lewis makes this additional move in chapter 4, 25–31.

10. Richard L. Purtill, *C. S. Lewis's Case for the Christian Faith* (San Francisco: Harper and Row, 1981), 23.

11. Purtill, *C. S. Lewis's Case*, 25, 26.

12. Peter Kreeft and Ronald K. Tacelli, *Handbook of Christian Apologetics* (Downers Grove, Ill.: InterVarsity Press, 1994), 66.

13. Stephen E. Parrish, *God and Necessity: A Defense of Classical Theism* (Lanham, Md.: University Press of America, 1997), 214–15.

14. Parrish, *God and Necessity*, cf. 172–73.

15. See Alvin Plantinga, *Warrant and Proper Function* (Oxford: Oxford University Press, 1993), 216–37.

16. Much interest in this argument is due to the publications of William Lane Craig, including: *The Kalam Cosmological Argument* (New York: Barnes and Noble, 1979), *The Cosmological Argument from Plato to Leibniz* (New York: Barnes and Noble, 1980); and popular volumes such as: *The Existence of God and the Beginning of the Universe* (San Bernardino, Calif.: Here's Life, 1979), *Reasonable Faith* (Wheaton, Ill: Crossway Books, 1994).

17. Kreeft and Tacelli, *Handbook of Christian Apologetics*, 58.

18. William Lane Craig and Quentin Smith, *Theism, Atheism, and Big Bang Cosmology* (Oxford: Clarendon Press, 1993), 57–63; Parrish, *God and Necessity*, 138–41; J. P. Moreland, *Scaling the Secular City: A Defense of Christianity* (Grand Rapids, Mich.: Baker Book House, 1987), 38–41.

19. William Lane Craig, "Philosophical and Scientific Pointers to Creatio ex Nihilo," *Journal of the American Scientific Affiliation* 32 (1980): 6–7; Moreland, *Scaling the Secular City*, 22–23.

20. Craig addresses some challenges in "Wallace Matson and the Crude Cosmological Argument," *Australasian Journal of Philosophy* 57 (1979): 163–70; Moreland articulates other examples and answers to objections (*Scaling the Secular City*, 28–33).

21. Moreland, *Scaling the Secular City*, 35.

22. One critic is J. L. Mackie, *The Miracle of Theism* (Oxford: Clarendon Press, 1982), 89–94. In addition to Craig's responses to Smith and Matson, listed above, see Craig's "Professor Mackie and the Kalam Cosmological Argument," *Religious Studies* 20 (1985), and "Dilley on the Cosmological Argument," *The New Scholasticism* 53 (1979).

23. Parrish, *God and Necessity*, 140.

24. Sir Fred Hoyle and Chandra Wickramasinghe, *Evolution from Space: A Theory of Cosmic Creationism* (New York: Simon and Schuster, 1981), chap. 9, "Convergence to God," esp. 130.

25. Report, "Hoyle on Evolution," *Nature* 294 (1981): 105.

26. Chandra Wickramasinghe, "Science and the Divine Origin of Life," in *The Intellectuals Speak Out about God*, ed. Roy Abraham Varghese (Chicago: Regnery Gateway, 1984), 27–36.

27. Robert Gange, *Origins and Destiny* (Waco, Tex.: Word Books, 1986), 73. Another excellent volume that reaches some similar conclusions is Charles B. Thaxton, Walter Bradley, and Roger L. Olsen, *The Mystery of Life's Origin: Reassessing Current Theories* (New York: Philosophical Library, 1984).

28. Gange, *Origins and Destiny*, 71; see also the appendix.

29. Michael Behe, *Darwin's Black Box* (New York: Free Press, 1992), 39–45, 69–72.

30. Hubert Yockey, "A Calculation of the Probability of Spontaneous Biogenesis by Information Theory," *Journal of Theoretical Biology* 67 (1977): 377. Similarly, see Hubert Yockey, "Self-Organization Origin of Life Scenarios and Information Theory," *Journal of Theoretical Biology* 91 (1981): 13–31.

31. Yockey, "Calculation," 396. Compare also Yockey's important study *Information Theory and Molecular Biology* (Cambridge: Cambridge University Press, 1992).

32. Owen Gingerich, "Where in the World is God?" in *Man and Creation: Perspectives on Science and Theology*, ed. Michael Bauman (Hillsdale, Mich.: Hillsdale College Press, 1993), 219–20.

33. William A. Dembski, *Intelligent Design: The Bridge between Science and Theology* (Downers Grove, Ill.: InterVarsity Press, 1999), 17.

34. Dembski, *Intelligent Design*, 112–13, 142.

35. Dembski, *Intelligent Design*, 17. In his more technical work on intelligent design, *The Design Inference* (Cambridge: Cambridge University Press, 1998), Dembski refers to specified complexity as the "specified small probability criterion."

36. For an in-depth discussion, see Dembski, *The Design Inference*, chaps. 1, 4–6; and *Intelligent Design*, 17–18, 106–7, 128–45.

37. Dembski, *Intelligent Design*, 149; cf. 147–50.

38. Dembski, *Intelligent Design*, 113.

39. Michael Behe, foreword to *Intelligent Design*, 10.

40. For some of this variety, see Moreland, *Scaling the Secular City*, chap. 2.

41. For well over a dozen evidenced NDE reports, see Gary R. Habermas and J. P. Moreland, *Beyond Death: Exploring the Evidence for Immortality* (Wheaton, Ill.: Crossway Books, 1998), chaps. 7–9. See also Gary R. Habermas, "Near-Death Experiences and the Evidence—A Review Essay" *Christian Scholars Review* 26 (1996): 78–85. Medical reports include: Michael Sabom, *Recollections of Death: A Medical Investigation* (New York: Harper and Row, 1982); Ian Stevenson and Bruce Greyson, "Near-Death Experiences: Relevance to the Question of Survival after Death," *Journal of the American Medical Association* 242 (1979): 265–67; Bruce Greyson and Ian Stevenson, "The Phenomenology of Near-Death Experiences," *American Journal of Psychiatry* 137 (1980): 1193–96; Melvin Morse, "Near Death Experiences and Death-Related Visions in Children: Implications for the Clinician," *Current Problems in Pediatrics* 24 (1994): 55–83; Kenneth Ring and Sharon Cooper, "Near-Death and Out-of-Body Experiences in the Blind: A Study of Apparent Sightless Vision," *Journal of Near-Death Studies* 16 (1997): 101–47; L. Houlberg, "Coming out of the Dark," *Nursing* (1992): 43.

42. Michael Sabom, *Light and Death* (Grand Rapids, Mich.: Zondervan, 1998), 37–51, 184–191. Another exceptionally well-attested case concerns a girl who was underwater for nineteen minutes, and was comatose, without brain activity. Just three days later she recovered and accurately described minute events both during her emergency room resuscitation and in her home, identifying what her family members were doing, including the meal of roast chicken and rice that her mother had prepared! This case is described by Melvin Morse, the pediatrician who resuscitated her, in his article, "A Near-Death Experience in a Seven-Year-Old Child," *American Journal of Diseases of Children* 137 (1983): 951–61. A popular report of the same case is included in Melvin Morse with Paul Perry, *Closer to the Light: Learning from Children's Near-Death Experiences* (New York: Random House, 1990), 3–9. I also had personal conversations with Melvin Morse, dated 15 November 1994 and 2 December 1994.

43. Fred Schoonmaker, "Near Death Experiences," *Anabiosis* 1 (1979): 35; John Audette, "Denver Cardiologist Discloses Findings After Eighteen Years of Near-Death

Research," *Anabiosis* 1 (1979): 1–2; Dina Ingber, "Visions of an Afterlife," *Science Digest* 89 (1981): 94–97, 142; Morse, "Near Death Experiences," 60, 70. I also had a personal conversation with Fred Schoonmaker, 1 June 1982. Incidentally, Schoonmaker did not employ temporal or deep cortical EEG leads.

44. A. J. Ayer, "What I Saw When I Was Dead: Intimations of Immortality," *National* Review, 14 October 1988, 39.

45. Antony Flew, personal correspondence, 9 September 2000.

46. From the data drawn from NDEs alone, I think we can argue only for what I have called "minimalistic" life after death (*Beyond Death*, 193–97). But the argument from NDEs to an afterlife still seems to be very powerful. For many details, see *Beyond Death*, esp. 184–97.

47. Alvin Plantinga, *God, Freedom, and Evil*, esp. 85–112. Cf., in particular, the essays by Charles Hartshorne, Norman Malcolm, and Alvin Plantinga in *The Ontological Argument*, ed. Plantinga (Garden City, N.Y.: Doubleday, 1965). See also Parrish, *God and Necessity*, chap. 4.

48. One major example is John D. Barrow and Frank J. Tipler, *The Anthropic Cosmological Principle* (New York: Oxford University Press, 1986).

49. Swinburne, *The Existence of God*, esp. chap. 14.

50. See Varghese, *Intellectuals Speak Out*. See the interviews with scientists Robert Jastrow (19–20), Henry Morgenau (39–45), Sir John Eccles (47–50), and Chandra Wickramasinghe (26–37); philosophers Alvin Plantinga (165–66), William Alston (153–58), Stanley Jaki (61–78), John E. Smith (160–61), Bernard Lonergan (175–84), and Ralph McInerny (169–74); and theologians, including Wolfhart Pannenberg (258–64).

51. Some of the key volumes are listed in note 3 above.

52. Alvin Plantinga, "Modern Philosophy and the Turn to Belief in God," in *Intellectuals Speak Out*, 165.

53. Dembski, *Intelligent Design*, 120.

54. Dembski, *Intelligent Design*, 120.

55. This option, however, is opposed by many problems. Regarding the resurrection alone, the failure of naturalistic theories that propose to account for this event, as even recognized by critical scholars, and the historical evidences for this event were mentioned in the last chapter.

56. Robert Larmer is one of a number of scholars who agrees both that miracles may serve as evidence for God's existence, and that such an approach amounts to a type of teleological argument. See his chapter, "Miracles as Evidence for God," in *God and Argument*, ed. William Sweet (Ottawa, University of Ottawa Press, 1999), 253–63.

57. For more details as to how the retrospective approach is not circular, see Habermas, "Closing Remarks," in in *Five Views on Apologetics*, ed. Steven B. Cowan (Grand Rapids, Mich.: Zondervan, 2000), 339–40.

58. A very similar definition was made famous by David Hume ("On Miracles," part I, in section X of *An Enquiry Concerning Human Understanding*, in *Hume on Religion*, ed. Richard Wollheim, Fontana Library of Theology and Phi-

losophy [London: Collins Sons and Company, 1963]). After pursuing a different definition of miracles, Swinburne decides to utilize Hume's definition (*The Concept of Miracle*, chap. 1, esp. 1, 11. See also his introduction to *Miracles*, ed. Richard Swinburne [New York: Macmillan, 1989], 2, 8–9).

59. For instance, R. F. Holland argues that Hume's definition is "unduly restrictive" ("The Miraculous" in *Logical Analysis*, 218); Lewis agrees (*Miracles* [1960 ed.], 5, 46, 59–60).

60. Mackie, *The Miracle of Theism*, 26; Antony Flew, introduction to *Of Miracles*, by David Hume (La Salle, Ill.: Open Court, 1985), 7–8.

61. Flew and I have debated on three separate occasions both the historicity of the resurrection and its relation to nature's laws. The first debate occurred in 1985 and was subsequently published by Harper and Row. This volume has been cited in each of the first two chapters. The second debate occurred in 2000 and is available on videotape from Impact, at www.impactapologetics.com.

62. See Swinburne, *The Concept of Miracle*, 26, and "Violation of a Law of Nature," in *Miracles*, 78–79. Swinburne points out that this is the notion also favored by Hume and others.

63. Swinburne, *The Concept of Miracle*, 26–27, 31–32; "Violation of a Law of Nature," 78–84.

64. Swinburne, *The Concept of Miracle*, 32; "Violation of a Law of Nature," 84.

65. Holland in *Logical Analysis*, esp. 218–21, 227–35.

66. Mackie, *The Miracle of Theism*, 24.

67. See Gary R. Habermas, "Resurrection Claims in Non-Christian Religions," *Religious Studies* 25 (1989): 167–77.

68. These same factors differentiate several ways in which Jesus's resurrection differs from the reports of others who were said to have returned to their former earthly lives after being raised from death, or who never died. We will return in chapter 6 to this question regarding the nature of the resurrection body.

69. Hume, "On Miracles," part I.

70. Mackie, *The Miracle of Theism*, 23; Flew in *Did Jesus Rise from the Dead?* 34–35.

71. It must be pointed out that complaints regarding the amount of necessary evidence, burdens of proof, and so on could be made concerning virtually *any* fact or position, whether scientific, historical, or otherwise. The knife in this objection, then, can cut in more than one direction (Mavrodes, *Belief in God*, 92–111). General arguments that simply assert that not enough evidence is present for a miracle are confronted by the specific evidences for the resurrection, such as those raised in the last chapter. Flew and I repeatedly dialogued concerning these points, especially in our second and third debates, mentioned above.

72. Patrick Nowell-Smith, "Miracles," in *New Essays in Philosophical Theology*, ed. Antony Flew and Alasdair MacIntyre (New York: Macmillan, 1964), 251–53.

73. Flew, introduction to *Of Miracles*, 18–19; Antony Flew, s.v. "Miracles," *The Encyclopedia of Philosophy*, 8 vols. (New York: Macmillan, 1967), 5:350, 352; George Chryssides, "Miracles and Agents," *Religious Studies* 11 (1975): 319–27.

74. Flew in *Did Jesus Rise from the Dead?* 34–35; S.V. "Miracle," in Antony Flew, editorial consultant, *A Dictionary of Philosophy*, rev. 2nd ed. (New York: St. Martin's Press, 1984), 234–35; Flew s.v. "Miracle," in *Encyclopedia of Philosophy*, 234–35; Christine Overall, "Miracles as Evidence against the Existence of God," *Southern Journal of Philosophy* 23 (1985): 347–53.

75. This is *not* to make the point that science and history are equally problematic, but rather that the gap between them is not one that would keep us from drawing proper historical conclusions.

76. David Hume, "Skeptical Solution of Those Doubts," in *An Enquiry Concerning Human Understanding*, V, part 1; A. J. Ayer, *Language, Truth, and Logic* (New York: Dover Publications, 1936), esp. 19; Bertrand Russell, "Truth and Falsehood," in *The Problems of Philosophy* (Oxford: Clarendon Press, 1912), esp. 284; Flew never hesitates to accept the veracity of historical data, even regarding the end of Jesus's life. For example, see Flew in *Did Jesus Rise from the Dead?* 79–81, 112–13.

77. Throughout my second debate with Antony Flew, we addressed a plausible explanation for the longer list of historical facts from chapter 1, all of which Flew also accepted.

78. Physician Randolf C. Byrd conducted a well-documented hospital study regarding the potential affects of prayer on the healing of cardiac patients. In a lengthy, double-blind study, 393 patients from a coronary care unit in San Francisco were monitored in twenty-six categories. The result was that patients receiving prayer fared statistically better in twenty-one of these categories than did those who did not receive prayer. Yet, the double-blind nature of the study would largely rule out "positive thinking" as a cause, since patients did not know whether they were receiving prayer. For the results, see Byrd's article, "Positive Therapeutic Effects of Intercessory Prayer in a Coronary Care Population," *Southern Medical Journal* 81 (1988): 826–29. The results are also reported in Randolph C. Byrd and John Sherrill, "On a Wing and a Prayer," *Physician* 5 (1993): 14–16.

79. Mackie, *The Miracle of Theism*, 28.

80. Antony Flew, *Hume's Philosophy of Belief* (London: Routledge and Kegan Paul, 1961), 193, 201; cf. also David Basinger, "Christian Theism and the Concept of Miracle: Some Epistemological Perplexities," *The Southern Journal of Philosophy* 28 (1980): 137–50.

81. Alasdair McKinnon, "Miracle," in *Miracles*, 49–53; Guy Robinson, "Miracles," *Ratio* 9 (1967): 155–66; Malcolm Diamond, "Miracles," *Religious Studies* 9 (1973), 320–21.

82. It should be noted here that I have appended the initial step concerning the failure of naturalistic responses to the two conditions already supplied by Mackie (*The Miracle of Theism*, 26) and Flew (introduction, *Of Miracles*, 7–8), as noted in the previous section above.

83. Swinburne, *The Concept of Miracle*, 26–32; "Violation of a Law of Nature," 75–84. For a related conclusion, see R. F. Holland, "The Miraculous," in *Miracles*, 53–69.

84. Nowell-Smith, "Miracles," 245–46, 251; Basinger, "Christian Theism," 140–41; David Basinger and Randall Basinger, *Philosophy and Miracle: The Contemporary Debate* (Lewiston, N.Y.: Edwin Mellen Press, 1986), esp. 59–71.

85. Swinburne, *The Concept of Miracle*, 31; "Violation of a Law of Nature," 82–84.

86. Swinburne, *The Concept of Miracle*, 32; "Violation of a Law of Nature," 84.

87. Michael Martin, "Why the Resurrection Is Initially Improbable," *Philo* 1 (1998): 63–73; David Owen, "Hume versus Price on Miracles and Prior Probabilities," in *Miracles*, 115–32; Jordan Howard Sobel, "On the Evidence of Testimony for Miracles: A Bayesian Interpretation of David Hume's Analysis," *Philosophical Quarterly* 37 (1987): 166–86, esp. 186.

88. Owen, "Hume versus Price," 129; Sobel, "On the Evidence," 186.

89. Parrish, *God and Necessity*, 156.

90. Parrish, *God and Necessity*, 172.

91. Owen, "Hume versus Price," 132.

92. For example, Rodney D. Holder, "Hume on Miracles: Bayesian Interpretation, Multiple Testimony, and the Existence of God," *British Journal for the Philosophy of Science* 49 (1998): esp. 60–62; George N. Schlesinger, "Miracles and Probabilities," *Nous* 21 (1987): esp. 219, 230–32; Schlesinger, "The Credibility of Extraordinary Events," *Analysis* 51 (1991): 125.

93. Richard Swinburne, *The Resurrection of God Incarnate* (New York: Oxford University Press, 2003), see esp. the appendix, where Swinburne provides the figures.

94. George I. Mavrodes, "David Hume and the Probability of Miracles," *International Journal for Philosophy of Religion* 43 (1998): 173.

95. Mavrodes, "David Hume," 176–77.

96. Mavrodes, "David Hume," 179–81. For other relevant thoughts, compare Benjamin F. Armstrong Jr., "Hume on Miracles: Begging-the-Question against Believers," *History of Philosophy Quarterly* 9 (1992): 319, 327; John Earman, "Bayes, Hume, and Miracles," *Faith and Philosophy* 10 (1993): esp. 293, 305–6; Roy A. Sorensen, "Hume's Scepticism Concerning Reports of Miracles," *Analysis* 43 (1983): 60.

97. Michael Grant, *Saint Paul* (Glasgow: William Collins Sons, 1976), 79.

98. Donald Goergen, *The Death and Resurrection of Jesus*, vol. 2 of *A Theology of Jesus* (Wilmington, Del.: Michael Glazier, 1980), 143–44.

99. Adrian Thatcher, "Resurrection and Rationality," in *The Resurrection of Jesus Christ*, ed. Paul Avis (London: Darton, Longman and Todd, 1993), 178; cf. also 177.

100. N. T. Wright, *What Saint Paul Really Said: Was Paul of Tarsus the Real Founder of Christianity?* (Grand Rapids, Mich.: Eerdmans, 1997), 93. Similarly, see Wright's *The New Testament and the People of God* (Minneapolis: Fortress Press, 1992), 370.

101. Stephen T. Davis, "Is It Possible to Know That Jesus Was Raised from the Dead?" *Faith and Philosophy* 1 (1984): 152.

102. William Lane Craig, "On Doubts about the Resurrection," *Modern Theology* 6 (1989): 71–72.

103. Again, it is this context that we will investigate in detail in the next chapter.

104. For instance, skeptic G. A. Wells rather intriguingly responds to me by claiming that my argument is contrary to New Testament teachings (Wells, *A Resurrection Debate* [London: Rationalistic Press Association, 1988], ix, 3)! But he seems to have missed a variety of biblical texts that argue from Jesus's resurrection to the truth of theism, including Jesus's own personal claims. Examples include Matt 12:38–40, 16:1–4; Jn 20:27–31; Acts 2:22–36, 17:22–31; Rom 1:3–4; 1 Cor 15:3–20; cf. Lk 7:18–23; among others. Don Cupitt objects that a similar argument employed by C. F. D. Moule is circular, without detailing the exact nature of his complaint. His dialogue with Moule is included in Cupitt's *Explorations in Theology* 6 (London: SCM Press, 1979), 30. It is very difficult to know the specific point that Cupitt is making, but we have responded above in some detail to the claim that arguing from the resurrection of Jesus to his deity is circular.

105. Besides those mentioned directly above, critical scholars who espouse similar positions include Flew in *Did Jesus Rise from the Dead?* 3, 39–42, 49–50; Wolfhart Pannenberg, *Jesus: God and Man*, 2nd ed., trans. Lewis L. Wilkins and Duane A. Priebe (Philadelphia: Westminster Press, 1977), 67–68, 108; N. T. Wright, *Jesus and the Victory of God*, vol. 2 of *Christian Origins and the Question of God* (Minneapolis: Fortress Press, 1996), 131–32; Gerald O'Collins, *The Resurrection of Jesus Christ: Some Contemporary Issues* (Milwaukee: Marquette University Press, 1993), 28–31; O'Collins, "The Resurrection: The State of the Questions," in *The Resurrection: An Interdisciplinary Symposium on the Resurrection of Jesus*, ed. Stephen T. Davis, Daniel Kendall, and Gerald O'Collins (Oxford: Oxford University Press, 1997), 25; Richard Bauckham, "God Who Raised the Dead: The Resurrection of Jesus and Early Christian Faith in God," in *The Resurrection of Jesus Christ*, 142–43; Stephen T. Davis, *Risen Indeed* (Grand Rapids, Mich.: Eerdmans, 1993), 200–201; Thorwald Lorenzen, *Resurrection and Discipleship: Interpretive Models, Biblical Reflections, Theological Consequences* (Maryknoll, N.Y.: Orbis Books, 1995), 264–65; Thomas C. Oden, *The Word of Life*, vol. 2 of *Systematic Theology* (Peabody, Mass.: Hendrickson, 1989), 466–67; Charles H. Talbert, "The Place of the Resurrection in the Theology of Luke," *Interpretation* 46 (1992): 21–22; Ralph Dawson, *Was There a Resurrection? The Challenge to Reason and Belief* (New York: Vantage Press, 1977), 114–15; J. P. Moreland and Kai Nielson, *Does God Exist? The Great Debate* (Nashville: Thomas Nelson, 1990), 232. For a supporting scientific comment on this issue, see Paul Davies, *God and the New Physics* (New York: Simon and Schuster, 1983), 190–91.

106. Mackie, *The Miracle of Theism*, 26; Flew, introduction to *Of Miracles*, 7–8. As mentioned above, these scholars obviously think that we do not have any actual examples of such events.

107. Flew in *Did Jesus Rise from the Dead?* 39; cf. also 3, 49–50.

CHAPTER THREE

The Person and Teachings of Jesus

In the first chapter I argued that Jesus actually rose from the dead in history. Alternative historical explanations fail to viably explain the data. In the second chapter I pointed out that there are many indications that naturalism has also failed to explain the universe, and that theism is more likely. Further, I argued that the two prerequisites for a miraculous event supplied by Mackie and Flew have been satisfied. The resurrection actually occurred, and it definitely contravened or overrode a natural law.[1] Other natural options have also failed here. In a theistic universe, it would be highly likely that God performed this event.

Since miracles are not self-interpreting, other contextual parameters need to be involved. In the last chapter I presented a few philosophical criteria for regarding the resurrection as a miracle, such as a theistic context, the inability to explain this event by adjusting nature's laws (besides the lack of a viable alternative theory, as pointed out in chapter 1), and the relation between the attributes of the God of traditional theism and the requirements of such an event. Critical objections do not disprove this connection.

In this chapter I argue that there are also specific criteria of a more theological nature that assist us in interpreting the data regarding the resurrection of Jesus. This will chiefly involve the context provided by the teachings of Jesus, the one who was raised.

Miracles as Confirmation of a Religious Message

Why were many of Jesus's listeners so enamored of his life and teachings? Some were moved by the nature of Jesus's teachings and the authority with which he spoke.[2] But undoubtedly, these teachings were powerfully augmented by the miracles that he seemed to be able to accomplish (Mk 1:27, 6:3; Mt 9:33). We are told that Jesus encouraged faith both because of the truth of his words (Jn 5:36–40; 14:11a), as well as because of his miracles (Mt 11:20–24/Lk 10:13–15; Mt 12:38–42/Lk 11:29–32; Jn 10:38, 14:11b). Why might the miracles have been such a powerful witness? It seems that these special actions were viewed as indicators of a divine seal on Jesus's ministry. There are several reasons why it was held that such events confirmed a religious message.

(1) Due to the very nature of miracles, especially their seeming inexplicable nature and the awe they produce, these occurrences tend to point beyond themselves. This attention seems to be placed squarely on the truth of the religious messenger as well as the teachings themselves. It is often thought that both are confirmed by the miracle, which makes sense if there is some reason to think that the miracle has divine attestation. Richard Swinburne argues that such a response is a distinctive feature of these events: "To be a miracle an event must contribute significantly towards a holy divine purpose for the world." Conversely, if occurrences are extraordinary but clearly lack any religious significance, then they are "more appropriately characterised [sic] as magical or psychic phenomena rather than as miracles."[3] Swinburne argues that one way a miracle might function in a religious context is to provide evidence for God's existence and activity.[4]

(2) More specifically, the Gospels report Jesus's claim that his miracles certified the truth of his message. After being accused of blasphemy, Jesus answered his critics by proclaiming that his healing a lame man let his hearers "know that the Son of Man has authority on earth to forgive sins" (Mk 2:10, RSV). Once he reportedly told the Jewish leaders that his miracles indicated that he was the Son of God (Jn 10:36–38). On two occasions, when asked for a sign, Jesus pointed to his resurrection as his chief vindication (Mt 12:38–42/Lk 11:29–32; Mt 16:1–4).

Few scholars have done more painstaking analyses of this subject than John Meier and Graham Twelftree. After judging that more then 40 percent of the miracle-claims in the Gospels correspond to specific historical even in Jesus's life, Meier concludes that, "In sum, the statement that Jesus acted as and was viewed as an exorcist and healer during his public ministry has as much historical corroboration as almost any other statement we can make about the Jesus of history. Indeed . . . it has much better attestation than many other assertions made about Jesus, assertions that people often take for granted."[5] Twelftree's percentage of the Gospel accounts of Jesus's miracles that correspond to specific historical events in Jesus's life is much higher. He concludes similarly: "there is hardly any aspect of the life of *the historical Jesus which is so well and widely attested as that he conducted un-parallel wonders."* These miracles *"were the most important aspect of Jesus's whole pre-Easter ministry."*[6]

That Jesus thought his miracles confirmed his message is conceded by perhaps a majority of critical scholars.[7] In fact, Twelftree remarks that the evidence indicates that *"because of his miracles,* Jesus appears to have been conscious that he was God's key figure."[8] Such critical recognition is not surprising, since the Gospel comments that indicate that Jesus thought in terms of miraculous confirmation of his message are reflected by very strong multiple attestations, being found in at least four sources: Mark, M, Q, and John.[9]

(3) Early believers, including some of those who heard Jesus, certainly agreed that his miracles confirmed the truth of his message. For example, the Gospels report that many believed after they saw Jesus's miracles.[10] In what the Book of Acts presents as its initial sermon, Peter reportedly declared that Jesus's miracles, and especially the resurrection, were the chief indication that God had approved Jesus's teachings (Acts 2:23–32). Later, we are told that Paul also used the resurrection as assurance that God had confirmed Jesus's teachings, challenging the Greek philosophers to repent (Acts 17:30–31). By citing an early creed that utilizes at least three Christological titles, Paul proclaimed that the resurrection was God's confirmation of Jesus Christ (Rom 1:3–4). Repeatedly, then, New Testament authors use Jesus's miracles, and his resurrection in particular, to indicate that Jesus's teachings were both true and ought to be recognized as such.

It is crucial that we view this entire situation from the perspective of ancient Judaism, which had guidelines for both establishing true prophets and exposing false ones. The former spoke God's words, and if they were disregarded, the people would be responsible before the Lord. The latter should be put to death for their false claims (Dt 18:18–22). Wolfhart Pannenberg argues that we have several indications that Jesus purposely linked himself with God. But if he was later resurrected, "this for a Jew can only mean that God himself has confirmed the pre-Easter activity of Jesus."[11] As repeatedly declared in the New Testament, the resurrection would have been taken as God's approval of Jesus's message.

Further, the Gospels claim that Jesus actually predicted his death and resurrection.[12] While the former is more understandable, if he predicted his resurrection, this would provide additional grounds favoring Jesus's perspective in revealing the meaning of this event. Critical scholars often agree that Jesus knew that he was going to die,[13] but usually deny that Jesus predicted his resurrection.[14]

There are at least four factors that favor the historicity of these predictions. First, these predictions are often denied because of their prophetic nature. But if Jesus's resurrection occurred (chapter 1), we should at least be open to the predictions of the event, especially since there are no sound reasons for rejecting them.

Second, the Gospels report that when Jesus spoke of his coming death and resurrection, the disciples misunderstood and even objected strenuously (Mk 8:31–33; 9:31–32; 14:27–31). They had to be reminded of this last prediction (Mk 16:7–8; Mt 28:7), since they still did not expect Jesus to be raised from the dead (Jn 20:9). According to the principle of embarrassment, the disciples' ignorance and lack of obedience is another indicator that Jesus's predictions are genuine, since the early church should arguably want the disciples to appear in a more positive light.[15]

Third, Jesus's predictions are multiply attested. They seem to be found in Mark, M, possibly Q, and John. Fourth, the predictions in Mark 8:31, 9:31, and 10:33–34 are part of the Son of Man passages. It is difficult to tell for sure, but this may point to their being genuine, just as I argue in this chapter for the authenticity of the Son of Man sayings.

So Jesus likely predicted his resurrection. If so, this would argue further that this event was not a coincidence or a chance occurrence, but a planned event. It also would be another indication that Jesus understood the event and its significance.

As I noted above, Jesus's listeners would most likely have concluded that his resurrection was an act that only God could perform. As such, it would constitute an incredible sign from God, confirming Jesus and his teachings. These convictions would also match Jesus's teachings concerning his own miracles, especially in that he regarded his resurrection as the chief sign. This would also be the best explanation of the apostolic proclamation that this event evidenced the Christian message.

It makes sense that Jesus was in the best position to interpret the meaning of the resurrection. He and his followers testified that, as his chief miracle, this direct act by the God of the universe verified his theistic perspective. In addition, if Jesus also made unique claims about his own divinity (a topic we need to explore in the remainder of this chapter), this would further extend God's approval, for it would appear that few subjects would more likely have qualified Jesus for the charge of heresy, especially in the Jewish context. The only time that an evidenced resurrection occurred in history,[16] it happened to an individual who appears to have made unique claims concerning himself and the nature of the world. But this leads us to an examination both of some possible objections, as well as of some of these claims.

Some Objections

As in chapter 2, sometimes a priori issues are raised that have comparably little to do with the actual state of the evidence. These concerns are largely related to the configuration of the argument, and question whether miracles provide any evidence for religious beliefs.

Linking Miracles to God

One frequent contention is that we can never know whether an event, no matter how strange or inexplicable, was caused by God. It might just be a very unusual set of circumstances. For example, perhaps an alternative explanation involving a "natural miracle" is plausible, a natural oddity such as a group hallucination.[17] This thoughtful challenge is opposed by several problems.

First, posing such an objection is not a problem. But if we *continue* to insist that we must *always* prefer and even invent natural scenarios for the resurrection, regardless of whether they are the best explanations, this is an ongoing *a priori* objection. The problem with the more radical approach is that it favors naturalism or another perspective that has not been proven. In other words, to assume that any but a supernatural universe is reality's default setting makes the same error in reverse, by assuming that God could not possibly be the Cause of any events. But if no metaphysical positions are assumed at the outset, it is difficult to see how the skeptic will succeed in ignoring the evidence for Jesus's resurrection.

Second, in chapter 2 I already mentioned a number of reasons for thinking that this is a theistic universe. If it is, then naturalistic and other nontheistic outlooks are improbable. So the way is clear to argue for a close connection between God and the resurrection.[18]

Third, natural oddities like mass hallucinations are not preferable to real miracles, and for several reasons. (1) None of these occurrences has ever been verifiably observed and they appear to be nonexistent. As such, they are simply suggestions without supporting data. (2) It does not appear that any single, natural option can explain all of the evidence for the resurrection, even from this adjusted angle. For example, adjusted hallucination theses would still leave unexplained facts like the empty tomb, the disciples's despair instead of excitement, the later transformation of the disciples, Paul's appearance, James's appearance, and others. So we would still be ignoring several of the critically acknowledged historical facts.[19]

(3) But even more problematic, this objection does not simply require a mass hallucination. It requires *several* of them! Incredibly, every group appearance of Jesus would require a separate one of these naturally unique

occasions. So we now need several consecutive natural oddities, all of which are foreign to modern psychology. (4) How should we categorize these events as they relate specifically to Jesus? Should we say that multiple mass hallucinations do not occur, except in the case of Jesus's followers, and then they did so repeatedly? Then, afterward, they simply *ceased*? Such an ad hoc solution would seem to be a highly problematic, even for skeptics, especially since it isolates Jesus as the only known exception in history. This itself appears to tightrope around a real miracle. Even a onetime resurrection looks better than these repeated natural contortions, especially if this is a theistic universe. Actually, such gymnastics point clearly to the a priori nature of their stance.

Fourth, I have developed, in addition to Jesus's resurrection, a set of criteria that point toward a theistic context for this event. In the last chapter I viewed some philosophical parameters, including the failure of naturalism, some probability for theism, the failure of physical laws to incorporate the resurrection, as well as the need for attributes like those of classical theism to explain this event. In this chapter I turn to theological parameters, claiming that never in history has there been such a unique *combination* of an event such as the resurrection and the teachings of the one involved, namely Jesus Christ. The close connection between the event and these criteria seem to invoke the action of God.

For reasons such as these, it would seem that indeed we do have several substantial criteria to ascertain when God is the Author of a particular event or teaching. These parameters apply to both the event and the interpretive context. Neither "natural miracles" nor other unusual circumstances explain this data.

Miracle-Claims in Other Religions

Some critics charge that rival miracle-claims in non-Christian religions are a threat to Christian claims. Perhaps they even nullify one another, leaving no viable examples. Further, what about other prominent religious personages who also make extraordinary claims, and then perform incredible actions that no one can explain? Should we also accept their teachings as truth?[20] Although questions regarding other religious traditions are common, there are a variety of factors opposing such challenges.

First, non-Christian miracle-claims can be quite compatible with Christian belief. There are several options here, too, from God actually performing a miracle elsewhere for his own purposes, to his allowing another to do so, to the event in question turning out, after an investigation, not to be a miracle at all. As C. S. Lewis points out, "I do not think that it is the duty of the Christian apologist (as many sceptics suppose) to disprove all stories of the miraculous which fall outside the Christian records. . . . I am in no way committed to the assertion that God has never worked miracles through and for Pagans."[21]

Second, the actual evidence in support of non-Christian miracles is actually quite scanty. For the founders of major world religions, the early supernatural claims are either nonexistent or made in documents that were written quite a long time afterward. Confucius and Lao-tzu, who were chiefly ethicists, did not make miracle-claims.[22] The Qur'an seems to state that, beyond the writing of the book itself, Muhammad performed no other miracles.[23] For Buddha, the texts detailing his life and teachings date from one or two hundred to four or five hundred years after the events themselves. For Krishna, this time also stretches to hundreds of years later. In fact, ancient historian Edwin Yamauchi argues that the Christian reports are unique: "we find that early accounts attribute miracles only to Jesus."[24] The point here is that non-Christian miracle-claims exhibit a rather startling lack of historical attestation. As such, they are hardly able to rule out or nullify well-evidenced Christian claims, such as those made for Jesus's resurrection. After all, if we follow our own principles here, only those miracles for which we have strong evidence should be discussed in this context.

Third, beyond the more obvious evidential inquiries, other sorts of questions also provide crucial distinctions. (1) Perhaps contrasting miracle-claims also exhibit moral differences. What is the ethical purpose of the particular miracles? Is the corresponding message one of moral repugnance or otherwise of an objectionable nature? (2) Do some miracles require more power than others? Perhaps some miracles are of a lesser nature, or do not demand the actions of an infinite being.

Fourth, we have repeatedly acknowledged that historical events need to be connected to other interpretive criteria in order to provide identifying causal marks. Therefore, a crucial question involves the extent to which other religious systems can also provide a unique context for their miracle-claims. If such a context is absent, these alternative declarations would lack the criteria that are necessary for identification as God's work.

Fifth, regarding the truth of someone's religious teachings when they perform incredible feats, several critical items need to be evaluated. (1) Only the performance of truly miraculous events can be entertained here, since this definitely does not apply to rare but readily explicable or repeatable natural phenomena. (2) It needs to be ascertained whether any naturalistic alternative hypotheses better explain the claims, just like those that critics have proposed regarding Jesus's resurrection. Can the non-Christian accounts produce strong arguments to refute *all* of these possibilities? (3) Surprisingly, serious claims of deity are rarely, if ever, made by those who have founded major world religions. In the absence of such teachings, of course, the deity of the individual would not even be a necessary consideration. (4) We would still have to apply every one of the other tests listed above. For example, is the miracle highly evidenced by a variety of arguments? What are the moral implications of the claimed event? What sort of power is reportedly required? Is there a strong, multi-faceted interpretive context for the event? As far as we know, no founder of a major world religion (or any other noteworthy religious figure, for that matter) even offers competition on all of these points. World religions scholar Stephen Neill asserts that, no matter how critically we take the Gospels, Jesus's teachings on these subjects are utterly unique among all of the other religious traditions. He summarizes his claims, "Jesus is not the least like anyone else who has ever lived."[25]

It would appear, then, that objections based on miracle-claims in other religious traditions simply fail to challenge Christian examples. Our arguments have been reached from a variety of angles, adding up to a formidable case.

Jesus's Teachings Regarding Himself

What did Jesus teach concerning himself? Did the early church change him from a prophet into some sort of divine personage? Here I continue the method that I developed in the first two chapters, namely, arguing from a critical perspective. I discuss only those Gospel texts that, for a variety of reasons, are widely accepted among scholars as preserving Jesus's own comments on this subject. The conclusions of the critical community will help serve as common denominators for my conclusions.[26] My purpose here is to continue my study of a context for Jesus's resurrection.

Recent Christological Studies

Commenting on the state of Christological studies, Raymond Brown surveys five common positions that have been widely held in recent years. He argues that the most popular position is what he terms "scholarly (moderate) conservatism." The distinguishing characteristic of these thinkers is that "they posit a christology in the ministry of Jesus himself," although they sometimes differ "on whether that christology was explicit or implicit." It should be carefully noted that there are a wide range of positions represented here regarding what is meant by Jesus's divinity, as well.[27]

I present an overview of several key New Testament texts along with some of the critical considerations that point to Jesus's divine self-consciousness. I concentrate chiefly on publications during the last two decades that argue that Jesus held an explicit Christology, and that this is largely determined by Jesus's use of divine titles. Regardless of whether those in Brown's camp of "moderate conservatism" hold that Jesus's Christology was explicit or implicit, these texts are highly respected, as Brown points out.

The strongest case is to be made by an inductive study that builds a cumulative argument. However, due to the voluminous detail of these discussions, I am absolutely forced to summarize areas in which an exceptionally large number of publications has appeared in recent decades. Some of the sources will provide far more details.

To further narrow my discussion, I chiefly study Jesus's use of two titles—Son of God and Son of Man—although a few other helpful considerations will be mentioned briefly. Scholars are split regarding which title is more likely the key to this discussion. For instance, Walter Kasper and George Ladd hold that Son of God is in some sense the central concept.[28] But Ben Witherington III and Seyoon Kim think that Son of Man is a more unifying and expressive title.[29]

Son of God

According to the synoptic Gospels, Jesus taught that he had a unique relationship with God, as seen in contexts where Jesus spoke of himself as the "Son" while addressing God as "Father." Most commentators seem more than willing to refer simply to whether Jesus referred to himself as the "Son of God."[30] Several passages are highly instructive.

Matthew 11:25–27/Luke 10:21–22

Many scholars think that this is perhaps the key reference expressing Jesus's self-consciousness as the Son of God, largely because it comes from the Q material, and thus is dated among the very earliest texts. In what is referred to as a Johannine thunderbolt (Witherington contends that "meteorite" is more accurate)[31], Jesus speaks of the Father in intimate terms, stating that only he knows the Father directly.

Commentators have noted the presence of "many Semitic features," such as the special way a father and son know each other.[32] Another critical factor is the way Jesus is said to have singled himself out as the only person who directly shares this confidentiality. Witherington notes the importance of the comment: "The unique relationship of Jesus with the Father is the basis for the claim of special knowledge and for the ability to be a special revealer of knowledge."[33]

Older, influential publications also note the force of this text. Reginald Fuller declares that this saying is "an explicit expression of the implicit Christology of Jesus's own use of Abba."[34] Oscar Cullmann more boldly announces that this text "points to Jesus's omniscience."[35] More recently, Donald Guthrie writes that this passage "seems to include the unique filial relation between Jesus and God. There can be no doubt that Jesus was conscious of that relationship."[36] I. H. Marshall affirms that "Jesus is applying 'a son' to himself, and is thus making an implicit claim to a unique relationship with God."[37]

Mark 14:36

Closely aligned with the idea of an intimate relation between father and son is Mark's testimony that Jesus utilized the Aramaic term "Abba" to refer to God. The presence of the Aramaic is widely held to represent one of our surest insights into an actual expression used by Jesus, thereby reflecting his own self-consciousness. It is significant that this was a familiar and intimate word for "Father." Joachim Jeremias, whose research brought this saying to the forefront of contemporary discussions, concludes "that *Abba* as an address to God is *ipsissima vox*, an authentic and original utterance of Jesus."[38]

Even though scholars often reject the popular notion that "Abba" means "Daddy,"[39] the critical community usually recognizes that the term still intimates a very familiar reference to God, which is highly unusual in ancient Judaism. Martin Hengel translates this reference to God as "dear Father" and includes Paul's two citations (Rom 8:15ff.; Gal 4:4ff.) as further indications that, like Matthew 11:27, this text indicates Jesus's filial consciousness.[40] Even Marcus Borg agrees that Jesus used this term, an indication that Jesus "clearly was aware of a relationship of special intimacy" with God.[41] Jeremias summarizes: "this *Abba* implies the claim of a unique revelation and a unique authority. . . . We are confronted with something new and unheard of which breaks through the limits of Judaism."[42]

Many other scholars generally agree on the nature and significance of this intimate, filial manner of referring to the God of the universe. It has the potential to provide us with another insight into Jesus's notion of his own person. Witherington states strongly that, "this form of address does imply a filial consciousness on the part of Jesus that involved a degree of intimacy with God unlike anything we know of in Judaism prior to Jesus's day. . . . [T]his material shows that Jesus saw himself as the unique mediator of a relationship with the Father."[43] Guthrie agrees: "the evidence supports most strongly the view that Jesus was conscious of a relationship to his Father which was unique."[44]

Mark 13:32

This is another saying in which Jesus most likely referred to himself as the Son. The chief argument for authenticity here is rather paradoxical, involving the principle of embarrassment. Intriguingly, that Jesus denied that he had knowledge of the time of his return makes it quite improbable that such a difficult remark was invented by the church. If the church had desired to contrive such a statement and place the title "Son" on Jesus's lips, it presumably would have done so without raising in the very same verse the vexing question of the extent of Jesus's knowledge!

Guthrie states the central issue this way: "it is impossible to suppose that a saying so Christologically embarrassing should have been invented. There is no strong reason to question its authenticity."[45] So it is not surprising that, according to Witherington, "Few scholars today are willing to dismiss the whole saying as inauthentic."[46] Cullmann had reached some similar conclusions a few decades ago: "On the other hand, it is questionable whether the early Church could have invented a saying of Jesus which in this way limits his unity with the Father at such an important point."[47] The best judgment is that Jesus actually made such a comment.[48]

Mark 12:1–12 (Matthew 21:33–46; Luke 20:9–19)

One other passage should be mentioned very briefly. In the parable of the wicked tenants, Mark reports Jesus's story that a man sent many of his servants to those who rented his vineyard, to collect what was due. After each servant was either beaten or killed, the man sent his "beloved son" (Mk 12:6), thinking that he would surely be treated better. But the renters killed the son, too.

Critical scholars usually treat Jesus's parables very seriously, as representing authentic glimpses of Jesus's teaching. The parable of the wicked tenants is no exception. Craig Evans comments that this is "a parable which increasingly scholars are coming to regard as authentic."[49] Another indication of authenticity is the absence of any Christian additions to the parable regarding the son, his representing Jesus, or his resurrection. Still, Jesus's intentions seem to be clear. Rather intriguingly, Witherington holds that the simplest version of this parable is found in *The Gospel of Thomas* 65.[50]

We could look at other texts that regard Jesus as the Son of God.[51] One major passage that appears to state in a rather straightforward manner that Jesus affirmed that he was "the Christ, the Son of the Blessed" (Mark 14:61–64, RSV) will be discussed in the next section.

Conclusion

Could Jesus's use of the title "Son of God" provide any indications that his self-understanding included some sense that he was divine? Such a conclusion would best be derived in an inductive manner, taking into account various facets such as those outlined above. It seems that, even after applying critical standards, it can be determined that Jesus did refer to himself as the "Son." Furthermore, he did so in a manner indicating that this designation should be taken in a special, filial sense of intimacy with his heavenly Father, which was shared directly by him alone.

Many scholars in the critical community have drawn similar conclusions. Cullmann declares that "Jesus's consciousness of being the Son of God refers both to his person and to his work."[52] It is not surprising, then, that the Jewish leaders usually responded to Jesus's self-understanding in a negative manner. So they "correctly interpret Jesus's claim to be 'Son' as identification with God."[53] Brown concludes that the relevant passages "make it *likely that Jesus spoke and thought of himself as 'the Son,' implying a very special relationship to God that is part of his identity and status.*"[54] Kasper reasons that even "[t]his exclusive 'my Father' implies a non-transferable, unique relationship between Jesus and God. . . . [H]e is Son in a special and unique way."[55] Critical comments like these contain many possible implications concerning Jesus's nature.

Additionally, Ladd finds that "Jesus thought of himself as the Son of God in a unique way, that he was set apart from all other men in that he shared a oneness with God impossible to ordinary men."[56] Witherington thinks that the Son of God texts indicate that the idea of Jesus's preexistence "was probably bound to arise."[57] Marshall concludes that the title "Son of God" involves "the divinity of Jesus; this emerged as the inescapable corollary of Jesus's position."[58] Other scholars agree with various aspects of this argument.[59]

Son of Man

The second title to discuss is the designation "Son of Man." Few New Testament topics have been treated in more publications, or with more details. So I must necessarily be very brief, relying heavily on summations and scholarly positioning.

Some Background

The Old Testament speaks in various ways of the "son of man." The title could be used as a general reference to human beings (Ps 8:4). It appears dozens of times in Ezekiel as a reference to the prophet (2:1, 3, 6, 8 for example). The major reference is Daniel 7:13–14; an enigmatic figure comes on the clouds and approaches the Ancient of Days, being given glory, power, and an everlasting Kingdom.

In some segments of Jewish thought in the first century A.D., the Son of Man appears again, as a specific person, with some additional divinelike emphases. In the Similitudes of Enoch, the Son of Man exists before creation (1 Enoch 46:2; 48:2–3; 62:7) and will be worshiped by all people on Earth (48:5;

62:6, 9). Further, he will be seated on a glorious throne (62:5; 69:29), judging sin (69:28). He seems to be identified as the Messiah (48:10; 52:4). 4 Ezra (2 Esd) may also be helpful here in its commentary on Daniel 7:13–14.

Earlier last century, scholars regularly dated these writings to the pre-Christian era. However, recent experts agree in dating them to the first century A.D., with 1 Enoch perhaps earlier than 4 Ezra.[60] James Charlesworth states: "Repeatedly the specialists on *1 Enoch* have come out in favor of the *Jewish* nature of this section of *1 Enoch* and its first-century C.E. origin and probable pre-70 date. The list of specialists on *1 Enoch* arguing for this position has become overwhelmingly impressive. . . . [N]o specialist now argues that *1 Enoch* 37–71 is Christian and postdates the first century."[61]

So in the first century A.D., there was some Jewish interest in apocalyptic subjects, sometimes centering on the figure of the Son of Man, and seemingly drawn from Daniel 7:13–14, at least as portrayed in these writings. Even if the compositions of 1 Enoch and 4 Ezra postdate Jesus, the ideas concerning the Son of Man "were already extant and probably familiar in Jesus's era."[62] That these concepts reveal a non-Christian tradition that appears "likely in circulation during the time of Jesus" is a view "which today enjoys widespread scholarly support."[63]

Many scholars have agreed that the notion of the Son of Man that appears at least in the Similitudes and 4 Ezra is that of a messianic personage who is preexistent, heavenly, and divine.[64] As we saw, the Son of Man sits on a glorious throne and is worshiped by all of the inhabitants of Earth. As Brown summarizes regarding 4 Ezra 13:3ff., a "superhuman figure" comes on the scene, "flies with the clouds of heaven," and destroys God's enemies.[65] Daniel 7:13–14 hints at some of these ideas and appears to be the impetus for the later Jewish writings.

The best way to ascertain the nature of the Son of Man expressions in the Gospels is to examine the references. Scholars are generally agreed that these sayings fall into three categories: the earthly ministry of Jesus; the suffering, death, and resurrection of the Son of Man; and the future coming of the Son of Man in exaltation and judgment. The last category is particularly close to the Danielic text, especially in Mark 13:26 and 14:62, which appear to be even partial citations. Witherington notes, however, that "the case for Daniel 7 lying in the background of a good many of the Son of man sayings, and at least some from all three categories or types of sayings, is a strong one."[66] So at least some of these sayings, attributed to Jesus, should be seen against Daniel's background. A few of these Gospel texts even seem to speak of Jesus's divinity. But before turning to some instances, we need to ascertain whether these sayings can be linked to Jesus, or whether they come from another source, such as the early church.

Genuine Sayings of Jesus?

In one of the most intriguing topics in New Testament theology, there is widespread agreement among recent critical scholars that at least some of the Gospels' Son of Man sayings can be attributed only to Jesus.[67] Three highly impressive reasons for this conclusion may be provided: the Son of Man sayings are found in all strata of the Gospel traditions, in multiple sources and multiple forms. Further, the sayings satisfy the criterion of dissimilarity.

Explaining in a little more detail, Robert Stein answers denials that Jesus made any of the Son of Man comments: "such attempts founder on the fact that this title is found in all the Gospel strata (Mark, Q, M, L, and John) and satisfies perfectly the 'criterion of dissimilarity,' which states that if a saying or title like this could not have arisen out of Judaism or out of the early church, it must be authentic."[68]

Of the three groups of Son of Man sayings in the Gospels, only the second is not multiply attested. The third, apocalyptic category that comes closest to the Danielic model is found in all four of the Synoptic categories.[69] Bock argues specifically concerning Jesus as the apocalyptic Son of Man: "If the criterion of multiple attestation means anything or has any useful purpose, then the idea that Jesus spoke of himself in these terms should not be doubted."[70]

The Son of Man sayings also appear in texts that exhibit multiple literary forms, including parabolic, miraculous, and teaching narrative. From these two considerations, we learn that these sayings are exceptionally well evidenced.

But could the title have been attributed to Jesus by others, like Jews or early Christians? This charge is also answered by the principle of dissimilarity, since neither Judaism nor the church can account adequately for this title being applied to Jesus. As discussed above, a similar concept is definitely found in Judaism at about the same time as the Gospels. But non-Christian Jews, of course, would not have applied this title to Jesus!

Since "Son of Man" was Jesus's favorite self-designation, it would make some initial sense to charge that this simply indicates that it was a popular Christian title at the time when the Gospels were written. However, this does not explain the attribution of the title to Jesus, either, since Jesus is never given this designation in any of the New Testament epistles. In other words, if it is in effect the church's favorite title for Jesus, so that it shows up repeatedly in all of the Gospel strata, then why is it entirely absent in the epistles, especially where other titles are popular? And in the Gospels, no one else applied the title to Jesus, except when Jesus was simply asked what he meant by it (Jn 12:34). Outside the Gospels, it only appears with the definite article in Acts 7:56. But even here it refers not to the earthly Jesus, but only to the heavenly, exalted Jesus, which seems to reflect Daniel 7.[71]

So how could early Christians be responsible for originating the "Son of Man" title as Jesus's favorite self-description, when the texts never attribute it to Jesus during his earthly ministry or in the epistles? Even the glorified Jesus is very rarely referred to in this manner. Cullmann asserts that this issue is "completely inexplicable" as argued by the older critical thesis. The only sensible option is that the Gospels reliably reported that Jesus used the title and applied it to himself.[72] Other scholars argue that to deny the authenticity of this self-given title is to do so on a priori rather than exegetical grounds.[73] That the title "Son of Man" is Jesus's self-designation is by far the strongest conclusion, and is exceptionally well supported by three separate arguments. It is multiply attested in each of the Gospel strata, as well as being located in multiple Gospel literary forms. Moreover, it is Jesus's favorite designation in the Gospels, yet it is nowhere else applied to his earthly ministry, and used very sparingly in referring to his exalted, glorified state. This title is virtually inexplicable unless Jesus applied it to himself.

A Title of Divinity?

Does the title "Son of Man" provide any crucial insights into Jesus's self-consciousness? In particular, did Jesus thereby refer to his own divinity? I look at a couple of texts.

Mark 2:1–12

In this passage, Jesus declared that the Son of Man had the authority to forgive a paralyzed man's sins. The Jewish leaders in attendance charged Jesus with committing blasphemy, objecting that forgiving sin was God's prerogative alone. Jesus responded that, by healing the man, he would evidence his claim that he was able to forgive sin.

In his study of Jesus's miracles, Twelftree "judged with high confidence" that this healing miracle reflects a historical incident in the life of Jesus. In particular, he found textual support from both enemy attestation and the element of surprise in the account of breaking through the roof of the house, especially since this is consistent with the nature of homes in Palestine.[74] John Meier agrees concerning the force of the last point.[75] Although these considerations do not demonstrate this particular case, they at least provide some critical considerations in favor of this narrative.

A few scholars agree that this situation is significant in terms of Jesus's self-consciousness. Marshall points out, "We have here a fact about the conduct of Jesus which is beyond critical cavil."[76] Guthrie moves further: "Jesus as Son of man was exercising authority which he himself knew was legitimate only for God."[77] Cullmann concludes in still stronger terms: "this meant a conscious identification with God."[78]

Mark 14:61–64

Several powerful indications that Jesus thought of himself as divine are garnered from an instance in the third category of Son of Man sayings: his future coming with the clouds of heaven in exaltation and judgment. Of these texts, the most crucial is Jesus's session before the high priest, leading to the charge of blasphemy being leveled against him.[79] At least Mark seems to conclude that this was the motive for Jesus's crucifixion. When asked if he was "the Christ, the Son of the Blessed?" (RSV), Jesus answered unambiguously: "I am" (ἐγώ εἰμι).

Then Jesus turned his statement that he was the Messiah, the Son of God into a comment revealing that he was also the Son of Man. His response precipitated the final Jewish charge of blasphemy (Mk 14:62–64), and led to Jesus's execution. Perhaps surprisingly, scholars usually agree that the claim to be the Messiah, as climactic as it was, would not by itself constitute sacrilege.

So what exactly did Jesus say that required the high priest to charge him with blasphemy? This has been a focal point in a number of recent studies involving Jesus's self-consciousness, and the answer seems to be garnering some agreement. Brown argues that Jesus's claim to be the "apocalyptic Son of Man" crossed the line of blasphemy, because it revealed "arrogant intentions infringing on divine prerogatives."[80]

Scholars frequently agree on the next point. In his weighty study of this text, Evans asserts that, when he claimed that he would sit on God's right hand (14:62), "Jesus anticipated sharing God's chariot throne. Such a claim would have been scandalous, for the idea of a mortal sitting on God's throne was unthinkable." Evans concludes: "for surely Jesus's claim to share God's throne . . . would have prompted the High Priest to accuse Jesus of blasphemy."[81]

N. T. Wright explains that Jesus was referring to both Daniel 7:13–14 and Psalm 110, thereby explaining the "enthronement" passages in 1 Enoch. The combination yields an extraordinary claim by Jesus to "an enthronement in which the Messiah, or the 'son of man,' would share the very throne of Israel's god."[82] Witherington holds that Psalm 80:17 may also be added to the mix, along with Daniel 7:13–14 and Psalm 110:1, indicating that Jesus "deliberately" combined these texts to produce a "definite enthronement" theme reminiscent of 1 Enoch.[83]

After Jesus announced that he would be seated on the right hand of God, he also said that he would come with the clouds of heaven. Even this seemingly harmless comment adds to the nature of Jesus's claim. John Collins maintains "that the entourage of clouds normally denotes divine status in ancient Israel." Citing Emerton, Collins reports: "If Dan. vii:13 does not refer to a divine being, then it is the only exception out of about seventy passages in the O.T."[84]

Perhaps the most detailed study of this passage has been written by Darrell Bock. One of his chief contributions is to place Mark's text against virtually every relevant passage from ancient Judaism, in order to establish the most likely meaning. He also concludes that Jesus was condemned for a combination of reasons, both theological and political. In addition to responding affirmatively to the high priest's question of whether he was the Christ, the Son of God, Jesus used the imagery of coming on the clouds, which is "a right only deity possesses." Then, by combining two Old Testament texts, Jesus put himself in God's place by claiming to be the enthroned regal figure of Psalm 110:1 and the authoritative figure of a Son of Man in Daniel 7:13–14. He thereby shared God's throne and authority. Further, Jesus attacked the Jewish priests, who were "God's authorities" on Earth.[85]

Regarding the authenticity of this text, Bock mentions a few considerations favoring its accuracy in depicting a historical scene from Jesus's life. On several occasions, Mark uses the title "Son of God," but not "Son of the Blessed One," while it was a popular Jewish practice to avoid the proper name for God. Further, there is dissimilarity between this phrase in Mark and Christian titles for Jesus, which argues that it was probably not derived from other Christian circles, either. The term "Power" is not used elsewhere in the New Testament as a title for God. Especially since critical challenges fail to provide better explanations at these points, Bock concludes, "There is a far greater likelihood that this text, with all of its sensitivity to Jewish background, goes back to Jesus, or, at the least, reflects an earlier setting than Mark or the early church with which he was associated."[86]

Therefore, the best response to the text in Mark 14:61–64 is that Jesus was condemned for making a combination of blasphemous comments, what Witherington calls "a creative conglomerate."[87] He clearly gave an affirmative answer to the question regarding whether he was the Christ, the Son of the Blessed One. Next, combining at least two Old Testament texts, he asserted that he would be seated on God's throne and would come again with clouds in judgment, each of which includes special divine overtones. The high priest had heard enough to decree that Jesus had indeed committed blasphemy. Jesus had claimed divine prerogatives. Tearing his own clothing, indicating the formal charge, the priest declared that no further witnesses were necessary.

Thus, numerous scholars have recognized that Jesus's personalizing the title "Son of Man" indicates an indirect claim to divinity as the heavenly, preexistent, glorified divine figure of Daniel 7:14. Cullmann concludes: "by means of this very term Jesus spoke of his divine heavenly character."[88] Brown notes that Jesus's teachings were taken as "arrogant pretensions infringing on divine prerogatives."[89] Ladd agrees that the appropriation of this title "carried overtones of essential supernatural character and origin."[90] Witherington thinks that this text "suggests that Jesus had a messianic or transcendent self-understanding."[91] Bock holds that Jesus made it "apparent that more than a purely human and earthly messianic claim is present," thereby evoking the charge of heresy, indicated by the high priest tearing his own clothes.[92] Many other scholars basically agree with these conclusions.[93]

Conclusion

Although there is no scholarly unanimity regarding Jesus's self-designations "Son of God" and "Son of Man," there are some important trends. An overview of a few critically attested Gospel texts indicates that, on several occasions, Jesus apparently claimed divine prerogatives. He acknowledged a unique filial relationship to the God of the universe, including privileged knowledge of God and the authority to forgive sins. He also affirmed specifically that he was both the Son of God and the Son of Man, and that, as such, he would occupy God's throne, and come with the clouds of heaven.

Other Indications of Jesus's Divine Self-Consciousness

We have other indications that Jesus held either an explicit or implicit Christology. But I can mention them here only very briefly. For instance, Jesus clearly taught that he was the sole avenue to personal salvation. He challenged others with God's message and presence. Moreover, he taught that their response to him would determine their eternal destiny.[94] This is admitted in some sense by most critical scholars. According to Bultmann, Jesus taught that his person, deeds, and message signaled the in-breaking of God's Kingdom.[95]

Jesus's temptation, baptism, performance of miracles, exorcisms, and the inscription placed on the cross are often mentioned by scholars as other pointers to the divinity of Jesus.[96] Further, the very earliest witnesses to Jesus's teachings include dozens of critically acclaimed creedal texts that also testify to the belief that Jesus was divine.[97] As the earliest witnesses we have, it makes sense that they reflect at least some of Jesus's own thoughts. I have said more than once that the exact sense of Jesus's divinity differs among critical scholars, but some general agreement on this point using critical methodology is still quite remarkable.

Looking even more critically at the Gospel data may indicate a new twist on Jesus's self-consciousness. Gruenler developed an argument that utilizes only a minimal list of Jesus's best-evidenced sayings, as assembled and accepted by radical New Testament critics. These Synoptic passages contain no explicit Christological utterances, and critics almost unanimously believe that they preserve the authentic words of Jesus. Yet, Gruenler argues, it can be shown from these texts alone that Jesus was conscious of his own divinity. Consequently, there are no adequate reasons for differentiating between the Jesus of the minimal authentic sayings and the Jesus who makes the lofty, divine claims found in all four Gospels. Based on either approach, Jesus claimed divine prerogatives.[98]

I have mentioned many other scholars who agree that applying critical research standards to the Gospels indicates that Jesus claimed to be divine. Witherington concludes his important Christological study by composing an impressive list of thirteen items that must be included in any scholarly estimation of Jesus's thoughts concerning himself. The inventory includes Jesus's references to himself as the Son of Man and Son of God, his conviction regarding God's presence in his ministry, his use of "Abba" and "Amen," his pronouncements about being the sole means of entering God's Kingdom, his miracles and what he thought about them, as well as other expressions of authority. Witherington concludes that "these factors are fully accounted for only if Jesus saw himself as God's *mashiach*, God's royal Son . . . and that he had been endowed with the necessary divine knowledge, power, and authority."[99]

Similarly, Marshall thinks that these conclusions follow, in spite of more radical criticism being applied to the Gospels. Given this New Testament data, the issue of Jesus's preexistence also arose in the early church. From an implicit, functional Christology, we can still move on to an explicit Christology and to "the divinity of Jesus; this emerged as the inescapable corollary of Jesus's position."[100] Kasper likewise agrees: "essential Christology and functional Christology, cannot be opposed. They cannot even be separated; they are mutually dependent. . . . [F]unctional Christology implies an essential Christology."[101]

In a simply amazing remark that extends beyond much of what I have been saying here, Raymond Brown states, "I would not object to the thesis that if Jesus reappeared about the year 100 . . . and could have read John, he would have found in that Gospel a suitable (but not an adequate) expression of his own identity."[102] This is where I must leave the matter of Jesus's teachings concerning himself.

A Key Principle

In chapter 1 I outlined a case for Jesus's historical resurrection from the dead. In chapter 2 I attempted to place this event in a *philosophical* context, and set forth criteria that link this event to God. In this chapter I have outlined a specific *theological* context for interpreting the resurrection, further connecting this event with Jesus.

The philosophical context included arguments for theism being more likely than naturalism, the inability to adjust nature's laws to explain the resurrection naturally, the lack of a viable alternative theory, and a connection between the attributes of the God of traditional theism and the requirements for such an event. The theological context was provided by the confirming nature of miracles, especially in an ancient Jewish context, Jesus's view of his own miracles, as well as some of Jesus's major teachings regarding himself and his mission.

More specifically, in this chapter, I have argued for several conclusions. Miracles tend to point beyond themselves to a religious message. Jesus claimed that his miracles were a sign that God had approved his teachings. There are good reasons to hold that he predicted that his resurrection would be his supreme vindication. Still, he did point to his miracles as the evidence for his message, and the resurrection event was the greatest of the miracles. Among his chief teachings, Jesus taught from more than one angle that he was divine and that he was God's chosen messenger, especially regarding the message of God's Kingdom (to which I will turn in the next chapter). In him, God was confronting humankind with a choice. Many critical scholars accept this scenario, particularly regarding Jesus as God's spokesperson.

Given the convergence of all these philosophical and theological indicators, it appears that Jesus's resurrection is strong evidence for the truth of his teachings. As the greatest miracle, it was the ultimate vindication of his message by God. By raising Jesus from the dead, God placed his special approval on Jesus's message, thereby validating Jesus's theistic view of the universe.

In other words, against the general backdrop of miracles and their meaning, Jesus taught that his miracles, including his resurrection, were the accrediting signs that verified his claims. He also taught that he was divine, and that he was God's chosen messenger and agent for the coming Kingdom. Then he was raised from the dead. Negatively, especially in a Jewish context, it is highly unlikely that God would have raised a heretic from the dead. Positively, the best explanation for the resurrection is that, in this act, God placed his stamp of approval on Jesus's teachings.

The Christian theistic framework makes better sense of the data, besides being more internally consistent than other scenarios. Based on this thesis, as an incredible miracle, Jesus's resurrection serves to approve his theistic perspective. God raised Jesus, indicating the truth of both his personal claims to divinity and the central thrust of his mission. Not only was this Jesus's own position, but it is the repeated teaching of the earliest New Testament witness. As Marshall informs us, Jesus's resurrection was "the decisive stimulus" in the early Christian recognition that Jesus was deity.[103]

Conversely, other positions are confronted by numerous hurdles. For example, naturalists as well as others need to explain Jesus's miracles, along with his other teachings. They also need to draft a viable alternative hypothesis to explain the resurrection and/or make major adjustments to nature's laws. If some unknown, even nonreligious person had been raised, some would call this a freak event of nature. But since it occurred only to the very individual who made these unique claims, this favors the retrospective corroboration of Jesus's theistic claims. As Neill asserts, "Jesus is not the least like anyone else who has ever lived. The things he says about God are not the same as the sayings of any other religious teacher. The claims that he makes for himself are not the same as those that have been made by any other religious teacher."[104]

Other options regarding God's action in raising Jesus are all less likely. If Jesus were mistaken in his teachings, or if there are other paths to God, why was only Jesus raised from the dead? Further exasperating the critics' problem here is the exclusive nature of Jesus's message. It would have been helpful if the other major religious founders were also raised from the dead, to similarly indicate that their messages were true. So God's raising Jesus is best viewed as confirmation of his message, in opposition to these alternate scenarios.

Could God have been acting purposely in order to confuse us? There are several reasons for rejecting such views. Initially, these alternatives would be contrary to what we saw in chapter 2 regarding God's existence and attributes, such as the knowledge of truth, the character of the universe, and so on, not to mention the nature of morality and aesthetics. There is an entire cadre of reasons here that argue very strongly that we are not being deceived. Additionally, the internal consistency of Christian theism involving God's actions in raising Jesus to confirm his theistic worldview opposes such motives. Further, many who have responded to Jesus's promises have indicated that God keeps His promises. Lastly, these views make little sense and are only idle ventures, since no evidence supports such claims.

We have to base decisions on the available data, and several intersecting factors indicate that these alternative options fail to adequately account for the facts. The character of God, as shown by our theistic considerations as well as by our other studies, combined with Jesus's convictions regarding his miracles, the uniqueness of Jesus's message, and God's subsequent corroboration in the resurrection, provide a formidable case for Christian theism. Testimonies from believers who have acted on these claims and have found God to be faithful only confirm the promises, demonstrating the futility of alternative explanations, not to mention that reasons are very seldom even provided for such alternate hypotheses.

God had a specific purpose in raising Jesus from the dead. This event was not a coincidence or a freak occurrence of nature, nor was its purpose confirming conflicting messages. It makes the most sense that God agreed with Jesus's teaching.

So I arrive at a key principle. *By raising Jesus from the dead, God placed His stamp of approval on Jesus's entire message, both concerning himself and his other teachings, because God would not have raised a heretic from the dead.*

There are several reasons for accepting this principle. From what appears to be God's perspective, He acted positively according to His nature when He raised Jesus. Both the prospective and retrospective arguments presented in the last two chapters confirm this conclusion. It makes the most sense that God's action signified His approval of Jesus's total message, particularly those portions applying to Jesus's major teachings, such as what he said about himself and his call to commitment. Negatively, confirming someone who proclaimed a false message would be contrary to God's nature, especially in such central areas of theology. If Jesus was a false teacher, it makes no sense for God to have raised him from the dead.

We may add Jesus's viewpoint on the matter, as well. In light of all his unique teachings about the confirming value of his miracles, his own identity, and his call for an eternal decision, it certainly makes sense that he was in the best position to know the meaning of the resurrection. Jesus taught that it was the chief sign that he was teaching and acting on God's behalf. Besides, since Jesus had died, how else can we account for the resurrection unless God was involved? A dead man could hardly raise himself! It makes sense that, as his chief miracle, it was the greatest indication that his Father, the God of the universe, had specifically verified *his* message. Briefly stated, history's most unique messenger was the focus of history's most unique event.

So this principle has the twofold benefit of verification from two perspectives: from that of the Father and the Son. This is significant because it both grounds Jesus's message and opens it for further study. Determining what follows from this principle is my goal for the remainder of the first section of this book.

Jesus's Resurrection and Contemporary Scholarship

Although similar arguments have impressed many scholars, we need to be cautious because Jesus's resurrection is an area in which, as I have remarked more than once, different scholars hold differing senses of the terms being used. This especially applies to the subject of the divinity of Jesus. Still, an overview may provide some hints.

Philosopher Richard Swinburne remarks that numerous claims pertaining to Jesus are unique when compared to the claims of other major theistic religions and that extraordinary miraculous events potentially serve as a means of evidencing these teachings.[105] Philosopher Stephen Davis comments similarly: "In a world in which messiahs and gurus proliferate, we who need spiritual guidance are forced to ask how we can tell whom to believe."[106] So how do we differentiate between the conflicting claims? Davis answers: "Jesus made extraordinary claims. . . . The resurrection of Jesus, then, is God's decisive proof that Jesus is not just a great religious teacher among all the great religious teachers in history. It is God's sign that Jesus . . . alone is Lord. . . . [H]e alone was resurrected from the dead."[107]

After developing a detailed, systematic argument to back his thesis, theologian Wolfhart Pannenberg concludes that, "The resurrection of Jesus confirmed not merely his message and work . . . but Jesus himself."[108] Brian Hebblethwaite agrees that the resurrection cannot by itself show that Jesus was divine. But he combines this event with a half dozen other indicators, including Jesus's special authority claims, in order to arrive at an ontological Christology.[109] Donald Hagner explains, "For it is the resurrection that vindicates all that Jesus said, believed, and did, and so is the definitive answer to the cross. It is obvious, as well, that the resurrection served as the impetus for the christological thinking of the early church."[110] Ben Witherington asks, "What sort of bridge can be built between Jesus's resurrection and claims about his divinity? . . . [T]he resurrection shows that God vindicated Jesus."[111]

In spite of their obvious differences with Christian theism, even skeptics occasionally grant the tenor of the argument here. Philosopher Antony Flew agrees that if Jesus's resurrection actually happened, then naturalists would have to be open to considering Jesus's teachings concerning Christianity, including Jesus's own deity, even to the extent of changing their naturalistic position.[112] Historian Michael Grant remarks, regarding the Christian belief that Jesus appeared after his death: "These appearances, then, have been described, and quite rightly described, as the nearest Christians can ever get to providing proof that Jesus was Christ."[113] And for "those who believed in Jesus's Resurrection, it conferred utterly satisfying evidence of the divine power's sovereign penetration and destruction of the whole man-made fabric of the history of the world."[114] Historian J. K. Elliott holds the New Testament "is full of the theological implications of the resurrection," providing some examples.[115]

Many additional critical scholars have also cited the value, at some level, of reasoning from the resurrection to the truth of Jesus's teachings.[116] Granted, many scholars do not like to argue from the resurrection to other truths. Among their reasons for doing so, some reject (or remain agnostic concerning) the event itself, but, strangely enough, still see value in the resurrection as some sort of indication of the general truth of Jesus's teachings.[117] But others, who readily believe in the resurrection, think that this event and other doctrines that follow from it all emerge from a stance of faith rather than from any pattern of argumentation. This position seems to fail for several reasons, including its opposition to the New Testament witness under the guise of defending it, as well as its refusal to adequately ground faith.

Conclusion

Miracles, by their nature, point beyond themselves to a message of religious significance. Jesus claimed that his miracles were indications that his message was true. This would especially apply to his resurrection. Objections fail to alter this stance.

Jesus made some rather exalted personal statements, chiefly by using the titles "Son of God" and "Son of Man," among other teachings. Further, he claimed to be God's unique agent in establishing the Kingdom. The eternal destiny of his hearers depended on their response to his call.

I pointed out many reasons why God raising Jesus from the dead is best understood as His placing His stamp of approval on Jesus's entire message. This is by far the best conclusion regarding the meaning of this event. Other options inadequately address the historicity of the resurrection, the evidence for theism, and/or Jesus's message.

For these reasons, then, we may affirm the truth of Jesus's teachings. We have already seen two examples, Jesus's teachings concerning himself and his message of the Kingdom. I noted briefly that the latter comprised Jesus's central preaching, especially regarding the requirements for salvation, in the form of a required decision. Jesus called his listeners to respond to him and his message, since he was God's personal agent of salvation. This is the subject matter of my next three chapters. In chapter 4 I treat more extensively the nature of the Kingdom of God. In chapter 5 my topic is the decision that Jesus required as grounds for entering the Kingdom. In chapter 6 I examine the life of the Kingdom—eternal life. As Jesus's chief message, these teachings would especially be vindicated by Jesus's resurrection.

Notes

1. J. L. Mackie, *The Miracle of Theism* (Oxford: Clarendon Press, 1982), 26; Antony Flew, introduction to *Of Miracles*, by David Hume (La Salle, Ill.: Open Court, 1985), 7–8.

2. As in Mk 1:22, 27; 6:2; 11:18; 12:17, 37; Mt 22:46.

3. Richard Swinburne, *The Concept of Miracle* (New York: St. Martin's Press, 1970), 7–10; cf. Swinburne, introduction to *Miracles*, ed. Swinburne (New York: Macmillan, 1989), 6–9.

4. Richard Swinburne, *The Existence of God*, rev. ed. (Oxford: Clarendon Press, 1991), chap. 12; cf. Swinburne, "Historical Evidence," in *Miracles*, 151.

5. John Meier, *A Marginal Jew: Rethinking the Historical Jesus*, 3 vols. (New York: Doubleday, 1987–2001), 2:970. For Meier's conclusions regarding the historicity of Jesus's miracle-claims, see 968–70.

6. Graham H. Twelftree, *Jesus the Miracle Worker: A Historical and Theological Study* (Downers Grove, Ill.: InterVarsity Press, 1999), 345. For Twelftree's historical analysis and conclusions, see 328–30.

7. For instance, see Rudolf Bultmann, *Theology of the New Testament*, 2 vols., trans. Kendrick Grobel (New York: Scribner's Sons, 1951, 1955), 1:7; Reginald H. Fuller, *The Foundations of New Testament Christology* (New York: Scribner's Sons, 1965), 107; Wolfhart Pannenberg, *Jesus: God and Man*, 2nd ed., trans. Lewis L. Wilkins and Duane A. Priebe (Philadelphia: Westminster Press, 1977), 63–64; Raymond E. Brown, *An Introduction to New Testament Christology* (Mahweh, N.J.: Paulist, 1994), 61–67; Howard Clark Kee, *What Can We Know about Jesus?* (Cambridge: Cambridge University Press, 1990), 112; Meier, *A Marginal Jew*, 2:967–70; Twelftree, *Jesus the Miracle Worker*, 328–30, 343–48.

8. Twelftree, *Jesus the Miracle Worker*, 346–47.

9. In addition to the examples given above, see Mt 11:2–6/Lk 7:18–23; Mt 12:28/Lk 11:20; Jn 5:36–37, 11:41–44, 14:11, 15:24.

10. Mk 2:12; Mt 8:27, 14:32–33; Jn 3:2, 11:45.

11. Pannenberg, *Jesus: God and Man*, 67–68.

12. See Mk 8:31, 9:31, 10:33–34, 14:27–28, 14:61–64; Mt 12:38–40/Lk 11:29–32, 16:1–4; Jn 2:18–22, 10:17–18.

13. For instance, Martin Hengel thinks that the probability of Jesus knowing about his death "should no longer be doubted" (*The Atonement* [Philadelphia: Fortress Press, 1981], 70–71). For just a few of the other critical scholars who agree that Jesus knew (or probably knew) about his impending death, see Fuller, *Foundations*, 107–8; Günther Bornkamm, *Jesus of Nazareth*, trans. Irene and Fraser McLuskey with James M. Robinson (New York: Harper and Row, 1960), 154–55; Titus Oluwafidipe Oluwafemi, "Jesus's Resurrection as the Ultimate 'Sign' of His Messianic Authority (A Special Reference Study of the Jonah-Sign in Mathew-Luke and the Temple-Sign in John)," (Ph.D. diss., Baylor University, 1979), abstract; Hans Küng, *Eternal Life? Life after Death as a Medical, Philosophical, and Theological Problem*, trans. Edward Quinn (Garden City, N.Y.: Doubleday, 1984), 94; Thomas Sheehan, *The First Coming: How the Kingdom of God Became Christianity* (New York: Random House, 1986), 103; Dale C. Allison Jr., *The End of the Ages Has Come: An Early Interpretation of the Passion and Resurrection of Jesus* (Philadelphia: Fortress Press, 1985), 100, 116–18, 137–41; Kee, *What Can We Know?* 112;

Hans F. Bayer, *Jesus's Predictions of Vindication and Resurrection* (Tübingen, Germany: Mohr Verlag, 1986); Marcus Borg, "The Truth of Easter," in *The Meaning of Jesus: Two Visions*, by Borg and N. T. Wright (San Francisco: Harper Collins, 1999), 87, cf. 99; Pheme Perkins, "The Resurrection of Jesus of Nazareth," in *Studying the Historical Jesus: Evaluations of the State of Current Research*, ed. Bruce Chilton and Craig A. Evans (Leiden, Netherlands: E. J. Brill, 1994), 431; Raymond E. Brown, *The Death of the Messiah*, 2 vols. (Garden City, N.Y.: Doubleday, 1994), 2:1487–88; John Meier, "Dividing Lines in Jesus Research Today: Through Dialectical Negation to a Positive Sketch," *Interpretation* 50 (1996): 369; Rudolf Pesch, "Die Passion des Menschensohnes: Eine Studie zu den Menschensohnworten der vormarkinischen Passionsgeschichte," in *Jesus und der Menschensohn*, ed. Pesch and Rudolf Schnackenburg (Freiburg, Germany: Herder, 1975), esp. 189–92.

14. Still, a significant number of key critical scholars also hold that Jesus predicted (or probably predicted) his resurrection or vindication after death. Some examples include Perkins, "The Resurrection of Jesus," 431; Gerald O'Collins, *Interpreting Jesus* (Mahweh, N.J.: Paulist Press, 1983), 85–87; Craig A. Evans, "Did Jesus Predict His Death and Resurrection?" in *Resurrection*, ed. Stanley E. Porter, Michael A. Hayes, and David Tombs, *Journal for the Study of the New Testament* Supplement Series 186 (Sheffield, England: Sheffield Academic Press, 1999), 91–97; Barnabas Lindars, "The Resurrection and the Empty Tomb," in *The Resurrection of Jesus Christ*, ed. Paul Avis (London: Darton, Longman and Todd, 1993), 125–26; William Lane Craig, "The Guard at the Tomb," *New Testament Studies* 30 (1984): 276–77; John Frederick Jansen, *The Resurrection of Jesus Christ in New Testament Theology* (Philadelphia: Westminster Press, 1980), 38; Bayer, *Jesus's Predictions*; Oluwafemi, "Jesus's Resurrection," abstract; George Eldon Ladd, *I Believe in the Resurrection of Jesus* (Grand Rapids, Mich.: Eerdmans, 1975), 34.

15. Perhaps the Gospels placed the disciples in a negative light in order to emphasize Jesus or his predictions, but this would be a high price to pay, since these men were the leaders in the early church. Interestingly, the leader of the disciples, Peter, plays a particularly negative role in these texts. Moreover, Jesus's resurrection predictions serve no real apologetic or theological purpose in the early church.

16. For this conclusion, see Gary R. Habermas, "Resurrection Claims in Non-Christian Religions," *Religious Studies* 25 (1989): 167–77.

17. Patrick Nowell-Smith, "Miracles," in *New Essays in Philosophical Theology*, ed. Antony Flew and Alasdair MacIntyre (New York: Macmillan, 1964), 245–46, 251; Antony Flew, s.v. "Miracles," in *The Encyclopedia of Philosophy*, ed. Paul Edwards (New York: Macmillan, 1967), 5:347; David Basinger, "Christian Theism and the Concept of Miracle: Some Epistemological Perplexities," *The Southern Journal of Philosophy* 28 (1980): 139–49.

18. We have seen that even Flew admits this. See Habermas and Flew, *Did Jesus Rise from the Dead? The Resurrection Debate* (San Francisco: Harper and Row, 1987), 3, 39, 49–50.

19. Our brief treatment of hallucinations in chapter 1 lists additional problems. See also Gary R. Habermas, "Explaining Away Jesus' Resurrection: The Recent Revival of Hallucination Theories," *Christian Research Journal* 23 (2001): 26–31, 47–49.

20. David Hume, "On Miracles," part II, in section X of *An Enquiry Concerning Human Understanding*, in *Hume on Religion*, ed. Richard Wollheim, Fontana Library of Theology and Philosophy (London: Collins Sons and Company, 1963); Nowell-Smith, "Miracles," 245; J. C. A. Gaskin, "Contrary Miracles Concluded," *Hume Studies*, 10th anniversary issue, 1985 supplement, 1–14.

21. C. S. Lewis, *Miracles: A Preliminary Study* (New York: Macmillan, 1960), 132.

22. Archie J. Bahm, "Comments by the Author," in *Tao Teh King*, by Lao-tzu, 2nd ed., ed. Bahm (Albuquerque, N.M.: World Books, 1986), on both Confucius and Lao-tzu, see 89, 114–15.

23. See Surahs 2:23; 3:183–184; 10:38; 17:88–89.

24. Edwin Yamauchi, *Jesus, Zoroaster, Buddha, Socrates, Mohammad*, rev. ed. (Downers Grove, Ill.: InterVarsity Press, 1972), 40; cf. esp. 4–7, 18, 38–41.

25. Stephen Neill, *Christian Faith and Other Faiths: The Christian Dialogue with Other Religions*, 2nd ed. (London: Oxford University Press, 1970), 233.

26. We will note that the degree of critical attestation on the topic of Jesus's teachings concerning himself is not as great as that favoring the data for Jesus's resurrection that we investigated in chapter 1. However, it is also the case that the caliber of scholarly agreement represented here is still quite substantial.

27. Brown, *Introduction*, 4–15, 102.

28. Walter Kasper, *Jesus the Christ*, trans. V. Green (Mahweh, N.J.: Paulist Press, 1974), 109; George Eldon Ladd, *A Theology of the New Testament* (Grand Rapids, Mich.: Eerdmans, 1974), 159.

29. Ben Witherington III, *The Christology of Jesus* (Minneapolis: Fortress Press, 1990), follows C. K. Barrett here, 261, 269; Seyoon Kim, *The Son of Man and the Son of God* (Grand Rapids, Mich.: Eerdmans, 1985), 75.

30. Cf. Brown, *Introduction*, 89; Kasper, *Jesus the Christ*, 109.

31. Witherington, *The Christology of Jesus*, 221.

32. Examples include Brown, *Introduction*, 88–89; Witherington, *The Christology of Jesus*, 226–27; Kasper, *Jesus the Christ*, 109–10.

33. Witherington, *The Christology of Jesus*, 226.

34. Fuller, *Foundations*, 133 n. 20.

35. Oscar Cullmann, *The Christology of the New Testament*, rev. ed., trans. Shirley C. Guthrie and Charles A. M. Hall (Philadelphia: Westminster Press, 1963), 288.

36. Donald Guthrie, *New Testament Theology* (Downers Grove, Ill.: InterVarsity Press, 1981), 307.

37. I. Howard Marshall, *The Origins of New Testament Christology*, updated ed. (London: InterVarsity Press, 1990), 115; cf. also 123.

38. Joachim Jeremias, *The Central Message of the New Testament* (Philadelphia: Fortress Press, 1965), 30.

39. James Barr, "Abba Isn't Daddy," *Journal of Theological Studies* 39 (1988): 28–47.

40. Martin Hengel, *The Son of God*, trans. John Bowden (Philadelphia: Fortress Press, 1976), 63, 45; Gerald O'Collins translates "Abba" as "Father, dear" (*Interpreting Jesus*, 52).

41. Borg thinks "Abba" "has as its corollary the term 'son,'" Still, he does not consider these designations as expressions of deity (*Jesus: A New Vision: Spirit, Culture, and the Life of Discipleship* [San Francisco: Harper Collins, 1987], 49–50).

42. Jeremias, *Central Message*, 30

43. Witherington, *The Christology of Jesus*, 220.

44. Guthrie, *New Testament Theology*, 304. Marshall speaks similarly, and includes Jesus's term "Amen" in the discussion of Jesus's consciousness of his own uniqueness (*Origins*, 46).

45. Guthrie, *New Testament Theology*, 794 n. 14; see also 308.

46. Witherington, *The Christology of Jesus*, 229.

47. Cullmann, *Christology*, 288–89.

48. Brown, *Introduction*, 89; O'Collins, *Interpreting Jesus*, 52–53; cf. Marshall, *Origins*, 116.

49. Craig A. Evans, "In What Sense 'Blasphemy'? Jesus Before Caiphas in Mark 14:61–64," *Society of Biblical Literature Seminar Papers* 30 (1991): 231; see also Brown, *Introduction*, 89; Marshall, *Origins*, 115.

50. Witherington, *The Christology of Jesus*, 213–15.

51. John's references to Jesus as the only-begotten Son of God (μονογενής, see 1:14, 18; 3:16, 18; cf. 1 Jn 4:9), indicating Jesus's unique relationship to the Father, might provide some similar ideas to those we have explored in the synoptics. The baptismal, temptation, and transfiguration passages in the synoptics also give a prominent place to the theme of sonship (see Ladd, *Theology*, 164–65; Guthrie, *New Testament Theology*, 308–9).

52. Cullmann, *Christology*, 290.

53. Cullmann, *Christology*, 302; cf. 270.

54. Brown, *Introduction*, 89, even though he says that Jesus "never indisputably" uses the entire title "Son of God" for himself.

55. Kasper, *Jesus the Christ*, 109.

56. Ladd, *Theology*, 168–69.

57. Witherington, *The Christology of Jesus*, 233.

58. Marshall, *Origins*, 129; cf. 123.

59. Ladd makes the intriguing comment that probable first-century-A.D. Jewish writings such as Enoch 105:2 and 4 Ezra 7:28–29, 13:32, 37, 52, and 14:9 speak of a supernatural Messiah as "My Son" (Ladd, *Theology*, 161–62). Others link the title "Son of God" with Jesus's claims to be divine (Guthrie, *New Testament Theology*, 306; cf. Evans, "In What Sense 'Blasphemy'?" 231).

60. See C. F. D. Moule, *The Origin of Christology* (Cambridge: Cambridge University Press, 1977), 15–16; Brown, *Introduction*, 93–96; Darrell L. Bock, *Blasphemy*

and *Exaltation in Judaism: The Charge Against Jesus in Mark 14:53–65* (Grand Rapids, Mich.: Baker Books, 1998; reprint of vol. 106 of *Wissenschaftliche zum Neuen Testament*, 2nd ser., J. C. B. Mohr [Paul Siebeck]), 222–25; Witherington, *The Christology of Jesus*, 234–48; Marshall, *Origins*, 67; Evans, "In What Sense 'Blasphemy'?" 219; Guthrie, *New Testament Theology*, 273–75; Ladd, *Theology*, 161–62; cf. Kasper, *Jesus the Christ*, 107.

61. Charlesworth as quoted by Witherington, *The Christology of Jesus*, 234–35 (Charlesworth's emphasis).

62. Witherington, *The Christology of Jesus*, 235; Bock agrees (*Blasphemy and Exaltation*, 224–25).

63. Evans, "In What Sense 'Blasphemy'?" 219. Besides Witherington, *The Christology of Jesus*, 235, in agreement are Brown, *Introduction*, 95–96; Marshall, *Origins*, 67; Ladd, *Theology*, 149.

64. Agreeing with at least some of these various descriptions are Brown, *Introduction*, 95–96; Moule, *The Origin of Christology*, 11, 23; Witherington, *The Christology of Jesus*, 259; Marshall, *Origins*, 68; Adela Yarbro Collins, "The Influence of Daniel on the New Testament," in *Daniel: A Commentary on the Book of Daniel*, by John Collins (Minneapolis: Fortress Press, 1993), 90; Guthrie, *New Testament Theology*, 274–75; Ladd, *Theology*, 148–49; Royce Gruenler, "Son of Man" in *Evangelical Dictionary of Theology*, ed. Walter A. Elwell (Grand Rapids, Mich.: Baker Book House, 1984), 1035. Although much older, C. K. Barrett's comments are still helpful (*The New Testament Background: Selected Documents* [New York: Harper and Brothers, 1956], 254–55).

65. Brown, *Introduction*, 95.

66. Witherington, *The Christology of Jesus*, 247; cf. 262.

67. O'Collins points out that the majority of scholars have accepted this thesis recently in spite of objections that were lodged chiefly a few decades ago, but that are still influential in some quarters (*Interpreting Jesus*, 62–64). Peter Stuhlmacher agrees that this older critical position has failed (*Jesus of Nazareth—Christ of Faith*, trans. Siegfried S. Schatzmann [Peabody, Mass.: Hendrickson, 1993], 24).

68. Robert Stein, "Jesus Christ," in *Evangelical Dictionary of Theology*, 584.

69. Bock is especially strong on this point (*Blasphemy and Exaltation*, 226–27). Witherington lists several problems with the charge that Jesus never applied to himself the third, future category of the Son of Man sayings (*The Christology of Jesus*, 256–57). O'Collins also critiques this last position (*Interpreting Jesus*, 63–64).

70. Bock, *Blasphemy and Exaltation*, 226. Bock then adds, "Once the category of apocalyptic Son of Man is associated with Jesus, then a connection with Dan 7 cannot be very far away."

71. The anarthrous "Son of Man" also appears in Rv 1:13, 14:14, although neither these texts nor Acts 7:56 refers to the earthly Jesus.

72. Cullmann, *Christology*, 155.

73. Jeremias, *New Testament Theology*, 206; Stein, "Jesus Christ," 584; Gruenler, "Son of Man," 1034–35.

74. Twelftree, *Jesus the Miracle Worker*, 64–66, 293–94, 328.

75. Meier, *A Marginal Jew*, 2:680.

76. Marshall, *Origins*, 50.

77. Guthrie, *New Testament Theology*, 280.

78. Cullmann, *Christology*, 282.

79. As remarked earlier, this text also has important ramifications for our overview of Jesus's claims to be the Son of God.

80. Brown, *Introduction*, 96.

81. Evans, "In What Sense 'Blasphemy'?" 221, 222, respectively.

82. N. T. Wright, "Looking Again for Jesus," *Stimulus* 4 (1996): 34–35.

83. Witherington, *The Christology of Jesus*, 258–61.

84. John Collins, *Daniel*, 290. Cf. J. A. Emerton, "The Origin of the Son of Man Imagery," *Journal of Theological Studies* 9 (1958), 225–42.

85. Bock, *Blasphemy and Exaltation*, esp. 197–209, 220–37. Bock's book was originally published as *Blasphemy and Exaltation in Judaism and the Final Examination of Jesus*, vol. 106 of *Wissenschaftliche zum Neuen Testament*, 2nd ser. (Tübingen, Germany: J. C. B. Mohr [Paul Siebeck], 1998). For a similar assessment in an older work, see Morna Hooker, *The Son of Man in Mark* (London: S.P.C.K., 1967), esp. 173.

86. Bock, *Blasphemy and Exaltation*, 229; for the details, see 210–20, 233, 236.

87. Witherington, *The Christology of Jesus*, 261.

88. Cullmann, *Christology*, 162; cf. 142, 151.

89. Brown, *Introduction*, 96.

90. Ladd, *Theology*, 157–58.

91. Witherington, *The Christology of Jesus*, 262.

92. Bock, *Blasphemy and Exaltation*, 202.

93. See Stuhlmacher, *Jesus of Nazareth*, 26–28; Kasper, *Jesus the Christ*, 108; Stein, "Jesus Christ," 584; Guthrie, *New Testament Theology*, 279–81; Marshall, *Origins*, 68, 79; Gruenler, "Son of Man," 1035.

94. For just a few of these texts, see Mk 2:17; 8:34–38; 10:29–30, 45; Mt 19:28–29; Lk 19:10; Jn 10:10.

95. Bultmann, *Theology of the New Testament*, 1:7–9. Other contemporary scholars, like Fuller, agree (*Foundations*, 105–6). Though these two scholars reject Jesus's ontological deity, they readily recognize Jesus's special claims to authority. Marshall also mentions the significance of Jesus's call to salvation: "Response to Jesus was the qualification for entering the kingdom and receiving its benefits." The authority of Jesus's message here is "beyond dispute" (*Origins*, 50).

96. On these topics, see Stuhlmacher, *Jesus of Nazareth*, 28; Witherington, *The Christology of Jesus*, 270; Marshall, *Origins*, 50, 116–17; Guthrie, *New Testament Theology*, 308–9; Ladd, *Theology*, 163–65.

97. O'Collins, *Interpreting Jesus*, 14, 92; Marshall, *Origins*, 121, 126. Just a few of the most important creeds that mention some of Jesus's titles, along with other relevant data pertaining to his divinity, are Acts 2:31–33, 36; 3:15; 10:36; Rom 1:3–4;

4:24–25; 8:32, 34; 10:9; 14:9; 1 Cor 11:23; 15:3; 2 Cor 4:14; 5:14–15; Phil. 2:6–11; 1 Thes 1:9–10; 1 Pt 3:18.

98. Royce Gordon Gruenler, *New Approaches to Jesus and the Gospels: A Phenomenological and Exegetical Study of Synoptic Christology* (Grand Rapids, Mich.: Baker Book House, 1982). Gruenler thinks that Jesus made no explicit claims in the fourth Gospel that are inconsistent with what is already known from his implicit claims derived from this minimal data in the synoptic Gospels.

99. See Witherington, *The Christology of Jesus*, 268, for this list; cf. 274.

100. Marshall, *Origins*, 128–29; cf. 47, 51–52, 56.

101. Kasper, *Jesus the Christ*, 110–11.

102. Brown, *Introduction*, 203 n. 304. Brown elsewhere makes a similar comment regarding the New Testament proclamation that Jesus was God. See Raymond E. Brown, "Did Jesus Know He Was God?" *Biblical Theology Bulletin* 15 (1985): 74–79.

103. Marshall, *Origins*, 128–29.

104. Neill, *Christian Faith*, 233. Even if the *uniqueness* of Jesus's claims were challenged, this would not affect the corroboration of what Jesus *did* teach.

105. Swinburne, *The Existence of God*, 222, 225–26, 233–34, 241–43.

106. Davis, *Risen Indeed*, 194.

107. Davis, *Risen Indeed*, 195, 197–98, respectively.

108. Wolfhart Pannenberg, *Systematic Theology*, vol. 2, trans. Geoffrey W. Bromily (Grand Rapids, Mich.: Eerdmans, 1991), 365. For similar thoughts, see also Pannenberg, *Jesus: God and Man*, 73; Pannenberg, "The Historicity of the Resurrection. The Identity of Christ," in *The Intellectuals Speak Out about God*, ed. Roy Abraham Varghese (Chicago: Regnery Gateway, 1984), 263–64.

109. Brian Hebblethwaite, "The Resurrection and the Incarnation," in *The Resurrection of Jesus Christ*, 156–65.

110. Donald A. Hagner, "Gospel, Kingdom, and Resurrection in the Synoptic Gospels," in *Life in the Face of Death*, ed. Richard N. Longenecker (Grand Rapids, Mich.: Eerdmans, 1998), 119.

111. Ben Witherington III, "Resurrection Redux," in *Will the Real Jesus Please Stand Up? A Debate between William Lane Craig and John Dominic Crossan*, ed. Paul Copan (Grand Rapids, Mich.: Baker Books, 1998), 130–31.

112. Flew, *Did Jesus Rise from the Dead?* 49–50; cf. also 3.

113. Michael Grant, *Saint Paul* (Glasgow: William Collins Sons, 1976), 85–86.

114. Grant, *Saint Paul*, 79.

115. J. K. Elliott, "The First Easter," *History Today* 29 (1979): 210.

116. Besides the scholars already mentioned, see Hengel, *The Atonement*, 65–66, 72–74; Peter Stuhlmacher, "The Resurrection of Jesus and the Resurrection of the Dead," trans. Jonathan M. Whitlock, *Ex Auditu* 9 (1993): 47–48; N. T. Wright, *Jesus and the Victory of God*, vol. 2 of *Christian Origins and the Question of God* (Minneapolis: Fortress Press, 1996), 488, 660; Brown, *Introduction*, 112, 115; Francis X. Durrwell, *La Résurrection de Jésus: Mystère de Salut* (Paris: Les Éditions du Cerf, 1976), 89–126; Walter Künneth, *Theologie der Auferstehung*, 6th ed.

(Giessen, Germany: Brunnen, 1982), part II, 112–53; C. F. D. Moule, "Response to Don Cupitt," in *Explorations in Theology* 6 (London: SCM Press, 1979), 36–37; E. P. Sanders, *The Historical Figure of Jesus* (London: Penguin Books, 1993), 13–14; Gerald O'Collins, "The Resurrection: The State of the Questions" in *The Resurrection: An Interdisciplinary Symposium on the Resurrection of Jesus*, ed. Stephen T. Davis, Daniel Kendall, and Gerald O'Collins (Oxford: Oxford University Press, 1997), 11, 25; Pheme Perkins, "Reconciling the Resurrection," *Commonweal* 112 (1985): 203; Thomas Torrance, *Space, Time and Resurrection* (Grand Rapids, Mich.: Eerdmans, 1976), 161; Thomas C. Oden, *The Word of Life*, vol. 2 of *Systematic Theology* (Peabody, Mass.: Hendrickson, 1989), 460, 496; Ben F. Meyer, *The Aims of Jesus* (London: SCM Press, 1979), 63; William Lane Craig, "Rebuttal," in *Will the Real Jesus?* 40; Peter Selby, *Look for the Living: The Corporate Nature of Resurrection Faith* (Philadelphia: Fortress Press, 1976), 95–100, 179–80; Jansen, *Resurrection of Jesus Christ in New Testament Theology*, 46–52; John Drane, *Introducing the New Testament* (San Francisco: Harper and Row, 1986), 108; Ladd, *I Believe*, 146; Donald G. Bloesch, *Essentials of Evangelical Theology: God, Authority, and Salvation* (San Francisco: Harper and Row, 1978), 126; Carey Newman, "Resurrection as Glory: Divine Presence and Christian Origins," in *The Resurrection*, 78–82, cf. 88–89; Murray Harris, *Raised Immortal: Resurrection and Immortality in the New Testament* (Grand Rapids, Mich.: Eerdmans, 1983), 72–76; David Peterson in *Resurrection: Truth and Reality*, ed. Paul Barnett, Peter Jensen, and Peterson (Sydney: Aquila Press, 1994), 16; Grant Osborne, *The Resurrection Narratives: A Redactional Study* (Grand Rapids, Mich.: Baker Books, 1984), 283–86, 293–94; J. I. Packer, "Response," in *Did Jesus Rise from the Dead?* 146; Paul Barnett, *Jesus and the Logic of History* (Grand Rapids, Mich.: Eerdmans, 1997), 94; Sunand Sumithra, review of *Jesus's Predictions of Vindication and Resurrection*, by Hans J. Bayer, *Evangelical Review of Theology* 11 (1987): 275; Helmut Merklein, "Die Auferweckung Jesu und die Anfänge der Christologie (Messias bzw. Sohn Gottes und Menschensohn)," *Zeitschrift für die Neutestamentliche Wissenschaft und die Kunde der Älteren Kirche* 72 (1981): 1; Malonga V. N'Zilamba, "Divinité et Résurrection de Jésus: Essai sur la Christologie de Jean Guitton," (Th.D. diss., Pontificia Universitas Gregoriana [Vatican], 1992), abstract.

117. Willi Marxsen (*The Resurrection of Jesus of Nazareth*, trans. Margaret Kohl [Philadelphia: Fortress Press, 1970], 125, 169) speaks for many critical theologians by looking for significance in the resurrection and deciding that God "endorsed" Jesus and his teachings through it. In fact, Marxsen rather incredibly says: "What happened . . . was that God endorsed Jesus *as the person that he was*: during his earthly lifetime Jesus pronounced the forgiveness of sins to men in the name of God. He demanded that they commit their lives entirely to God. . . . I could easily add a whole catalog of other statements" (125). Similarly, he ends his later treatment of the resurrection with "Jesus' invitation to faith" (*Jesus and Easter: Did God Raise the Historical Jesus from the Dead?* trans. Victor Paul Furnish [Nashville: Abingdon Press, 1990], 92). But since Marxsen rejects the historicity of Jesus's res-

urrection, it is not surprising that he also rejects the truth of some of Jesus's theology. Here critical theology is confronted with a dilemma. One might reject the divinity of Jesus, along with some of his other teachings, since his historical resurrection has also been rejected. But if the resurrection actually occurred, this would seem to place us on firmer grounds with these other doctrines, too, since the New Testament witness is that the doctrine relies on the event. Marcus Borg (with N. T. Wright, *The Meaning of Jesus*, 137–42) is another example of the many critical scholars who realize that multiple truths follow from the death and resurrection of Jesus, but, perhaps because they reject or question the historical resurrection, the corresponding truths are held in less-than-literal terms.

CHAPTER FOUR

The Kingdom of God

So far, I have argued that the resurrection of Jesus occurred in history. Further, the evidence indicates that this is probably a theistic universe. As such, God would most likely have raised Jesus from the dead. Additionally, the resurrection indicates from a different perspective that God approved the truth of Jesus's message, especially regarding his central concerns. Since Jesus claimed to be divine, this is another argument for the theistic nature of the world. In this chapter, I look at the major emphasis in Jesus's teaching.

Jesus's Central Teaching

Few scholars today doubt that Jesus's central message was the Kingdom of God and the response that Jesus required for individual admittance into the Kingdom and participation in its blessings. But unpacking some of these ideas has not always been easy. My chief concern in this chapter is a broad outline of Jesus's teaching concerning the Kingdom. In the next chapter I view the entrance requirements and the personal decision required by Jesus.

By far the majority position among contemporary scholars is that Jesus's central teaching concerned the Kingdom of God and the personal response required for admittance. Sanders lists the matter as "almost beyond dispute."[1] Wright thinks that "we actually know more securely that Jesus of Nazareth was a Jewish prophet announcing the kingdom of God than we know almost anything."[2] O'Collins states, "Hardly anything is more certain."[3] Charlesworth calls the amount of agreement "one of the strongest consensuses in New Testament research."[4] Even John Dominic Crossan, who, along with many members of the Jesus Seminar, is among the lone dissenters here, admits, "Now the majority clearly say that what Jesus talked about was . . . the kingdom of God (or God's will for the earth)."[5] In this matter, then, we find broad concurrence among contemporary scholars.[6]

But this does not mean that there is unanimity of interpretation concerning some of the details. In fact, Meier finds that scholarship is "strongly divided" regarding what is perhaps the foremost issue—the timing of the Kingdom, and whether Jesus taught that it was primarily a present or a future reality.[7]

One of the most influential approaches to this question, consistent eschatology, is usually associated with Johannes Weiss and Albert Schweitzer in the late nineteenth and early twentieth centuries. Emphasizing the importance of the future, apocalyptic nature of Jesus's preaching, Weiss holds that, for Jesus, the coming of the Kingdom was imminent and would be brought about, not by himself or by others, but only by a supernatural act of God. Expecting the Kingdom to arrive soon, Jesus initially hoped that he would be alive when it was established. He gradually realized that he would first have to die, but was still convinced that he would return and set up God's Kingdom. Judgment would take place, the dead would be raised, and a new world would emerge. Jesus and his followers would rule on God's behalf.[8]

Schweitzer thinks that Weiss marked one of the major trends in nineteenth-century theology, in that Weiss had the distinction of being the only scholar (aside from Reimarus, in the previous century) who recognized that Jesus's message was "purely eschatological" and "wholly future" in its orientation.[9] But for Schweitzer, Jesus's view of his ministry and the coming Kingdom are not authoritative for modern faith. Schweitzer thinks not only that Jesus was mistaken in these theological views, but that faith should not be placed in scholarly reconstructions of the historical Jesus.[10]

The views of Weiss and Schweitzer show that, for Jesus, his death and vindication were crucial, as were his ethical teachings and his messianic consciousness as the Son of Man, the one who would serve as judge and rule God's Kingdom. Additionally, the Kingdom of God was proclaimed as a future act of God, although imminent. It would not arrive due to human efforts.

But the view of Weiss and Schweitzer fail to account for several factors. First, it is one-sided in not allowing for the present aspect of the Kingdom. Weiss thinks that Matthew 16:17f. is the only attested passage in which Jesus founds the Kingdom.[11] Schweitzer mentions Matthew 12:25–28 as the only sense in which Jesus thinks that the Kingdom has arrived, and even here Jesus does not establish its presence.[12] As noted below, this ignores many critically attested texts in which, in some sense, Jesus teaches that the Kingdom had arrived in his person and actions. Admittedly, uncritical elements like these in the exegesis practiced by Weiss and Schweitzer are also due to the perspective of an ensuing century of scholarship.

Second, Jesus's teachings were not floating around freely in space, unanchored to reality. That he was actually raised from the dead provides confirmation for his message, in the form of God's corroboration, thus indicating that Jesus was correct. This especially applies to Jesus's teachings regarding the Kingdom of God, as his central message, as we will see below.

Third, the position of Weiss and Schweitzer is also fatally flawed in that both based their thesis on the premise that Jesus was mistaken regarding the timing of the Kingdom. But Jesus declared that even he did not know when he would return (Mk 13:32), a comment that, as was shown in the last chapter, meets critical muster. I return below to this question.

Fourth, I point out in the next chapter that New Testament faith was rooted in Jesus's person and actions in history. In missing crucially significant items like these, the approaches taken by Weiss and Schweitzer are based on a sadly defective picture of Jesus. Schweitzer ends his monumental work on the historical Jesus with one of the most forlorn conclusions imaginable.[13] It is simply amazing that a historical resurrection and a different perspective on Jesus's teachings can make such an enormous difference!

A few decades after Schweitzer wrote his best-known work, C. H. Dodd's "realized eschatology" emphasized the presence of the Kingdom of God. Dodd thinks that there was no unfulfilled compendium of events that was yet to occur in the future. He reacted to views that some apocalyptic cataclysm would break into history, shortly after Jesus's day or otherwise, and bring world history to a close. In perhaps his best-known work, *The Parables of the Kingdom*, Dodd holds that Jesus never taught that the Kingdom was to occur shortly. Instead, in our earliest traditions, Jesus proclaimed that it was already present, as an integral part of our realized experience. For Dodd, the Kingdom is actually the fulfillment of God's promises in history.[14]

For example, Dodd explains that Scripture utilizes traditional imagery in order to depict great theological truths like the Kingdom of God, the coming of the Son of Man, judgment, the millennium, and so on. This imagery includes "symbols of supra-sensible, supra-historical realities" that actually find "their corresponding actuality within history." So "there is no coming of the Son of Man 'after' His coming in Galilee and Jerusalem, whether soon or late, for there is no before and after in the eternal order. The Kingdom of God is not something which will happen after other things have happened." These items are symbolized by great word pictures such as flashes of lightening.[15] Jesus "employed the traditional symbolism of apocalypse" to teach about the

Kingdom of God, as represented in his Kingdom parables.[16] But this approach does not totally nullify future blessings. Dodd concludes that the present order of time and space will never exhaust our destiny in God's eternal order.[17]

Dodd has frequently been criticized for this view. Perhaps most regularly, commentators remark that he largely ignored the portions of Jesus's message that clearly indicate a future consummation for the Kingdom of God, like the passages mentioned below. Jeremias's work on Jesus's parables[18] provides much groundbreaking work in the Jewish background of these teachings, sometimes proving difficult for Dodd's interpretation. John Riches explains that the "Jewish apocalyptic, by contrast, taught that [the Kingdom] was still to come in the future." The result was that, "Dodd, under pressure from the exegetically much more detailed and powerful work of Jeremias . . . was eventually to concede that Jesus did indeed still envisage some future stage of fulfillment."[19] Perhaps this is also what is behind Norman Perrin's comment that Dodd's realized eschatology is limited by an "unduly one-sided understanding of the eschatology of Jesus."[20]

Another concern, expressed by Ladd, who cites Perrin for support, is that Dodd's position is also faulty regarding its claim to historicize biblical imagery. However, this cannot be done completely, for even Dodd thinks that the final "consummation of the Kingdom will not occur in history but in this transcendent order beyond time and space."[21]

Both consistent and realized eschatology exhibit some strengths. But perhaps their chief weakness is that they support positions that perceptibly fail to present balanced approaches to Jesus's teachings. In particular, they largely ignore either the present or the future aspects of the Kingdom of God. Thus, if both aspects are taught by Jesus, as most scholars conclude, then any treatment of his position should also address both concepts.

To show that Jesus taught that the Kingdom of God had both present and future aspects, one excellent study was conducted by G. R. Beasley-Murray. In his detailed volume, he treats twenty-one Gospel passages (plus parallels) that teach that the Kingdom was present, and thirteen Gospel texts (plus parallels) that mention the future aspect. Amazingly, *each* category is multiply attested by all four synoptic categories, Mark, Q, M, and L.[22] Concerning only the former, Witherington remarks in his own study on the subject: "By the criterion of multiple attestation alone, this idea of the present *basileia* must surely go back to Jesus."[23] I am able to mention only a few examples of each category.

More texts present the Kingdom of God as present. Certainly one of the major examples is the Q saying in Luke 11:20/Matthew 12:28, where Jesus asserts that his exorcisms are signs that the Kingdom has already arrived. Given the impressive textual evidence favoring Jesus's miracles, along with the corresponding scholarly attention to these occurrences in the life of the historical Jesus, as well as the strong textual confirmation for this particular saying, it is not difficult to understand why it is treated so seriously. Even Perrin argues that its authenticity "may be regarded as established beyond reasonable doubt."[24] Other present Kingdom comments in Q include Matthew 11:11/Luke 7:28 and Matthew 11:12/Luke 16:16. Mark records other important sayings (1:15; 4:11–12). Jesus's parables include other crucial perspectives on the present Kingdom of God (Mk 2:18–22, 4:26–29; Mt 13:1–9, 31–32, 44–46).

It seems clear that Jesus equated the present in-breaking of the Kingdom with his personal ministry, preaching, and miracles. Notably, Matthew 12:24–27 reports Jesus implying that the Pharisees' followers did not inaugurate the coming of the Kingdom when they cast out demons, in contrast to his doing so (v. 28). Jesus's presence and activity were the deciding factor (Mt 11:4–6/Lk 7:22–23; Mt 13:16–17/Lk 10:23–24).[25] When the Pharisees questioned Jesus regarding the timing for the Kingdom, he responded that it was already among them (Lk 17:20–21). To be sure, it is difficult to ascertain the exact sense in which the Kingdom had arrived, indicated by the term ἐντὸς.[26] But the Kingdom's presence is still apparent.

The future aspect of the Kingdom of God also appears frequently in Jesus's teachings. Many significant passages are located in Mark (with parallels), including a number of key sayings about entering the Kingdom, such as Mark 9:42–50, 10:15,[27] 10:23–31. Well-known passages from Q are also represented, like the Lord's prayer (especially Mt 6:10/Lk 11:2), the Beatitudes (Mt 5:3–12/Lk 6:20–23), and the great feast in God's Kingdom (Mt 8:11–12/Lk 7:28–29). During his last meal with his disciples, Mark relates Jesus's testimony that he would not drink of the fruit of the vine until he did so in the future Kingdom of God (Mk 14:25). Matthew 25:31–46 is an incredible account contrasting the coming judgment in the last days and the eternal life of the Kingdom.

Jesus's parables also depict future aspects of the Kingdom of God. Mark 4 (usually with parallels) reports several examples regarding the growth of the Kingdom (4:2–20, 26–29, 30–32). Luke presents the unjust steward (16:1–12) and the tenacious widow (18:1–8). From Q we get the parables of the thief (Mt 24:42–44/Lk 12:39–40) and the talents or pounds (Mt 25:14–30/Lk 19:11–27).

The dialogue between realized and consistent eschatologies gradually produced the recognition that Jesus clearly spoke of both future as well as present aspects of the Kingdom of God. Even in the older studies, scholars tried to work out these relationships. For Bultmann, Jesus conceived of the Kingdom of God chiefly as a future, apocalyptic invasion of history, but Bultmann conceded that there were some present eruptions.[28] In spite of this admission, Bultmann asserted that realized eschatologies were not supported by a single saying by Jesus.[29] Fuller theorized that Jesus taught the proleptic presence of the yet-future revelation of the Kingdom. However, it was presently hidden, awaiting its final actualization.[30]

Bornkamm also affirms what he terms the "remarkable tension" between present and future aspects of the Kingdom of God. We must reject approaches like Dodd's that postulate only present ramifications, but neither can we hold that Jesus taught only a future revelation of God's reign. These two dimensions ought not be either separated or spiritualized. The present dawning of God's Kingdom indicates future salvation and judgment, while the future unlocks and enlightens the present by calling for a decision.[31]

Ladd wrote several detailed studies on this subject. Briefly, through Jesus the Kingdom of God was actually present in the historical realm, though only in a veiled form. The future, glorious coming at the consummation of history would fulfill what had already begun.[32]

Arguably the primary difference between Ladd's position and that of Bultmann, Fuller, and others is that Ladd postulates a literal, still-future arrival of God's Kingdom. Bultmann, for instance, thinks that Jesus was mistaken regarding the Kingdom, and attempts to reinterpret it, along with Jesus's teachings as a whole, in terms of human existence.[33] For Ladd, this is an improper interpretation of both the Jewish hope and Jesus's own teachings on this subject. The future manifestation of the Kingdom of God is historical, just like Jesus's first coming. This teaching is still relevant even for the present.[34]

Increasingly, contemporary theologians moved toward recognizing both the present and future aspects of the Kingdom of God. As Ladd explained a few decades ago, the vigorous debate produced much progress, and, "There is a growing consensus in New Testament scholarship that the Kingdom of God is both present and future."[35] This has continued to be the case, so that Witherington could still say, "It is widely agreed among scholars that Jesus likely spoke of a future *basileia* and of the *basileia* being at work in the present."[36]

The present aspect of the Kingdom is revealed in the person, actions, and message of Jesus. In particular, the rule of God was made known through Jesus's miracles, exorcisms, and in his preaching of a radical call to decision.

But a future manifestation of the Kingdom of God can also be discerned in many of Jesus's teachings. He thought that the Kingdom would be initiated by events such as the coming of the Son of Man, the resurrection of the dead, the conquering of evil, and the ushering in of an eternal blessedness for those who responded to his message.

As Beasley-Murray reminds us, many scholars hold that the latter are all mythical events. Also, it is true that much symbolism accompanies Jesus's teachings here. So a major question is whether Jesus's teachings have literal meaning for today, or whether they need to be reinterpreted in some other fashion.[37] Ladd's defense of Jesus's concepts against contemporary challenges has already been noted briefly above.

Earlier, I stated the principle that, since God raised Jesus from the dead, He thereby placed his stamp of approval on Jesus's teachings here and elsewhere. I argued that this especially guaranteed the truth of Jesus's central teachings regarding the Kingdom of God. Even if many contemporary scholars cannot accept the literal truth of a future Kingdom, this does not make these beliefs untrue. A historical resurrection of Jesus is also difficult for many, yet the data indicate that it really occurred. Further, I argued that the historicity of Jesus's resurrection provides special assurance that Jesus's teachings concerning the Kingdom of God are also true, since they were Jesus's central teachings. If God had thereby confirmed any teachings by raising Jesus from the dead, it would seem that this would especially extend to Jesus's chief message.

Was Jesus Mistaken concerning the Time of His Coming?

However, perhaps there is a roadblock at this point. One continuing influence of consistent eschatology is that some scholars still think that Jesus believed in the immanent coming of God's Kingdom, and that he mistakenly held that it would culminate very shortly. The support for this view is usually an appeal to Mark 9:1, 13:30, and/or Matthew 10:23.

For example, Schweitzer, about a century ago, proclaimed that Jesus expected that the Kingdom would appear imminently. Schweitzer thought that, for Jesus, the coming of the Son of Man was "temporally identical with the dawn of the Kingdom," and that these events would transpire quickly. He concluded, "The whole of 'Christianity' down to the present day . . . is based on the delay of the Parousia, the non-occurrence of the Parousia."[38] We have already seen that Bultmann concludes similarly: "Jesus' expectation of the near end of the world turned out to be an illusion."[39]

This objection may be addressed variously. Initially, as Witherington points out repeatedly, *none* of the passages unequivocally teach that the coming of either Jesus or the Kingdom of God *must* be soon. At most, these texts indicate that the Kingdom *could* come at any time, or even a long time hence.[40] While it is impossible here to do more than make a few summarizing comments, it is obvious that many other scholars in recent decades agree with Witherington. Jesus's remark in Mark 9:1 (cf. Mt 16:28; Lk 9:27) is often taken to refer either to the transfiguration, which follows directly in each of these narratives, or to the resurrection.[41]

It is difficult to take Mark 13:30 as Jesus's comment that his generation would definitely witness his return, since, just two verses later (13:32), Jesus specifically asserts that he did not even know when he would return. One of the most common responses is that Jesus is addressing two major questions in this discourse, the fall of the Jerusalem and the temple, and his return (Mt 24:1–3). The answer to the first is that it will occur in this present generation (Mk 13:30), while the answer to the second question regarding his coming is that Jesus did not know the time (Mk 13:32).[42]

Concerning Matthew 10:23, it is often noted that it would have been physically impossible for the disciples to have ministered in every city of Israel even during the remainder of Jesus's earthly life, let alone before the end of this particular missionary trip. Further, few knew better than the author of the first Gospel that Jesus did *not* return before the deaths of at least most of the apostles. If so, then why would he have reproduced such a spurious report, and on an incisive topic? So it is likely that Jesus's instruction here refers not simply to his immediate disciples and this particular trip, but extends to future Christian missionary work.[43]

At least two other considerations make it very unlikely that Jesus taught that the Kingdom *must* come shortly. First, there are many texts that clearly indicate that this event would *not* come quickly, but at a much later time. The disciples would die for their faith (Mt 24:9; Jn 16:2), the Gospel message would be preached to the whole world (Mk 13:10), Jerusalem would be under the control of the Gentiles for an unspecified amount of time, and the Jewish people would be dispersed throughout the world (Lk 21:24). Obviously, most of these items could not take place in a short time span. In more than one parable, we are also told that the master delayed his coming for a long time (Mt 24:48; 25:19). One intriguing saying reports both that there was *more than one* day of the Son of Man, and that, while the disciples would long to experience one, they would not do so (Lk 17:22). So in addition to alternative meanings of the texts in question, other passages make it very difficult to conclude that Jesus could *only* have meant that the Kingdom *would* come immediately.

Second and very crucially, according to the dating of the vast majority of critical scholars, the Gospels of Matthew and Luke were written about five or six decades after Jesus's proclamations concerning the time of the Kingdom. On the interpretation that Jesus was mistaken regarding the imminent coming of the Kingdom, it certainly should have appeared at least between his death and the fall of Jerusalem in A.D. 70, especially since these events are somehow linked (Mt 24:1–3; Lk 21:20–32). Given that the Kingdom never arrived, Matthew and Luke would knowingly have been declaring (even repeatedly so) that Jesus was mistaken. This is an exceedingly problematic position, especially given the prominence of the Kingdom in their Gospels.[44] Moreover, even highly critical scholars have generally held that especially Luke historicized Mark's interpretation and placed Jesus's coming in the indefinite future. So at least the third Gospel, in particular, would not have interpreted these same texts to mean that Jesus had wrongly predicted the timing of the Kingdom.[45] It would seemingly be quite troublesome for Matthew, as well, and so is probably not the intent of either of these Gospel writers.

If even these critical scholars think that these texts in Luke and perhaps Matthew do not mean that Jesus would return soon, why must even Mark include the mistaken teaching? After all, not only was Mark written near the close of the generation, as well, and so probably was aware of the same troublesome issues, but he (and probably Mt 24:36) is the author who specifically explained that Jesus disavowed knowledge of when he would return (13:32)! So it seems exceptionally difficult to press the point that the Gospels must have taught that Jesus would return soon.

From a totally different perspective, in the next two chapters I examine the life of the future Kingdom, which is eternal in nature (Mk 9:43–48; 10:17, 29–31; cf. Lk 20:36). Even so, such life is still not synonymous with the Kingdom. According to Jesus, an afterlife was a reality for saints who lived before his preaching (Mk 12:26–27; Lk 16:19–31), and it was a present truth (Lk 23:43; cf. Jn 11:25–26). It was also proclaimed in the early church as a present reality (2 Cor 5:1–8; Phil 1:21–23; 1 Jn 5:13), before the future dawning of God's Kingdom. So the timing of the Kingdom would especially not invalidate the truth of eternal life, which actually preceded it, and was rather directly evidenced by Jesus's resurrection.

But even if eternal life exists apart from the Kingdom, I have argued that Jesus's message, and especially his central teaching regarding the Kingdom, was confirmed by his resurrection. Since Jesus specifically declared that even he did not know when the final phase of God's Kingdom would begin (Mk 13:32; cf. Acts 1:6–7), the precise time factor is not the crucial portion of his message. Rather, as I have repeatedly said, the content regarding the Kingdom and its entrance requirements must occupy this central position. In short, through the resurrection, God especially verified the content of Jesus's message regarding the Kingdom, not the specific time factor, since Jesus carefully taught that he did not know that information.

Critical scholars have agreed with this last argument. Pannenberg explains:

Neither the two-thousand-year interval from the time of Jesus' earthly appearance nor its continuing quantitative growth is sufficient in itself to let the connection between the activity and fate of Jesus and the expected end of all things discovered then to become untenable. . . . [T]he question as to how much time might elapse between the appearance of Jesus and the coming of the Son of Man is completely irrelevant. The important thing in it is the material correspondence of the coming judgment with the present attitude of men toward Jesus. . . . The delay of the end events, which now amounts to almost two thousand years, is not a refutation of the Christian hope and of the Christian perception of revelation as long as the unity between what happened in Jesus and the eschatological future is maintained.[46]

This unity between Jesus and the future is primarily represented by the "divine confirmation of Jesus" as seen in his resurrection.[47]

Torrance adds that, due to misunderstandings of the notion of imminence, this entire issue "looks rather like a legend of the critics!"[48] Wright adds that, "the old scholarly warhorse of the 'delay of the Parousia' has had its day at last, and can be put out to grass once and for all."[49] It is no surprise that Beasley-Murray declares that probably even most historical Jesus scholars "are not greatly concerned with the question of whether Jesus was mistaken regarding the time of the end."[50]

Conclusion

For Jesus, the Kingdom is God's entrance into history to reign over His creation. The present, "hidden" aspect was inaugurated by Jesus's preaching, miracles, and exorcisms. In his person and salvation message, he challenged his listeners with a decision to respond to the reign of God. Jesus also taught that the future form of the Kingdom of God would enter history on a grander scale, identified by his return, the resurrection of the dead, and judgment. Those who refused God's reign would be banished. Those who embraced the Kingdom by responding to Jesus's message would gain eternal blessedness in a body like Jesus's resurrected body.[51]

In this chapter, I argued that the resurrection provides the assurance of the reality of the Kingdom of God as taught by Jesus. There is little scholarly disagreement that the center of Jesus's teaching was confronting his listeners with the Kingdom and the possibility of entering its blessings. Most think that there were present and future aspects of Jesus's message, as well. That this was Jesus's major emphasis is crucial, in that it highlights the area that would most warrant God's approval. To be sure, it would certainly seem that God approved Jesus's other teachings, as well. However, the point here is that, since the Kingdom of God and the corresponding preaching of salvation occupied the central position in Jesus's teachings, it most indicates God's agreement. By raising Jesus from the dead, God would especially be emphasizing Jesus's primary message, for He would not have raised a heretic from the dead. It would make little sense if the resurrection confirmed some lesser truth if the greater message of the Kingdom was mistaken.

So Jesus's message regarding the Kingdom of God demands our utmost respect. It is not a doctrine to be taken lightly, even if it may be contrary to our contemporary mind-set. Jesus demanded an individual response, on which I will concentrate in the next chapter. Briefly, those who refuse Jesus's instruction do so contrary to God's most pointed approval.

Notes

1. E. P. Sanders, *The Historical Figure of Jesus* (London: Penguin Books, 1993), 10; also *Jesus and Judaism* (Philadelphia: Fortress Press, 1985), 326.

2. N. T. Wright in *The Meaning of Jesus: Two Visions*, by Marcus Borg and Wright (San Francisco: Harper Collins, 1999), 23.

3. Gerald O'Collins, *Interpreting Jesus* (Mahweh, N.J.: Paulist Press, 1983), 49.

4. Quoted by Paul Eddy, "Response to William Lane Craig," in *The Resurrection: An Interdisciplinary Symposium on the Resurrection of Jesus*, ed. Stephen T. Davis, Daniel Kendall, and Gerald O'Collins (Oxford: Oxford University Press, 1997), 273 n. 2.

5. Crossan, "Rebuttal," in *Will the Real Jesus Please Stand Up? A Debate between William Lane Craig and John Dominic Crossan*, ed. Paul Copan (Grand Rapids, Mich.: Baker Books, 1998), 46.

6. In addition to those just cited above, scholars who hold this position include Reginald H. Fuller, *The Foundations of New Testament Christology* (New York: Scribner's Sons, 1965), 103–6; Rudolf Bultmann, *Jesus Christ and Mythology* (New York: Scribner's Sons, 1958), 11; Bultmann, *Theology of the New Testament*, 2 vols., trans. Kendrick Grobel (New York: Scribner's Sons, 1951, 1955), 1:4–11; Günther Bornkamm, *Jesus of Nazareth*, trans. Irene and Fraser McLuskey with James M. Robinson (New York: Harper and Row, 1960), 64–95; Wolfhart Pannenberg, *Theology and the Kingdom of God*, ed. Richard John Neuhaus (Philadelphia: Westminster Press, 1969), 51; Raymond E. Brown, *Jesus: God and Man* (Milwaukee: Bruce, 1967), 101–4; Raymond E. Brown, *An Introduction to New Testament Christology* (Mahweh, N.J.: Paulist Press, 1994), 100–101; Geza Vermes, *Jesus and the World of Judaism* (Philadelphia: Fortress Press, 1983), 28; John Meier, "Dividing Lines in Jesus Research Today: Through Dialectical Negation to a Positive Sketch," *Interpretation* 50

(1996): 438, 624, 626; Hugh Jackson, "The Resurrection Belief of the Earliest Church: A Response to the Failure of Prophecy," *The Journal of Religion* 55 (1975): 418; George Eldon Ladd, *I Believe in the Resurrection of Jesus* (Grand Rapids, Mich.: Eerdmans, 1975), 144, 150; Michael Grant, *Jesus: An Historian's Review of the Gospels* (New York: Scribner, 1977), esp. 10–11, 44–45, 52, 76, 94; Walter Kasper, *Jesus the Christ*, new ed., trans. V. Green (Mahweh, N.J.: Paulist Press, 1976), 74–78; Ben Meyer, *The Aims of Jesus* (London: SCM Press, 1979), 82; Martin Hengel, *The Atonement* (Philadelphia: Fortress Press, 1981), 34; Francis Watson, "'Historical Evidence' and the Resurrection of Jesus," *Theology* 90 (1987): 367; Barnabas Lindars, "The Apocalyptic Myth and the Death of Christ," *Bulletin of the John Rylands University Library of Manchester* 57 (1975): 368; Howard Clark Kee, *What Can We Know about Jesus?* (Cambridge: Cambridge University Press, 1990), 65–66; Pheme Perkins, "The Resurrection of Jesus of Nazareth," in *Studying the Historical Jesus: Evaluations of the State of Current Research*, ed. Bruce Chilton and Craig A. Evans (Leiden, Netherlands: E. J. Brill, 1994), 430; G. B. Caird, *New Testament Theology*, ed. L. D. Hurst (Oxford: Clarendon Press, 1994), 404; Luke Timothy Johnson, *The Living Jesus: Learning the Heart of the Gospel* (San Francisco: Harper Collins, 1999), 183.

7. Meier, "Dividing Lines," 359. Kasper agrees regarding this being the main area of difference (*Jesus the Christ*, 776–77). George Ladd offers a brief survey of various approaches in *The Pattern of New Testament Truth* (Grand Rapids, Mich.: Eerdmans, 1968), 47–63.

8. Johannes Weiss's small work *Die Predigt Jesu vom Reiche Gottes* was published in Göttingen, Germany, in 1892. The much larger second edition appeared in 1900. For details of his position, see Johannes Weiss, *Jesus' Proclamation of the Kingdom of God* (Philadelphia: Fortress Press, 1971), esp. chap. 11, in which Weiss summarizes his view in ten steps.

9. Albert Schweitzer, *The Quest of the Historical Jesus: A Critical Study of its Progress from Reimarus to Wrede*, trans. W. Montgomery (1906; reprint, New York: Macmillan, 1968), 238–41.

10. Schweitzer, *Quest*, 398–403.

11. Weiss, *Jesus' Proclamation of the Kingdom of God*, chap. 5.

12. Schweitzer, *Quest*, 239.

13. Schweitzer, *Quest*, chap. 20.

14. C. H. Dodd, *The Parables of the Kingdom* (London: Nisbet and Company, 1935), cf. 46–55, 197–207. Dodd supplied the name ("realized eschatology") by which this approach is still best known (51, 203).

15. Dodd, *Parables of the Kingdom*, 106–8.

16. Dodd, *Parables of the Kingdom*, 197, 207.

17. Dodd, *Parables of the Kingdom*, 209–10.

18. Joachim Jeremias, *The Parables of Jesus*, 2nd rev. ed., trans. S. H. Hooke (Upper Saddle River, N.J.: Prentice-Hall, 1972).

19. John K. Riches, *A Century of New Testament Study* (Valley Forge, Pa.: Trinity Press International, 1993), 66.

20. Norman Perrin, *Rediscovering the Teaching of Jesus* (New York: Harper and Row, 1967), 257–58.

21. For details, see Ladd, *Pattern of New Testament Truth*, 48–49.

22. See G. R. Beasley-Murray, *Jesus and the Kingdom of God* (Grand Rapids, Mich.: Eerdmans, 1986). The present Kingdom texts are treated on pages 71–146, while the future citations are discussed on pages 147–218.

23. Ben Witherington III, *Jesus, Paul and the End of the World: A Comparative Study in New Testament Eschatology* (Downers Grove, Ill.: InterVarsity Press, 1992), 68.

24. Perrin, *Rediscovering the Teaching of Jesus*, 65; cf. the discussion on this text, 63–67.

25. Fuller, *Foundations*, 104.

26. Witherington lists three possible meanings—within you, among you, and within your grasp (*Jesus, Paul*, 71–72).

27. Witherington thinks Mk 10:15 may well be independently attested in Jn 3:3, 5 (*Jesus, Paul*, 64).

28. Bultmann, *Theology of the New Testament*, 1:4–11.

29. Bultmann, *Theology of the New Testament*, 1:22.

30. Fuller, *Foundations*, 104.

31. Bornkamm, *Jesus of Nazareth*, esp. 90–95.

32. Ladd, *Pattern of New Testament Truth*, esp. 61, 63.

33. Bultmann, *Theology of the New Testament*, 1:22–23.

34. For Ladd's critique of other positions, see *The Pattern of New Testament Truth*, 49–63, which is a summary of a more in-depth criticism contained in Ladd's major study of the subject, *The Presence of the Future: The Eschatology of Biblical Realism* (Grand Rapids, Mich.: Eerdmans, 1974), esp. sec. III.

35. See Ladd, *The Presence of the Future*, 3. Chapter 1 summarizes the debate in some detail.

36. Witherington, *Jesus, Paul*, 68.

37. Beasley-Murray, *Jesus and the Kingdom*, 339–41.

38. Schweitzer, *The Quest of the Historical Jesus*, 358–60.

39. Bultmann, *Theology of the New Testament*, 1:22.

40. Witherington, *Jesus, Paul*, 36, 44, 48.

41. For just a small sampling, see Dodd, *Parables of the Kingdom*, 53–54; E. J. Tinsley, *The Gospel According to Luke* (Cambridge: Cambridge University Press, 1965), 102; A. R. C. Leaney, *The Gospel According to St. Luke* (London: Adam and Charles Black, 1966), 166; W. F. Albright and C. S. Mann, *Matthew*, The Anchor Bible (Garden City, N.Y.: Doubleday, 1971), 201; G. B. Caird, *Saint Luke* (Philadelphia: Westminster Press, 1963), 130; Ladd, *The Presence of the Future*, 323; Joseph A. Fitzmyer, *The Gospel According to Luke*, The Anchor Bible (Garden City, N.Y.: Doubleday, 1981), 786–90; Witherington, *Jesus, Paul*, 37–39; Craig S. Keener, *A Commentary on the Gospel of Matthew* (Grand Rapids, Mich.: Eerdmans, 1999), 436.

42. Favoring this response are scholars like Caird, *Saint Luke*, 198–200; C. E. B. Cranfield, *The Gospel According to St. Mark* (Cambridge: Cambridge University Press,

1966), 409; William Lane Craig, *The Gospel According to Mark* (Grand Rapids, Mich.: Eerdmans, 1974), 479–82; Ladd, *The Presence of the Future*, 310–11; F. F. Bruce, *The Hard Sayings of Jesus* (Downers Grove, Ill.: InterVarsity Press, 1983), 225–30; Witherington, *Jesus, Paul*, 42; Caird and Hurst, *New Testament Theology*, 255–56.

43. For a few examples of those who take these approaches, see T. W. Manson, *The Sayings of Jesus* (Grand Rapids, Mich.: Eerdmans, 1957), 182; R. V. G. Tasker, *The Gospel According to St. Matthew* (Grand Rapids, Mich.: Eerdmans, 1961), 103, 108; A. W. Argyle, *The Gospel According to Matthew* (Cambridge: Cambridge University Press, 1963), 81; Albright and Mann, *Matthew*, 125; George Eldon Ladd, *A Theology of the New Testament* (Grand Rapids, Mich.: Eerdmans, 1974), 200; Robert H. Gundry, *Matthew: A Commentary on His Literary and Theological Art* (Grand Rapids, Mich.: Eerdmans, 1982), 194; Bruce, *The Hard Sayings of Jesus*, 109; Keener, *Commentary*, 324–25.

44. Even given the thesis, supported by some scholars, that Matthew and Luke were composed in the 60s A.D., we would still have some serious problems here. These writings still would be at (or very nearly at) the end of the generation to whom Jesus preached, without Jesus having returned (Mt 24:34; Lk 21:32). As the disciples began dying, it would seem that these Gospel authors would be even more apprehensive about repeating such teachings. But more importantly, on the earlier date, why would Luke (as in 21:12–24) need to historicize Mark at all (see the next note below) if the events in question had not even occurred yet? Then there would be a real conflict here between Luke not feeling any pressure from coming to the end of the generation, as indicated by 21:32, but historicizing Jesus's teachings, and both in the same text! On the supposition that Luke (and perhaps Matthew) *did* detect the problem and meant for the entire subject to be historicized, we are precisely back at the points I am making in the text.

45. Especially Hans Conzelmann, *The Theology of Luke*, trans. Geoffrey Buswell (New York: Harper and Row, 1961), 105; and Willi Marxsen, *Mark the Evangelist: Studies on the Redaction History of the Gospel*, trans. James Boyce, Donald Juel, William Poehlmann, with Roy A. Harrisville (Nashville: Abingdon Press, 1969). For similarly supportive views, see Leaney, *Gospel According to St. Luke*, 166, 263; Tinsley, *The Gospel According to Luke*, 185–86; Gerald O'Collins, *The Easter Jesus*, 2nd ed. (London: Darton, Longman and Todd, 1980), 87.

46. Wolfhart Pannenberg, *Jesus: God and Man*, 2nd ed., trans. Lewis L. Wilkins and Duane A. Priebe (Philadelphia: Westminster Press, 1977), 107–8.

47. Pannenberg, *Jesus: God and Man*, 108.

48. Thomas Torrance, *Space, Time and Resurrection* (Grand Rapids, Mich.: Eerdmans, 1976), 154.

49. N. T. Wright, *Christian Origins and the Question of God* (Minneapolis: Fortress Press, 1996), 462–63.

50. Beasley-Murray, *Jesus and the Kingdom*, 190. Cf. also C. F. D. Moule, *The Birth of the New Testament*, 3rd rev. ed. (San Francisco: Harper and Row, 1982), 143–45; Wright, *Christian Origins*, 463.

51. Ladd, *Pattern of New Testament Truth*, 63.

CHAPTER FIVE

Salvation and Radical Commitment

The resurrection of Jesus most likely indicates God's activity in the world. Through this event, God vindicated Jesus's teachings, since He would not have raised a heretic from the dead. In particular, this approval would chiefly apply to Jesus's central message regarding the Kingdom of God, in both its present and future aspects.

Jesus's Central Teaching

This chapter addresses the reverse side of Jesus's central teaching. Having already outlined the general nature of God's Kingdom, I turn now to the personal decision that Jesus required for admittance into the Kingdom and participation in the blessings of eternal life. I have termed this subject the "entrance requirements" to the Kingdom. As William Strawson points out, to speak of Jesus's view of the afterlife "assumes there must be some conditions to be fulfilled if life hereafter is to be gained." Strawson adds, "If there is one aspect of the matter which is supremely important it is that Jesus urges upon all men the absolute necessity of meeting the conditions required to obtain future blessedness."[1]

I have remarked that critical scholars in recent decades have widely recognized that Jesus challenged his listeners to exercise radical commitment to God. Rather uniquely, Jesus thought that, in his own person, he confronted his audience with a decision for salvation, obedience, and even judgment. How people responded to him determined whether or not they inherited the Kingdom of God.[2] Even Lüdemann claims that Jesus "issued a radical call to discipleship."[3] Neill adds, "The demands he makes on his followers are more searching than those put forward by any other religious teacher."[4]

What was the content of Jesus's message of salvation? Jesus frequently mentioned the reality of sin and its remedy (Mk 8:38; 9:42–48). He taught that he was the answer to this dilemma (Mt 12:38–42/Lk 11:29–32). Speaking of John 20:19–20, Fuller explains that the language of the risen Jesus is "that of release, liberation from sin as a burden and enslaving power" that "calls for decision. If it is accepted, then men and women who come to faith participate in the victory of Christ; their sins are remitted, they are released from this power."[5] Hodgson agrees that the resurrection event can be characterized as an experience that "is above all one of freedom—a setting free from the bondage of sin and evil."[6] Other critical scholars have made similar comments.[7]

Meyer points out that "Jesus himself offered numerous clues to his view of the human dilemma," which involved "an inevitable state of sin and death." Jesus proposed a rather radical solution to the problem of sin—his death as some sort of expiatory payment for sin.[8] This solution—his atoning for the sins of the world—would be the pinnacle of his mission (Mk 10:45; 14:24). As Hengel explains, "We are probably to understand Mark 14.25 . . . as meaning that Jesus wanted to prepare the way for the coming of the kingdom of God through his sacrificial death." This justified hypothesis would be "the ultimate mystery of Jesus' career."[9] Further, Hengel asserts, "the Christian message fundamentally broke apart the customary conceptions of atonement in the ancient world and did so at many points."[10] Caird adds that, although for moderns, sacrifice is a foreign notion, "For Jesus, however, sacrifice was a vital concept."[11] A surprising number of influential thinkers postulate that this teaching of atonement derives from Jesus.[12] This doctrine also became, from a very early date, the center of New Testament Christology.[13]

Why was an atonement necessary? Many would claim that such a notion is outdated, at best. Emil Brunner denounces this challenge as the product of rationalistic presuppositions. For Brunner, there must have been a real atonement because sin and guilt are real. "Communion with God has been destroyed by sin. . . . Between us and God lies the burden of guilt." So the removal of sin must be equally real, necessitating Jesus's death for our sins. For those who reject the atonement, "that guilt is glossed over, and this breeds a still greater guilt. . . . [F]ellowship with God is impossible, save through the intervention in the human situation." Here God made the path, and it involves the atoning death of His Son.[14]

In light of the problem of sin and Jesus's own remedy, he confronted his hearers with a decision. He preached the necessity of repentance (Mk 1:15a; Lk 13:1–5), involving a complete turnaround from old lifestyles.[15] In particular,

Jesus proclaimed the need to exercise faith in God, as well as in his own person and teaching, as God's chosen messenger (Mk 1:15b; 10:15, 26–31; Mt 10:40) who suffered, died, and rose from the dead (Lk 24:46–47). Jesus offered forgiveness in light of the future judgment. The result was a changed life of total commitment (Lk 14:25–35). The call to discipleship issued by Jesus was, first of all, a challenge to love God with all that we are: heart, soul, mind, and strength (Mk 12:28–30). Right behind it was the second greatest command: to love our neighbors as ourselves (Mk 12:31).[16]

The earliest church also proclaimed a similar message, as indicated by many early confessional texts, as well as other teachings.[17] Everyone has sinned (Rom 3:9–11, 23; Jas 1:19–21), and God's remedy for sin is Jesus Christ (Rom 6:23; 1 Pt 2:24). Several early creedal passages ascribed titles of deity to Jesus (Rom 1:3–4, 10:9; Phil 2:6–11; Heb 1:3). Jesus Christ died a subsititutionary death (1 Cor 15:3; Rom 5:8; 1 Pt 3:18), his shed blood providing the means of forgiveness (1 Pt 1:18–19; Heb 9:12–14). His resurrection completed God's provision for salvation (Rom 10:9; 1 Cor 15:3–4; 1 Pt 1:3–5, 21). The result is God's work, and is unattainable by good works or by human power (Eph 2:8–10; Ti 3:5). Repentance (Acts 2:38; 3:19) and faith in Jesus Christ were essentials for salvation (Acts 16:31; 13:38–39). The result was a transformed life involving commitment and obedience (1 Pt 2:21, 4:1; 1 Jn 2:3–5). This new life was to be radically lived out with regard to others, as well (1 Jn 3:16–24; Jas 2:15–17).

I have said that the earliest apostolic preaching is recorded in the pre–New Testament creeds that are found largely in Paul's epistles and the brief, kerygmatic statements in Acts.[18] These texts include self-contained synopses of the earliest Gospel that was preached to others. Although additional items are occasionally mentioned, at least three doctrines always appear whenever the Gospel is actually defined. Time and again Jesus is given titles of deity, and we are told that he died, and that he was raised from the dead.[19]

From the teachings of both Jesus and the early church, two terms deserve brief explanations. First, "repentance" was more than remorse for sin. The Greek word μετανοέω denotes a complete change of mind, an "about-face." Such a change primarily indicates the renouncing of sin and living a life of commitment to God.[20] Second, "belief" or "faith" is usually a very strong word, in contrast to its English counterpart, where it more often expresses simple agreement. The Greek term πιστεύω usually expresses being persuaded to the extent of placing one's confidence, reliance, credence, or trust in someone or something. Especially when used with the preposition εἰς, with God or Jesus as its object, it almost always involves commitment and surrender to their person and message.[21]

Brunner argues that if Jesus had only proclaimed the Kingdom of God and the need for a decision of obedience in order to share in its benefits, he would not have distinguished himself from one of the prophets. But Jesus went beyond this, confronting persons with the decision to respond to himself by faith, providing a personal invitation to participation in God's Kingdom.[22]

Raymond Brown asserts that "an irreducible historical minimum" is Jesus's proclamation that in his preaching, miracles, and person, he was God's unique presentation of the Kingdom message. God's rule was established through him, by faith in him, as a committed response to Jesus's call.[23]

We need to issue an important caution at this point. My brief survey of a number of influential contemporary theologians indicates some general agreement regarding Jesus's teachings on the subject of salvation, or his call to decision in favor of the Kingdom of God. However, it must be emphasized that even similar language shared among these scholars frequently fails to indicate what are often significant differences between them. A good instance is the agreement that sin corrupts, while different conceptions are held on the nature of sin itself. Further, mainline scholars often agree on the general nature of Jesus's teachings, while often rejecting the theological doctrine itself. An example here is "atonement," which is sometimes defined differently than Jesus or the New Testament authors treated this word, often by downplaying or rejecting the notion of Jesus's substitutionary death.[24]

But if Jesus's resurrection actually occurred in history, it would seem that contemporary theologians may face a dilemma here. Why should Jesus's deity or his atonement be rejected or spiritualized if Jesus really rose from the dead? We have seen that many scholars recognize that Jesus's teachings rely in some sense on the truth of his resurrection. If the latter actually occurred, this should best indicate a literal interpretation of the former, as well. I have argued that God especially vindicated Jesus's message of salvation, since it was his central teaching, as providing entrance to God's Kingdom.

As I pointed out in the last chapter, compliance with Jesus's message gains an individual admittance to God's Kingdom and participation in eternal life. It is clear that Jesus thought that the life of the Kingdom was eternal, with blessings for the faithful.[25] Based on the teachings of Jesus, the early church also taught the blessings of eternal life.[26] Such is the consequence of a positive decision in answer to Jesus's challenge to faith and commitment.

God's Confirmation

Jesus's message of the Kingdom of God involves certain personal requirements that were necessary for entrance into eternal life. As Strawson remarks, "We assume then that there are conditions to be met if we are to obtain everlasting life."[27] Jesus's salvation teaching was that he came to do what we could not do for ourselves. He thought that his death, in some sense, dealt with the reality of sin. This act of love reached its zenith in his resurrection from the dead. In light of all this, he demanded unconditional commitment to God as revealed in his person. His call to follow him was one of radical discipleship.

Jesus demanded a change of mind (repentance) from his hearers, characterized by turning to God through faith in his chosen messenger. This reliance and commitment apply especially to Jesus himself. Certainly, such surrender is only possible because Jesus was the Son of God, and because he performed unique actions: he taught that his death was a payment for personal sin and his resurrection was the life-giving event that foreshadowed eternal life in the Kingdom of God. A true act of commitment is made to another; trust is best placed in a person. To be sure, such trust is given in light of what is known about that person, but it is nonetheless placed primarily in persons, not ideas or events. Jesus called others to himself—to leave all, come, and follow him. The result of such a commitment to Jesus Christ includes a radically changed life and outlook, according to which we reach out to others and love them as ourselves.

We have seen that this preaching of the Gospel was taught both by Jesus and in the early church. Today such a message is often considered to be outdated. But a couple of considerations seem to indicate that Jesus's message, especially in this particular area, is not only true, but equally binding even today.

A major theme in this book has been the New Testament message that, by raising Jesus from the dead, God approved of Jesus's teachings. Two corollaries of this theme bear on the present issue. The first concerns the event of Jesus's resurrection itself; the second deals with Jesus's central teaching of salvation as the entrance into God's Kingdom.

Contemporary theologians widely recognize that these doctrines were taught by both Jesus and the early church, although their literal truth is still questioned by many. A historical resurrection is often questioned, as well.

However, if Jesus actually rose from the dead in history, then it would appear that Jesus's Kingdom message should also be accepted in a straightforward manner. Jesus's teachings are often rejected because the confirming event on which the New Testament bases its truth is affirmed in a manner that is not historical. But if the resurrection really occurred, the foundation for Jesus's teachings appears to be firm; the event ensures the doctrine.

Further, I have mentioned several times that Jesus's teachings regarding the Kingdom of God and the required conditions of salvation are at the very center of his message. They are two sides of the same point. So it would seem that any approval provided by God in raising Jesus would particularly extend to this central teaching. It makes little sense for God to confirm other teachings, but not this crucial doctrine.

So Jesus's Kingdom message should be taken above all as God's word even for us. Jesus spoke for God on the topic of salvation. This appears to be required by the resurrection, since God would especially be emphasizing the message that Jesus indicated was at the core of his mission (Mk 2:17, 10:45; Lk 19:10). It does not make much sense to hypothesize that God raised a heretic from the dead, particularly a heretic in such a crucial matter.

Raymond Brown offers some pertinent thoughts here. Jesus required faith in God as revealed in himself, in light of the coming Kingdom. Jesus's authority is especially evident here, as he imparted God's will on this issue. As such, it follows that his message is true for every century. No age, even ours, ought to reject Jesus's demands as outdated, because he spoke for God. Therefore, faith in Jesus continues to be necessary for salvation.[28]

There appears to be a solid grounding on which to affirm Jesus's salvation message. Although its truth may be questioned, God provided confirmation of Jesus's central teaching by resurrecting him from the dead.

Radical Commitment

Regarding the depth of commitment to which Jesus challenged his followers, many contemporary theologians have followed the lead of Søren Kierkegaard. Breaking strongly with the popular notions in his day, Kierkegaard taught that faith was not merely one's agreement with a creed, but a radically changed life of total obedience to God.

In his volume *Attack Upon "Christendom,"* Kierkegaard developed an especially trenchant criticism of those who believed that they could become Christians by intellectual assent apart from personal commitment. He especially rejected the common view of Christian faith that he found in his own country of Denmark, where it was customarily believed that by being a good Danish citizen one would also be a good Christian.[29]

Kierkegaard argued that Christianity involved a radical response to the call of Jesus Christ. There was a cost to be paid to be a Christian. Often the price was personal suffering for one's stand. Nonetheless, a true Christian was one who was absolutely surrendered and committed to the teachings of Jesus Christ. Applying this to what he observed, Kierkegaard complained that contemporary Christians, and especially religious leaders, desired a version of observance that involved no following of Jesus and no suffering. They claimed that sacrifice should be made, but failed to live it. Because their faith was a matter of play, Jesus would have kicked them out of the temple.[30]

Bultmann notes that, according to the New Testament view of faith, an "obedient self-commitment and inward detachment from the world is only possible when it is faith in Jesus Christ."[31] In many texts, like Matthew 6:19–24 and 13:44–46, Mark 10:25, and Luke 9:61–62 and 14:15–32, Jesus demanded that his hearers choose between serving God and accumulating earthly, material possessions. Jesus taught that God should be favored above riches and even above one's family.[32]

Bornkamm also emphasizes Jesus's call for true discipleship. A commitment to follow Jesus signifies "the determination to abandon everything." Texts like Luke 9:59–62 and 14:26–33, and Matthew 13:45–46 are sayings "of extreme vigor; they demand the utmost."[33] In these and related passages, we find Jesus's call to a decision.

Perhaps the most challenging volume written on this topic is Dietrich Bonhoeffer's *The Cost of Discipleship*, which is a stern rebuke to those whose Christian faith costs them nothing. To the contrary, real faith costs something. Bonhoeffer explains, "The call to follow implies that there is only one way of believing on Jesus Christ, and that is by leaving all and going with the incarnate Son of God."[34]

For Bonhoeffer, faith definitely involves the next step of obedience to Jesus Christ. On this emphasis he is adamant. Faith challenges the whole person and demands a response. It wholeheartedly embraces Jesus's person and teachings. Summarizing this emphasis, Bonhoeffer makes a demanding declaration: "When Christ calls a man, he bids him come and die."[35]

Few works on the topic of commitment to Jesus Christ are as hard hitting or have been as influential as Bonhoeffer's *The Cost of Discipleship*. Bonhoeffer pursues related themes in other texts, as well, in spite of the brevity of his life, cut short in a Nazi prison camp. His little volume *Life Together* is a fascinating study of fellowship and Christian discipline.[36] His unfinished *Ethics* is a longer treatment that contains discussions of a number of related items.[37]

More recently, other critical scholars have also published challenging studies on the theme of following Jesus Christ.[38] Motivated by the writings of Kierkegaard, Vernard Eller issues a summons to a life of commitment to Jesus's chief principle: "absolute personal loyalty to God must take precedence over anything and everything else."[39] James D. G. Dunn emphasizes Jesus's message as life-transforming repentance, faith as seeking God's Kingdom above all else, and abandoning ourselves to follow Jesus's teachings.[40] N. T. Wright reviews the messages of several New Testament writings, asking how they contribute to following Jesus.[41] Others, like Martin Hengel and Craig Blomberg, have written convicting treatises on the use of one's possessions to facilitate Jesus's call to discipleship.[42]

The strength of such studies is in explicating Jesus's radical call for believers, even today. Especially due to his resurrection, we need to embrace total commitment to God through the Lord Jesus Christ.[43] Jesus frequently proclaimed a message of radical obedience. Many of the key biblical texts I cite below are the same as those used by Bultmann, Bornkamm, and other scholars.

For instance, in Luke 14:25–35, Jesus demands that he be placed first. Believers should love him before their own family members (vv. 25–26; cf. Mt 10:37; cf. *The Gospel of Thomas* 55a, 101), before their own lives (vv. 26, 27; cf. Mt 10:38–39, 16:24–26; cf. *Thomas* 55b), and before their possessions (v. 33; cf. Lk 12:33). Jesus's call is to love him preeminently.

This commitment begins by placing God first in our lives. As Jesus commanded, "Seek first the Kingdom and His righteousness" (Mt 6:33, translated from the Greek). This is our spiritual priority. Everything else is subordinate (Lk 9:57–62). God's Kingdom is like the buried treasure found in a field (Mt 13:44), or the priceless pearl (Mt 13:45–46), to obtain which we sell everything we own. Similarly, we should sell our possessions in order to lay up treasures in heaven (Lk 12:33–34; cf. Mt 6:19–21).

When asked about the greatest commandment of all, Jesus listed the requirement that we love God with all we have—with our heart, soul, mind, and strength. The near repetition here probably indicates that such commitment involves our entire selves. The second greatest command is that we love our neighbors even as we love ourselves (Mk 12:28–31). In Luke 10:25–37, the parable of the Good Samaritan is added. At the risk of his own life, the Samaritan sacrificed his time and finances to care for a wounded man, a Jew whom custom dictated that he should avoid. We are told that we should similarly make sacrifices for others (10:37).

Radical commitment is certainly taught by Jesus, as well as by other New Testament authors. Those who have followed Jesus in repentance and commitment are commanded to submit to him completely. The extent of one's personal obedience, especially regarding time and finances, will of course vary and should be worked out in dependence on God and openness to Him. But it is clear that Jesus's call to discipleship involves good stewardship of God's provisions, so that as much as possible is freed for God's Kingdom work, meeting spiritual as well as physical needs.[44]

Conclusion

Jesus taught that sin marked humanity. In some sense, he also taught that his death would serve a substitutionary purpose, with the shedding of his blood paying for human sin. His resurrection completed this provision for sin and human need. Entrance into the Kingdom of God depends on one's repentance, or turning from sin, and personal commitment to Jesus in light of his person and work on our behalf.[45] God especially verified Jesus's central Kingdom message of salvation by raising him from the dead.

Radical commitment to love God through Jesus Christ, and to do so with our whole being, is a challenge to all believers. It is our highest priority. Jesus commanded us to place himself above our loved ones, ourselves, and our possessions. The second greatest command should then follow: to practice the love of our neighbors to the extent that we also love ourselves. Personal sacrifice is demanded on *both* fronts. Christians are called to total self-surrender in accordance with God's leading us in our lives; such surrender involves our time and resources, and a pursuit of the eternal life of God's Kingdom as the greatest treasure we could ever find.

Notes

1. William Strawson, *Jesus and the Future Life* (London: Epworth Press, 1970), 227–28; cf. 196.

2. For these and related ideas, see Rudolf Bultmann, *Theology of the New Testament*, 2 vols., trans. Kendrick Grobel (New York: Scribner's Sons, 1951, 1955), 1:4–11; Reginald H. Fuller, *The Foundations of New Testament Christology* (New York: Scribner's Sons, 1965), 105–6; Wolfhart Pannenberg, "Dogmatic Theses on the Doctrine of Revelation," in *Revelation as History*, ed. Pannenberg, trans. David Granskou (New York: Macmillan, 1968), 139–45; Thomas Torrance, *Space, Time and Resurrection* (Grand Rapids, Mich.: Eerdmans, 1976), 20; Joseph M. Hallman, "The Resurrection of the Human Jesus," *Process Studies* 8 (1978): 257; George W. E. Nickelsburg, "The Genre and Function of the Markan Passion Narrative," *Harvard Theological Review* 73 (1980): 182; Hans Küng, *Eternal Life? Life after Death as a Medical, Philosophical, and Theological Problem*, trans. Edward Quinn (Garden City, N.Y.: Doubleday, 1984), 107; Robert H. Smith, *Easter Gospels: The Resurrection of Jesus According to the Four Evangelists* (Minneapolis: Augsburg, 1983), 49–50, 54; Gerald O'Collins, *The Easter Jesus*, 2nd ed. (London: Darton, Longman and Todd, 1980), 122–25; Brian Hebblethwaite, "The Resurrection and the Incarnation," in *The Resurrection of Jesus Christ*, ed. Paul Avis (London: Darton, Longman and Todd, 1993), 169; Jürgen Moltmann, *Jesus Christ for Today's World*, trans. Margaret Kohl (Minneapolis: Fortress Press, 1994), 47; Thorwald Lorenzen, *Resurrection and Discipleship: Interpretive Models, Biblical Reflections, Theological Consequences* (Maryknoll, N.Y.: Orbis Books, 1995), 143, 232–35; Luke Timothy Johnson, *Living Jesus: Learning the Heart of the Gospel* (San Francisco: Harper Collins, 1999), 46, 97, 193, 199–200; Pheme Perkins, "The Resurrection of Jesus of Nazareth," in *Studying the Historical Jesus: Evaluations of the State of Current Research*, ed. Bruce Chilton and Craig A. Evans (Leiden, Netherlands: E. J. Brill, 1994), 442.

3. Gerd Lüdemann, "Closing Response," in *Jesus's Resurrection: Fact or Figment? A Debate between William Lane Craig and Gerd Lüdemann*, ed. Paul Copan and Ronald K. Tacelli (Downers Grove, Ill.: InterVarsity Press, 2000), 159–60.

4. Stephen Neill, *Christian Faith and Other Faiths: The Christian Dialogue with Other Religions*, 2nd ed. (London: Oxford University Press, 1970), 233.

5. Reginald H. Fuller, "John 20:19–23," *Interpretation* 32 (1978): 184.

6. Peter C. Hodgson, *Winds of the Spirit: A Constructive Christian Theology* (Louisville, Ky.: Westminster John Knox Press, 1994), 268.

7. For some examples, see Karl Barth, *Church Dogmatics*, 13 vols., ed. G. W. Bromiley and T. F. Torrance (Edinburgh: T. and T. Clark, 1961), vol. 4, part I:252–56, 358; Emil Brunner, *The Christian Doctrine of Creation and Redemption*, vol. 2 of *Dogmatics*, 3 vols. (Philadelphia: Westminster Press, 1952), 89ff.; O'Collins, *The Easter Jesus*, 122; G. Walter Hansen, "Resurrection and the Christian Life in Paul's Letters," in *Life in the Face of Death: The Resurrection Message of the New Testament*, ed. Richard Longenecker (Grand Rapids: Eerdmans, 1998), 212; Jürgen Moltmann, *The Way of Jesus Christ: Christology in Messianic Dimensions*, trans. Margaret Kohl (Minneapolis: Fortress Press, 1993), 241.

8. Ben F. Meyer, "Resurrection as Humanly Intelligible Destiny," *Ex Auditu* 9 (1993): 22.

9. Martin Hengel, *The Atonement* (Philadelphia: Fortress Press, 1981), 72; cf. 65–75.

10. Hengel, *The Atonement*, 31–32 (including some examples). Paul Barnett agrees, providing four ways Jesus's death was distinctive (*Jesus and the Logic of History* [Grand Rapids, Mich.: Eerdmans, 1997], 159–61, 165).

11. G. B. Caird, *New Testament Theology*, ed. L. D. Hurst (Oxford, Clarendon Press, 1994), 411.

12. For some influential, though older, studies, see Vincent Taylor, *The Atonement in New Testament Teaching*, 3rd ed. (London: Epworth Press, 1963), esp. 5; Vincent Taylor, *The Gospel According to St. Mark* (London: Macmillan, 1963), esp. 445–46; Barth, *Church Dogmatics*, vol. 4, part I:211–83; Brunner, *Christian Doctrine*, 2:249, 281–307; Oscar Cullmann, *The Christology of the New Testament*, rev. ed., trans. Shirley C. Guthrie and Charles A. M. Hall (Philadelphia: Westminster Press, 1963), 65, 110; James Denney, *The Death of Christ*, ed. R. V. G. Tasker (London: Tyndale Press, 1951), chap. 6; Leon Morris, *The Apostolic Preaching of the Cross* (Grand Rapids, Mich.: Eerdmans, 1956), chap. 3. More recent studies include Meyer, "Resurrection"; Hengel, *The Atonement*; Caird, *New Testament Theology*; as well as Gerald O'Collins, *Interpreting Jesus* (Mahweh, N.J.: Paulist Press, 1983), 92; Donald Senior, "Crucible of Truth: Passion and Resurrection in the Gospel of Mark," in *The Passion, Death and Resurrection of the Lord: A Commentary on the Four Gospels*, ed. Reginald H. Fuller et al. (Mundelein, Ill.: Chicago Studies, 1985), 24; N. T. Wright in *The Meaning of Jesus: Two Visions*, by Marcus Borg and Wright (San Francisco: Harper Collins, 1999), esp. 104. Borg disagrees with Wright here (90–91).

13. Besides virtually all of the scholars in the previous note, see Jürgen Moltmann, *Jesus Christ for Today's World*, trans. Margaret Kohl (Minneapolis: Free Press, 1994), 40–42, 68; O'Collins lists three "various levels" of meaning of Jesus's dying for others in *The Easter Jesus*, 121–22; Johnson, *Living Jesus*, 82–83, 96, 108; Joost Holleman,

Resurrection and Parousia: A Traditio-Historical Study of Paul's Eschatology in 1 Corinthians 15 (Leiden, Netherlands: E. J. Brill, 1996), 184.

14. Brunner, *Christian Doctrine*, 2:291–92.

15. Cf. Bultmann, *Theology of the New Testament*, 1:20–21; Willi Marxsen, *The Resurrection of Jesus of Nazareth*, trans. Margaret Kohl (Philadelphia: Fortress Press, 1970), 169.

16. Cf. Brunner, *Christian Doctrine*, 2:298–305; Raymond E. Brown, *Jesus: God and Man* (Milwaukee: Bruce, 1967), 96–99, 101; Barth, *Church Dogmatics*, vol. 4, I:248–51; Fuller, *Foundations of New Testament Christology*, 105–6; Rudolf Bultmann, "New Testament and Mythology," in *Kerygma and Myth: A Theological Debate*, ed. Hans Werner Bartsch (New York: Harper and Row, 1961), 22; Günther Bornkamm, *Jesus of Nazareth*, trans. Irene and Fraser McLuskey with James M. Robinson (New York: Harper and Row, 1960), 92–94; Pheme Perkins, *Resurrection: New Testament Witness and Contemporary Reflection* (Garden City, N.Y.: Doubleday, 1984), 295–96; Johnson, *Living Jesus*, 45, 97, 194; Francis X. Durrwell, *La Résurrection de Jésus: Mystère de Salut* (Paris: Les Éditions du Cerf, 1976), 216–21; Walter Künneth, *Theologie der Auferstehung*, 6th ed. (Giessen, Germany: Brunnen, 1982), 287–89; Peter Stuhlmacher, "The Resurrection of Jesus and the Resurrection of the Dead," trans. Jonathan M. Whitlock, *Ex Auditu* 9 (1993): 53–54; Peter Stuhlmacher, *Was geschah auf Golgatha? Zur Heilsbedeutung von Kreuz, Tod und Auferweckung Jesu* (Stuttgart, Germany: Calwer Verlag, 1998), 69–88.

17. The majority of the following texts are widely thought to be early, pre–New Testament passages.

18. Further details can be found in chapter 1 and in the sources listed there.

19. Of the many examples here, I will list what are often thought to be the specific creedal portions. The extended contexts should be consulted for the mention of the Gospel along with other relevant teachings: Rom 1:3–4, 10:9–10; 1 Cor 15:3–5; Acts 2:22–24, 31–33, 36; 3:13b–15; 4:10b; 5:29b–31; 10:36, 39b–43. For other related creedal texts in Paul, see Rom 3:23–26, 4:24–25, 6:4, 8:10–11, 8:34, 14:9; 1 Cor 6:14. C. H. Dodd argues that at least the Petrine speeches in Acts "are based on material which proceeded from the Aramaic-speaking Church at Jerusalem, and was substantially earlier than the period at which the book was written" (*The Apostolic Preaching and Its Developments* [1936; reprint, Grand Rapids, Mich.: Baker Books, 1980], 20). When he summarizes the features of the setting and content of this early kerygma, Dodd also includes the death and resurrection of Jesus, noting that "by virtue of the resurrection, Jesus has been exalted to the right hand of God" as Lord and Christ (21–22). Regarding the Pauline kerygma, Dodd argues that the "coincidence between the apostolic Preaching as attested by the speeches in Acts, and as attested by Paul, enables us to carry back its essential elements to a date far earlier than a critical analysis of Acts by itself could justify; for as we have seen, Paul must have received the tradition very soon after the death of Jesus" (26). This essential "coincidence" or agreement between the Petrine speeches and Paul's citations of the kerygma provides some crucial corroboration from two early directions (16).

20. Walter Bauer, *A Greek-English Lexicon of New Testament and Other Early Christian Literature*, 2nd ed., trans. and rev. by William R. Arndt, F. Wilbur Gingerich, and Frederick W. Danker (Chicago: University of Chicago Press, 1979), 511–12.

21. Bauer, *Greek-English Lexicon*, 660–62.

22. Brunner, *Christian Doctrine*, 2:298–305.

23. Brown, *Jesus: God and Man*, 96–99, 101. Brown carries on the same emphasis in his much more recent volume, *An Introduction to New Testament Christology* (Mahweh, N.J.: Paulist, 1994), 68–70, for example.

24. Overviews reveal many of these doctrinal nuances. See Bernard Ramm, *A Handbook of Contemporary Theology* (Grand Rapids, Mich.: Eerdmans, 1966), cf. 8–9, 16–18, 117–19; James C. Livingston, *The Twentieth Century*, vol. 2 of *Modern Christian Thought*, 2nd ed. (Upper Saddle River, N.J.: Prentice-Hall, 1997), chaps. 1–2, 15.

25. See, for example, Mk 9:43–47, 10:29–31, 12:25; Mt 6:19–20/Lk 12:33; Mt 7:13–14/Lk 13:23–24; Mt 8:11/ Lk 13:28–30. Cf. Bultmann, *Theology of the New Testament*, 1:5–6. But as I remarked in the last chapter, eternal life is not synonymous with the future Kingdom. According to Jesus, the saints who lived before him had already experienced the afterlife (Mk 12:26–27; cf. Lk 16:19–31), and it was a present truth, as well (Lk 23:43; cf. Jn 11:25–26). The early church also proclaimed the afterlife as a present reality (2 Cor 5:1–8; Phil 1:21–23; 1 Jn 5:13), before the future dawning of the Kingdom of God.

26. See 1 Cor 2:9, 15:50–53; 2 Cor 5:1–8; 1 Pt 1:3–5, 5:10; Rev 21–22 for examples. Cf. Rudolf Bultmann, *History and Eschatology: The Presence of Eternity* (New York: Harper and Row, 1957), 32–33.

27. Strawson, *Jesus and the Future Life*, 227. Earlier he says, "There are conditions under which the gift is given." (196).

28. Brown, *Jesus: God and Man*, 101; cf. Brown, *Introduction to New Testament Christology*, 100–101. See the similar conclusion by Strawson (*Jesus and the Future Life*, 230).

29. Søren Kierkegaard, *Attack upon "Christendom,"* trans. Walter Lowrie (Princeton: Princeton University Press, 1968), 132–33; 164–65.

30. Kierkegaard, *Attack upon "Christendom,"* 117–24, provides an example of a reoccurring theme.

31. Bultmann, "New Testament and Mythology," 22.

32. Bultmann, *Theology of the New Testament*, 1:9–11; cf. 324–25. On Bultmann's view of total commitment, see Thomas C. Oden, *Radical Obedience: The Ethics of Rudolf Bultmann* (Philadelphia: Westminster Press, 1964). Kierkegaard's influence on Bultmann is noted (80, 111). A "Response" from Bultmann is generally appreciative of Oden's treatment of his view of obedience (esp. 144, 147).

33. Bornkamm, *Jesus of Nazareth*, 144–52.

34. Dietrich Bonhoeffer, *The Cost of Discipleship*, trans. R. H. Fuller (New York: Macmillan, 1959), 67.

35. Bonhoeffer, *The Cost of Discipleship*, 99; see esp. 45–104 for a most stimulating treatment of radical obedience.

36. Dietrich Bonhoeffer, *Life Together: A Discussion of Christian Fellowship*, trans. John W. Doberstein (New York: Harper and Row, 1954).

37. Dietrich Bonhoeffer, *Ethics*, ed. Eberhard Bethge, trans. Neville Horton Smith (New York: Macmillan, 1955).

38. Most of the recent scholars listed in note 2 above also offer positive comments on this subject.

39. Vernard Eller, *The Simple Life: The Christian Stance toward Possessions* (Grand Rapids, Mich.: Eerdmans, 1973), 24.

40. James D. G. Dunn, *Jesus' Call to Discipleship* (Cambridge: Cambridge University Press, 1992), chap. 2.

41. N. T. Wright, *Following Jesus: Biblical Reflections on Discipleship* (Grand Rapids, Mich.: Eerdmans, 1994).

42. Martin Hengel, *Property and Riches in the Early Church* (Philadelphia: Fortress Press, 1974); Craig Blomberg, *Neither Poverty nor Riches: A Biblical Theology of Material Possessions* (Grand Rapids, Mich.: Eerdmans, 1999); Craig Blomberg, *Heart, Soul, and Money: A Christian View of Possessions* (Joplin, Mo.: College Press, 2000).

43. Interestingly, Wright also bases Jesus's call to discipleship on his resurrection (*Following Jesus*, chap. 7).

44. For some excellent and stimulating discussions of total commitment, see Bonhoeffer, *The Cost of Discipleship*; George Verwer, *Come! Live! Die! The Real Revolution* (Wheaton, Ill.: Tyndale House, 1972); William MacDonald, *True Discipleship* (Kansas City: Walterick, 1962); David Gill, "Radical Christian: Rethinking Our Financial Priorities," *Right On* 7 (1976); Ronald J. Sider, *Rich Christians in an Age of Hunger: A Biblical Study* (Downers Grove, Ill.: InterVarsity Press, 1977); Gene A. Getz, *A Biblical Theology of Material Possessions* (Chicago: Moody Press, 1990); John White, *Magnificent Obsession: The Joy of Christian Commitment* (Downers Grove, Ill.: InterVarsity Press, 1990).

45. Dunn summarizes Jesus's central message quite similarly—as the recognition of the reality of God's Kingdom, an urgent call to a decision, the requirement of repentance and faith (as a relationship with God) in the person of Jesus. See Dunn, *Jesus' Call to Discipleship*, 30–31.

CHAPTER SIX

Eternal Life

In the last two chapters I studied Jesus's central teaching, the Kingdom of God and its entrance requirements for salvation. In this chapter I concentrate on the life of the Kingdom—eternal life. After making some observations regarding the teachings of Jesus and the early church, I turn to some pastoral considerations concerning biblical metaphors of heaven and assurance of a blessed afterlife.

The Resurrection of the Body versus Immortality of the Soul

Several views of the afterlife, along with many additional nuances, were prominent in the ancient world. I especially summarize two of the broad categories: the immortality of the soul and the resurrection of the body. A brief contrast will provide some background for the teachings of Jesus and the early church.

Immortality of the Soul

The view that the human soul was immortal was especially prevalent in ancient Greek thought, as well as in areas affected by Hellenism. Platonic concepts were probably the most influential subspecies. Very briefly, the soul existed before the physical birth of the body, where it acquired knowledge in the eternal realm of Ideas. In contrast, the body was part of the sense world. Because persons were composed of both soul and body, they were born with vast knowledge gained from the eternal realm, though it was difficult to recall due to physical cravings.

The physical body was a temporary vehicle for the soul, hindering it rather severely. Especially in more radical forms of this view, as in certain types of Gnosticism, it was held that the body was evil, imprisoning the soul with its material nature and desires.[1] So while the soul was not wicked and could never be destroyed by evil, it could be impeded. One was therefore to control the body, avoiding its desires, so that the soul would not be unnecessarily hindered. Pure knowledge was still impossible in this life, due to these physical influences.

For Plato, only the body died, while the immortal soul was reborn, often over thousands of years. The just were rewarded and received a better destiny while the unjust were judged. Intriguingly, philosophers made the trek through the process much more quickly! Then the soul was finally freed to take its flight to the eternal realm, to dwell there. Personal immortality was the final state, characterized by bliss and by acquiring pure wisdom. Accordingly, the philosopher, as illustrated by Socrates instructing his disciples before his own death, knows these things and has no fear of death, in that a much better state is attained.[2]

Greek thought before and after the time of the church was heavily influenced by Plato, especially in teachings regarding the realm of Ideas and the soul's immortality. Gnosticism amalgamated some of these thoughts along with notions taken from the mystery religions and elsewhere, often emphasizing the evil qualities of the body. Neoplatonism took some of Plato's ideas in much more intuitive and mystical directions. These and similar ideas were very popular in the Mediterranean area for up to centuries after the time of Jesus.

The Afterlife: Old Testament Teachings

A cyclical concept of history was also widespread in ancient times, popularized by the Greeks and others. According to this view, history did not progress in a forward direction, but repetitiously followed the cycles of nature.

Contrary to this notion, the Jews conceived of history as more of a linear process. God worked in past history, illustrated especially by the Jewish exodus from Egypt and their habitation of the "Promised Land." These mighty historical acts of God were frequently narrated (Ps 78, 81, 106, for example). God was also active in the present and would continue to act in the future, when He established His reign in Israel (Jer 23:5–8; Is 25:6–9, 43:1–7).

The Jews also believed in an afterlife. In earlier writings, this was expressed as existence in Sheol, the land of shadows. It was a meager existence where life was unsatisfied (Prv 27:20), without an opportunity to return (Jb 7:9).

The wicked would be in Sheol (Ps 49:14), where there was no opportunity to praise or find fellowship with God (Is 38:18). Neither would there be any working, planning, or knowledge in that place (Eccl 9:10).

While such negative aspects of Sheol are often emphasized by commentators, more positive aspects usually go unmentioned. But God is present there, too (Ps 139:8), and He rescues persons from Sheol (Ps 16:8–11). It is even inferred that some sort of rest is found there (1 Sm 28:15).

Some Jews may have believed that separate places existed in Sheol for the righteous and the unrighteous. For example, Psalm 49:13–15 contrasts the difference between the wicked and the righteous. The first century A.D. Book of Enoch (22:9–13) teaches such a division of persons.

Jewish thought increasingly taught the prospect of a blessed existence after death for the righteous.[3] The predominant view was that the bodies of the righteous would be transformed and raised at the end of history. The unrighteous would experience judgment at this time as well.

While the instances of Enoch (Gn 5:24) and Elijah (2 Kgs 2:11) being taken physically to heaven fall short of bodily resurrection, there are still some important similarities. These examples could have contributed to the Jewish view that God blesses the righteous, even in a physical manner. Citing many additional texts (Dt 32:39; 1 Sm 2:6; 1 Kgs 17:17–24; 2 Kgs 4:18–37, 5:7), the *Encyclopaedia Judaica* adds, "components of the idea of resurrection were present in biblical thought from early times."[4]

In the Old Testament, the two texts that clearly teach a bodily resurrection are Isaiah 26:19 and Daniel 12:2–3. The former presents a time characterized by the joyous conquering of death (cf. Is 25:8). The latter envisages both a resurrection of the righteous to an eternal life of glory and as well as a resurrection to judgment and everlasting disgrace.

From the intertestamental times to the first century A.D., other Jewish writings differ widely in their presentation of the afterlife. Ecclesiastes lacks any clear teaching regarding a blessed future existence, seemingly holding to a Sheol-like existence (14:16; 22:11; 46:19; etc.). The Wisdom of Solomon (2:23; 3:1–10) and 4 Maccabees (18:20–23) appear to envision the immortality of the soul. 2 Maccabees clearly holds to a strong view of bodily resurrection, with the physical organs intact (especially 14:46; cf. 7:8–9; 12:43–45)! In other writings through the first century A.D., the predominant view also seems to be the resurrection of the body, although it is sometimes transformed.[5] As *Judaica* summarizes: "the belief that ultimately the dead will be revived in their bodies and live again on earth. . . . A major tenet of Jewish eschatology alongside the Messiah, belief in resurrection is firmly attested from Maccabean times.[6]

So the earlier Jewish position favored an afterlife in terms of Sheol. However, by the close of the Old Testament, the resurrection of the body emerged. From this time until Jesus, this continued to be the predominant view, although a diversity of opinions and emphases existed.[7] Wright concludes that, for pre-Christian Judaism, "Resurrection meant embodiment." And Jews believed that their martyrs would be "reembodied, raised to life in God's new world."[8]

The Afterlife: The Views of Jesus and His Contemporaries

In Jesus's day, Jewish opinion regarding the nature of the afterlife was also less than unanimous. The Sadducees denied the resurrection (Acts 23:8) and challenged Jesus's view on the resurrection of the dead (Mk 12:18–27).[9] Josephus adds his testimony concerning the Sadducees' denial of immortality as well as rewards and punishments after death.[10]

The Book of Acts informs us that the Pharisees taught the resurrection of the body (23:6–9). There appears to be some confusion in Josephus, since his language leaves it unclear whether he thinks that the Pharisees believed in bodily resurrection or immortality of the soul, though he does affirm their belief in rewards and punishments after death.[11] The Mishnah likewise affirms the resurrection of the body, where *Sanhedrin* 10:1 teaches that there will be an inheritance in the next world for all Israelites, except for those who deny the resurrection!

It is difficult to determine the view of the Essenes. Josephus seems quite clear that they, like the Greeks, believed in the immortality of the soul, as it flees the body at death.[12] Writing about a century later, Hippolytus also notes similarities between the Essenes and the Greeks. But it is difficult to determine whether he thinks the Essenes accepted the immortality of the soul or the resurrection of the body, since he also discusses the rising of the flesh.[13]

Overall, it may be concluded that, as in the century or two before Jesus, the Jewish teaching of bodily resurrection seems clearly to be the dominant position in Judaism in the first century or so A.D. This is indicated by the probable position of the Pharisees, along with writings like 1 Enoch, 2 Baruch, and 4 Ezra, not to mention the earlier texts listed above that must have exercised some influence at this time.

Jesus also taught bodily resurrection. In the discussion with the Sadducees mentioned above, Jesus affirmed that after the dead are raised, they will be like the angels. By this he does not mean that believers would be pure spirit beings, for that was not the contemporary view of angels.[14] Further, Jesus thought that the resurrection of the body was taught in the Old Testament, since God presides over the living rather than the dead (Mk 12:18–27). In a remarkable discussion, Meier argues powerfully that this dispute is authentic, based on several criteria of historicity. There are "a number of different" sorts of discontinuity between Jesus, Jewish thought, and the teaching of the early church, all of which support the text "to a remarkable degree." Further, there are some crucial signs of coherence with other teachings of Jesus regarding the future state and resurrection of the dead, as I mention immediately below. Additionally, these latter texts are themselves multiply attested in Mark, Q, L, and perhaps M. Accordingly, Meier concludes that the dispute goes back to Jesus's own teaching on the resurrection of the dead.[15]

Another exceptionally important saying that teaches the resurrection of the body in the Kingdom of Heaven/God is the Q saying in Matthew 8:11–12/Luke 13:28–30. Intriguingly, the principle of coherence is also evident here concerning both subject matter, as well as the involvement of the same three patriarchs as in Mark 12:26. Meier also reaches a positive conclusion regarding its nature as an authentic saying of Jesus, largely due to this coherence plus its strong source attestation.[16] In addition, Witherington mentions the highly Semitic context as another reason to accept the saying in Matthew 8:11–12/Luke 13:28–30 as belonging to Jesus.[17] Wright argues for authenticity based on the coherence of the agreement with Old Testament expectations of God's blessings on the nations.[18] Not surprisingly, Sanders notes that most scholars accept the authenticity of at least the portions concerning the banquet.[19]

A set of sayings in Mark and perhaps Q (Mk 9:43–47; Mt 5:29–30, 18:8–9) also clearly presuppose the resurrection of the body. In fact, the portrayal of hands, feet, and eyes speak of eternal life in the "most graphic and concrete terms."[20] In arguing for authenticity based on qualities such as the early and Jewish nature of the saying, plus its exceptionally shocking nature, Beasley-Murray also notes the corporeality inherent in Jesus's language.[21] Ladd makes similar points, as well as noticing the coherence of these sayings with others made by Jesus.[22]

In other texts, Jesus taught that all persons would be raised after death, some to eternal life and some to eternal punishment (Mt 25:31–46). Some of Jesus's Kingdom of Heaven/God parables also developed this theme of rewards and punishments (cf. Mt 25:1–13; Mt 25:14–30/Lk 19:12–27). Jesus briefly mentioned the nature of resurrection life, as well. It is life in God's Kingdom, specially prepared for the righteous since the world began (Mt 25:34). This life will be eternal (Lk 20:36) and involves personal fellowship (Mk 14:25) and blessings (Lk 14:14; Mt 25:10; Mt 25:21–23/Lk 19:17–19). We should be single-minded, accumulating treasures in heaven rather than on earth (Mt 6:19–24/Lk 12:33–34; Lk 16:13), seeking God and His Kingdom above all (Mt 6:33/Lk 12:31).

But far from advocating disengagement from the world, Jesus indicated that pursuit of the Kingdom of God involved intense, radical commitment to God and himself (Mk 10:25–31; Lk 9:57–62, 14:25–35), as we saw in the last chapter. When asked about obtaining eternal life, Jesus taught that the greatest command was wholehearted commitment to God. The second greatest command involving loving others as much as ourselves, followed by the convicting parable of the Good Samaritan, with the mandate to do likewise (Lk 10:25–37).

Sometimes, Jesus simply refers to the Kingdom as a state of blessedness, as ζωή, emphasizing the quality of life (Mk 9:43, 45; 10:30; Mt 7:13–14).[23] So Jesus clearly taught the resurrection of the body, including a few characteristics of a blessed Kingdom life awaiting the righteous,[24] along with the need for wholesale commitment.

It should be noted that if Jesus was raised bodily, then, following our key principle, God's approval would serve as confirmation of the Judeo-Christian concept of bodily resurrection, as opposed to other options. This confirmation would extend both to Jesus's teachings on this subject, as well as to the event itself.

The Resurrection of the Body: The New Testament

So Jesus taught bodily resurrection. Few dispute that the Gospels also portrayed Jesus's own resurrection in a bodily manner. All four Gospels attest that his tomb was found empty (Mk 16:1–6; Mt 28:1–7; Lk 24:1–8; Jn 20:1–9), strongly implying that whatever happened involved his body. Later we are told both that Jesus offered his followers the opportunity to touch his body (Lk 24:36–43; Jn 20:24–29), and that some did so (Mt 28:9; cf. Jn 20:17). While Mark probably ends at 16:8, even he plainly implies a bodily appearance by the prediction that, after his resurrection, Jesus would appear to his disciples in Galilee (14:28), a promise that was repeated again in 16:7.

The Book of Acts also teaches the resurrection of the body, a position that was contrasted with the views of both the Sadducees (4:2; 23:6–9) and the Greek philosophers at Athens (17:32). Jesus demonstrated to his followers that he was alive after his death (Acts 1:3). And there would be a future resurrection of both the righteous and the unrighteous (Acts 10:42; 24:15).

But the chief critical question concerns the teachings of the apostle Paul. In 1 Corinthians 15, Paul speaks in terms of a σῶμα πνευματικόν. Persons will be raised in bodies that are changed (15:44, 50–54). In contrast to earthly bodies, Paul describes the resurrection body as imperishable, glorified, powerful, and spiritual (15:42–44). It is a body that is changed (15:50).

Elsewhere, Paul speaks similarly. In Philippians 3:21, he mentions Jesus's σώματι τῆς δόξης. But Paul does state here that Jesus was raised as a σῶμα, not a πνεῦμα (cf. 1 Cor 15:44). He also supplies some other hints in the context. In Philippians 3:4–6, Paul describes his pre-Christian life. At least before meeting the risen Jesus, he refers to himself as a "Hebrew of the Hebrews," a zealous persecutor of Christians, and a Pharisee. As we have seen above, Pharisees probably believed in bodily resurrection. Another clue comes in 3:11, where Paul mentions the ἐξανάστασιν τὴν ἐκ νεκρῶν, the "resurrection out from among the dead ones." Paul uses a similar expression in 1 Corinthians 15:12: ἐκ νεκρῶν ἐγήγερται. These strong phrases indicate that the body that was buried in death is the one that emerges in its new, resurrected state—the latter does not arise in the spirit realm.

Therefore, in order to do justice to Paul's concept of a "spiritual" or "glorious" body, each aspect must be given its due. The resurrection body is a real body, although it is transformed. Still, Paul's exact meaning is a matter of debate that cannot be solved here. As Brown notes, a majority of commentators recognize both aspects: "bodily resurrection" is "a reality on which I think all the pertinent New Testament writers would agree."[25] But while the bodily side of the phrase has been underplayed often, a growing number of recent scholars has been balancing the two aspects. Even Lüdemann states: "I do not question the physical nature of Jesus' appearance from heaven. . . . Paul . . . asserts that Christians will receive a transformed physical body like the one that the heavenly man Christ has (cf. 1 Cor 15:35–49)."[26] Many other scholars agree.[27] Wright summarizes: "Jesus' body was transformed into the new mode of physicality."[28]

Repeatedly, Paul and other New Testament authors assert that Jesus's resurrection was a model of the believers' resurrected body (Acts 4:2; Rom 6:5; 1 Cor 15:20–22; 1 Thes 4:14). Believers would be transformed like Jesus's glorious body (1 Jn 3:2; Phil 3:20–21). This teaching is even attributed to Jesus himself (Jn 14:19).

But the power of Jesus's resurrection is not only future, but is present in the new life of the believer (1 Pt 1:3; Rom 6:6–10, 8:9–11). So the New Testament teaches both a new life and power in our present lives (Phil 3:10, 20–21; Jn 6:47), as well as a transformed resurrection body of glory for eternal life in the age to come (1 Cor 15:42–57; Jn 6:40).

The Nature of Eternal Life

Jesus made comparatively few comments concerning the nature of eternal life. But even if all we knew about the subject followed from his resurrection and these few teachings, we would still have some crucial hints about what might await believers. Beyond that, several New Testament writers provide additional comments. What sort of a picture emerges?

In chapter 4 we treated in some detail Jesus's teaching that he had inaugurated the initial phase of the Kingdom of God. Kingdom life was already a present possibility. But there would be a future phase, too. In this chapter we have studied some of those details. Jesus clearly taught bodily resurrection, with both blessings and punishments after death. Believers would be like the angels (without meaning pure spirit beings). Fellowship and other rewards were promised. Believers would have fellowship with him, too, and even Gentiles would be present in the Kingdom of Heaven. Often the emphasis was placed on the quality of such life, without further details. The aspect of duration is also present in Jesus's teaching: the life of the Kingdom is eternal life; its inhabitants will never die.[29] In the meantime, we should build our treasures in heaven, seeking God and His Kingdom above all else. Loving others as much as we love ourselves results from this commitment to God.

Further, Jesus's appearances were real. As the initial manifestation of Kingdom life, Jesus's resurrection indicates that the future Kingdom is not some imaginary realm or simply the product of children's tales. It is also a substantial place. It is not simply a state of mind, nor merely the realm of spirits. Jesus appeared in a transformed body, and the believer's hope is to receive the same. So God's eternal Kingdom is an actual place for substantial persons to inhabit.

Other New Testament writers taught these and other aspects. Kingdom life begins in the present (1 Pt 1:3; 1 Jn 5:13). Paul explains that believers are already citizens of heaven! So believers may experience a foretaste of such life before they die. Jesus's resurrection made all of this possible (Phil 3:20–21).

In full agreement with Jesus's words, in the future manifestation of the Kingdom, believers will live eternally (2 Cor 5:1; 1 Thes 4:17). There is a maximum difference, then, between this life and that of some mere utopia where people are happy, but still must get sick and die. Rather, negative features like these will be absent in the Kingdom of God (Is 25:7–9; Rv 7:15–17). Eternal life has overruled our old enemies—pain, suffering, and death have been banished forever (1 Cor 15:53–57; Rv 21:4).

What do these writers report that believers will do in the Kingdom? As Jesus taught, we will experience fellowship with him and see him face-to-face (1 Jn 3:2), both immediately after death (2 Cor 5:8; Phil 1:23), and later in heaven (Rv 22:4). In rather picturesque language, other heavenly occupations involve serving God as priests (Rv 5:10) and corporate praise to both Jesus Christ, as well as to his Father (Rv 5:9–14). As in some of Jesus's parables, believers occupy positions of honor and authority in the Kingdom of God, including reigning with Him (2 Tm 2:11–12; Rv 5:9–10). Paul particularly makes the point that believers will also be glorified, raised with Jesus, and exalted with him in heaven (Rom 8:11, 17, 30; cf. Eph 2:6).

It would be difficult to miss the collective perspective of heavenly activity. Jewish theology emphasized the resurrection of the entire nation—the righteous would rise together (Dn 12:1–3; Is 26:19). Paul continued this practice, always speaking in the plural regarding the resurrection of the dead. All believers, both dead and living, will be raised together in the ultimate reunion (1 Thes 4:14–18). Other passages likewise speak about the heavenly fellowship between believers (1 Cor 13:12; Rv 21:26–27).

Far from static living, one stimulating feature of heavenly life is the continued pursuit of truth and knowledge regarding God, others, and creation. We read that, throughout the future ages to come, believers will be shown "the immeasurable riches of his grace" (Eph 2:7, RSV). It would surely seem that if God is revealing information, then believers will have the opportunity to learn. The prospect of future, personal growth is additionally inferred strongly from the very nature of human beings. Even after the resurrection of the dead, humans are glorified, but still are not omniscient. As finite, sentient beings, it is our very nature to learn from our surroundings.

As exciting as are all of these prospects, we are told that fallen creation itself will be "redeemed," becoming God's new creation (Rom 8:19–23). This new earth will be inhabited only by righteousness (2 Pt 3:13; Rv 21:25–27). God's newly recreated world is the perfect complement for redeemed persons to inhabit and enjoy.

Almost incomprehensibly, Jesus's resurrection guarantees that the believer's heavenly inheritance "is imperishable, undefiled, and unfading, kept in heaven" for us (1 Pt 1:3–4, RSV). The three terms (ἄφθαρτον, ἀμίαντον, ἀμάραντον) that describe these qualities guarantee that heavenly blessings are incorruptible, indestructible, and without any flaws or blemishes. To be "kept" or "reserved" (τετηρημένην) for believers (1:4) is to be preserved or watched on our behalf. The treasures and blessings of heaven will neither be stolen nor corrupted. The believer's eternal inheritance is preserved by God.

Scholars agree that Jesus and the New Testament writers taught that life in the Kingdom of Heaven had both qualitative as well as quantitative dimensions. The former comes from the nature of ζωή, signifying God's quality of life. As Peter Kreeft points out about God, "We never come to the end of exploring Him."[30] The aspect of quantity comes from terms such as αἰώνιος and especially the various forms of ἀθανασία, in that believers will never again die.[31] Few scholars have studied these concepts in relation to resurrection more than Murray Harris. Regarding the differences between these terms, Harris explains, "eternal life refers primarily to quality . . . secondarily to quantity." Harris adds: "Immortality, on the other hand, refers primarily to quantity . . . and secondarily to quality."[32] Further, eternal life and immortality inform each other in several ways. Eternal life is personal, corporate, and bodily. Immortality is a state rather than an event, a permanent condition, and sustained by God.[33]

The Kingdom of God is as multifaceted as it is unfathomable, a glorious paradise. Few of its treasures have been disclosed (cf. 1 Cor 2:9–13, 13:12; 1 Jn 3:2), and those that are mentioned or described are often hidden in metaphors and other word pictures, as I explore in the next section. In fact, J. P. Moreland and I have suggested that we employ a "Christmas morning" view of heaven, so we can anticipate its glories and blessings without attempting to figure everything out.[34] To even know the little amount that we do is more than sufficient to cause us to long for an incomparable time of eternal fellowship, learning, and enjoyment with Jesus Christ and our believing loved ones. This knowledge should translate to making a difference here, in this world.

Biblical Images of Heaven

The frequent use of metaphors and other figures of speech throughout Scripture invoke deep sensations regarding the afterlife. These word pictures perhaps imply what awaits us more vividly than does straightforward prose. Sometimes these images are combined with prose to produce similar effects. So Scripture may actually have more affect on us *not* when it teaches about the nature of heaven, but when it tugs at our heart by speaking figuratively. As Gabriel Fackre testifies, the teaching of everlasting life "is ablaze with many scenes—personal, social, cosmic. . . . What a sight!"[35] Caird discusses Scripture's preference for "powerful images" of the afterlife.[36]

I have mentioned a "Christmas morning" view of heaven, suggesting that believers take a "wait and see" attitude regarding what heaven will be like. Like trusting children, we know enough concerning our Father to expect the best!

Jesus taught that God had prepared His Kingdom from the creation of the world (Mt 25:34). Here our minds are free to roam, within the parameters of Scripture. What could the God who created the entire universe have in store for us? The possibilities are endless.[37]

Can we learn about the afterlife from Scripture's images? How is our imagination stirred, kindled, and engaged? Many of the most profound and comforting thoughts that are woven throughout the text culminate in highly picturesque descriptions of heaven. Often, similar ideas can be traced through the Old Testament, the teachings of Jesus, and on to the Book of Revelation. These deep-seated, immensely provoking images illuminate our concepts of eternity.

For example, few longings run more deeply than our desire for peace. Accordingly, Psalm 23:1–3 is a popular biblical text, with the Lord portrayed as the Shepherd who cares for his people's innermost needs, leading them to green meadows, beside quiet waters, and providing peaceful rest.[38] This theme is also encountered in John 10:1–16, where Jesus is the Good Shepherd who calls his individual sheep by name, guiding them to good pasture. The sheep recognize and follow the Shepherd, who protects them, and gives his life on their behalf. And the sheep receive eternal life from the Shepherd (10:27–29).

Carrying the same imagery into the heavenly scene in Revelation 7:15–17, the Lamb leaves his throne to spread a tent over his people, becoming their Shepherd and leading them to springs of living water. His followers are protected from all ills and will no longer experience pain and suffering. Heaven has become the final culmination of their search for peace.

Closely related to our longing for peace is the desire for satisfying rest. Another Old Testament theme is that God removes daily His people's burdens (Ps 68:19; 81:6–7). Jesus also promises that if those "who are heavy laden" will respond to him, then "I will give you rest," repeating, "you will find rest for your souls" (Mt 11:28–29, RSV). The theme reappears in Hebrews 4, where the rest is most likely both temporal and eternal, as well as in the heavenly scene in Revelation 14:13: "Blessed are the dead who die in the Lord henceforth . . . they may rest from their labors" (RSV). Heaven is the final attainment of the rest that may begin in this earthly life.

Another favorite Old Testament theme simply filled with meaning involves several images of security and protection, like those found in Psalm 91:1–4. Here God provides shelter for His people, who are secure under His wings. In these verses, God also appears as a mighty fortress, a refuge for His people, a haven of protection and serenity.[39] In Matthew 23:37–39, Jesus pictures himself as a mother hen who desires that her chickens find protection under her wings. In Revelation 21, God unveils the ultimate fortress created for His people, and He lives among them (21:1–3). Heaven is pictured as the utmost fulfillment of our need for refuge and protection.

From the sparkling river, to the rushing waterfall, to the deep, silent woods, to the austere, snow-capped mountains, beauty intrigues us. The Bible begins with God's wondrous creation, including the gorgeous Garden of Eden, with its trees, rivers, and scenery that was "pleasant to the sight" (Gen 2:8–15, RSV). The Septuagint uses the term "paradise" to describe this garden scene in 2:8, as it does in Numbers 24:6 to present another graphic picture.

While Jesus was dying, he told one of the men crucified with him that on that very day, they would experience παραδείσῳ together. The same term reappears in Revelation 2:7, where God's new creation involves gardenlike scenery, also termed παραδεισω Then in Revelation 21–22, almost half of the descriptive verses that portray the New Jerusalem also depict beauty—the glory of God; the colors of the walls, city, and streets; and the twelve multi-colored foundations. Of course there are interpretive differences here in regard to the amount of literal description. But I am making a more basic point: the emphasis on beauty remains. Brilliant, eye-dazzling colors like these would make science-fiction special-effects movies pale by comparison! Beyond sight alone, the believer has been invited to *live* in such a place!

C. S. Lewis explains the incredible effect of beauty: "We want something else which can hardly be put into words—to be united with the beauty we see, to pass into it, to receive it into ourselves, to bathe in it, to become part of it." Then he adds: "Nature is only the image, the symbol; but it is the symbol Scripture invites me to use. We are summoned to pass in through Nature, beyond her, into that splendour [sic] which she fitfully reflects."[40]

Another concept appearing throughout Scripture is the joy of fellowship. Few activities are as rewarding as sharing with others. Several metaphors of this nature occur in the Old Testament. Popular images include the great feast, the merrymaking of a wedding ceremony, or the marriage relationship.[41] Fellowship is also a prominent theme in Jesus's teaching, as with the great feast in the Kingdom of God where people will attend from all over the world, eating with celebrities like Abraham, Isaac, and Jacob (Mt 8:11–12/Lk 13:28-29; cf. Lk 14:15–24). Finally, the Marriage Supper of the Lamb (Rv 19:7–9) is a joyous occasion.

But Jesus also mentions the greatest fellowship of all—the promise of intimate and personal communion with him. He told the disciples that he would not drink wine again until he dined with them in God's Kingdom (Mt 26:29). He also told them that he was going to heaven, where they would afterward be reunited (Jn 14:1–3). Later, Revelation 22:4 extends this hope to all believers, when they "will see his face."

All of these ideas and images, whether literal or not, portray highly desirable concepts. Peace, rest, security, protection, beauty, and intimate fellowship are all deeply seated longings that humans experience throughout their lives.[42] Scripture maintains that these states are partially attainable in this life, but that each one reaches its pinnacle only in heaven.

All of these desires may reflect a longing that is probably the deepest one of all. According to Ecclesiastes 3:11, God has placed in everyone a desire for eternity, although it cannot be fathomed in this life.[43] In Hebrews 11, a major characteristic of the biblical heroes who lived faithful lives is that they were strangers on earth while looking forward to future blessings (11:13, 26–27, 35). More specifically, "they desire a better country, that is, a heavenly one" (11:16, RSV).

Our highest desires find their ultimate expression and fulfillment in heaven. Scripture both mentions specific characteristics of heaven, as well as utilizing various images and word pictures to provide us with some hints regarding its nature. The latter may actually be more stimulating. In both cases, the results are not only intellectually rewarding, but they invigorate our hearts, too.[44]

Conclusion

The historicity of the resurrection of Jesus indicates that believers will rise, too. The argument from this event to the truth of heaven appears to be well-founded. No other doctrine in the New Testament was linked more often to Jesus's resurrection. And seemingly few conclusions have more support from the community of critical scholars.[45]

Jesus was raised from the dead. The Fourth Gospel reports Jesus saying that, because he lived, believers would live, too (Jn 14:19). The New Testament writers repeatedly proclaim that Jesus's resurrection means that believers will be raised, too (Acts 4:2; 2 Cor 4:14; 1 Pt 1:3–4). Further, Jesus's body is an example of the body that believers will possess after death (Phil 3:20–21; 1 Jn 3:2).

The Christian hope is that the doctrine of bodily resurrection rests on the reality of Jesus's resurrection (1 Cor 6:14; 15:20–21). So the historicity of the resurrection guarantees the truth of the Judeo-Christian concept of the resurrection of the body, as opposed to other notions. In this case, evidence that God raised Jesus from the dead actually produces evidence that believers will be raised, as well.

I have been working on a chief principle throughout the first six chapters of this book. For a variety of reasons that I have pointed out, Jesus's resurrection best indicates that the God of the universe confirmed both Jesus's person and teachings by raising him from the dead.

More particularly, the resurrection of Jesus provides two convincing evidences for the believer's eternal life after death. The first path is an indirect one. By raising Jesus from the dead, God's approved Jesus's person and teachings. God's strongest endorsement would apply especially to Jesus's message regarding the Kingdom of God and its entrance requirements of salvation, since this was at the very center of his message. Since the life of the future Kingdom is eternal life, Jesus's resurrection confirmed the believer's resurrection and immortality. Briefly, Jesus's resurrection was God's special seal on Jesus's central teachings of eternal life in the Kingdom of Heaven.

The second argument is much more direct. Jesus's resurrection is an actual *example* of our eternal life. It is the only miracle that, by its very nature, indicates the reality of the afterlife. As Jesus appeared to his followers, heaven had actually broken into the earthly realm. The simplest way to understand the disciples' experience is that the person standing in front of them was walking, talking eternal life. Eternal life was a reality. Since Jesus lives forever, so will believers.

Jesus's resurrection argues that death is not the end. As with Jesus, death is simply a transition to a new, everlasting life. For these reasons, the evidences for Jesus's resurrection are likewise evidences for believers' eternal life.

Clearly, the chief verification and forerunner of the believer's resurrection body is Jesus's example (1 Cor 15:45–57; cf. 1 Pt 1:3–5). The implied resurrection also provides the basis for our victory over the fear and bondage of death (Heb 2:14–15). While not the only strong evidence for an afterlife,[46] Jesus's resurrection is the chief demonstration that the believer's body will be resurrected, too.

But we have also seen in this chapter a crucial side of Jesus's resurrection that proceeds far beyond any arguments. Jesus and his followers both provided a few details regarding heaven's characteristics. But they also employed some incredible word pictures, not only providing us with additional hints regarding its nature, but stimulating our longing to seek God and His heavenly Kingdom above all else. The results should arouse our intellect, as well as invigorate our hearts. As Jesus taught, this should motivate us to live an active life in this world, as we seek to obey the two greatest commands that he taught us: loving God wholeheartedly and loving others as we love ourselves.

Notes

1. For example, *The Treatise on Resurrection* 47:1–24.

2. For these and related ideas, see especially Plato's *Phaedo* 65–68, 91–94; *Republic* X:609–21; *Phaedrus* 248–49; *Meno* 81.

3. Hans Conzelmann is an example of the many scholars who believe that this teaching derives from Persian influences (*I Corinthians* [Philadelphia: Fortress Press, 1975], 261). Neil Gillman agrees (*The Death of Death: Resurrection and Immortality in Jewish Thought* [Woodstock, Vt.: Jewish Lights, 1997], 96). But ancient historian Edwin Yamauchi argues forcefully that such an influence commits numerous factual and dating errors ("Life, Death, and the Afterlife in the Ancient Near East," in *Life in the Face of Death: The Resurrection Message of the New Testament*, ed. Richard Longenecker [Grand Rapids, Mich.: Eerdmans, 1998] 40–42, 47–49).

4. S.v. "Resurrection," *Encyclopaedia Judaica* (Jerusalem: Keter, 1971), 14:97.

5. Testament of Benjamin 10:2–9; 1 Enoch 51:1–2, 62:13–16, although the fifth book of 1 Enoch seems to teach the immortality of the soul (103:4); 2 Bar 30:1–5, 50:2–51:10; 4 Bar 6:5–10; 4 Ezra 7:32–42.

6. "Resurrection," 14:96.

7. For some pertinent distinctions, see George Eldon Ladd, *I Believe in the Resurrection of Jesus* (Grand Rapids, Mich.: Eerdmans, 1975), chap. 5.

8. N. T. Wright, "Christian Origins and the Resurrection of Jesus: The Resurrection of Jesus as a Historical Problem," *Sewanee Theological Review* 41 (1998): 111, 117; cf. also N. T. Wright, "The Resurrection of Resurrection," *Bible Review* 16 (2000): 63.

9. On the historicity of this debate, see the detailed discussion by John Meier, *A Marginal Jew: Rethinking the Historical Jesus*, 3 vols. (New York: Doubleday, 1987–2001), 3:411–44. For Meier's conclusion on the historical nature of this text, see esp. 431–44.

10. Josephus, *Wars of the Jews* 2:8:14; *Antiquities of the Jews* 18:1:4.

11. Cf. Josephus, *Wars of the Jews* 2:8:14; *Antiquities of the Jews* 18:1:3.

12. Cf. Josephus, *Wars of the Jews* 2:8:11; *Antiquities of the Jews* 18:1:5.

13. Hippolytus, *The Refutation of All Heresies* 9:22.

14. Meier, *A Marginal Jew*, 3:423–24.

15. Meier, *A Marginal Jew*, 3:411–44, esp. 434–44; cf. Craig S. Keener, *A Commentary on the Gospel of Matthew* (Grand Rapids, Mich.: Eerdmans, 1999), 526–30.

16. Meier, *A Marginal Jew*, 3:251, 428, 438, 442, 494, 528.

17. Ben Witherington III, *Jesus, Paul and the End of the World: A Comparative Study in New Testament Eschatology* (Downers Grove, Ill.: InterVarsity Press, 1992), 66–68, 137–38.

18. N. T. Wright, *Jesus and the Victory of God*, vol. 2 of *Christian Origins and the Question of God* (Minneapolis: Fortress Press, 1996), esp. 308–10.

19. E. P. Sanders, *Jesus and Judaism* (Philadelphia: Fortress Press, 1985), 394 n. 38; cf. 218–21.

20. Meier, *A Marginal Jew*, 3:441.

21. G. R. Beasley-Murray, *Jesus and the Kingdom of God* (Grand Rapids, Mich.: Eerdmans, 1986), 174–75.

22. George Eldon Ladd, *The Presence of the Future: The Eschatology of Biblical Realism* (Grand Rapids, Mich.: Eerdmans, 1974), 163–64.

23. In the Fourth Gospel, eternal life is both a present possession (Jn 3:36; 6:47; etc.) and a future reality (Jn 5:24; 11:25, 26; etc.). George Ladd notes the different emphasis from the synoptics, but thinks that the same truth is being taught (*The Pattern of New Testament Truth* [Grand Rapids, Mich.: Eerdmans, 1968], 64–86).

24. For Rudolf Bultmann's attestation here, using some of the same texts, see *Theology of the New Testament*, 2 vols., trans. Kendrick Grobel (New York: Scribner's Sons, 1951, 1955), 1:5–6 and *History and Eschatology: The Presence of Eternity* (New York: Harper and Row, 1957), 32–33.

25. Raymond E. Brown, *A Risen Christ in Eastertime: Essays on the Gospel Narratives of the Resurrection* (Collegeville, Minn.: Liturgical Press, 1991), 53.

26. Gerd Lüdemann, "Closing Response," in *Jesus's Resurrection: Fact or Figment? A Debate between William Lane Craig and Gerd Lüdemann*, ed. Paul Copan and Ronald K. Tacelli (Downers Grove, Ill.: InterVarsity Press, 2000), 151.

27. Arguably the strongest presentation here is Robert H. Gundry, *Soma in Biblical Theology: With Emphasis on Pauline Anthropology* (Cambridge: Cambridge University Press, 1976), esp. chap. 13. For other recent commentators, see also:

N. T. Wright, "Early Traditions and the Origin of Christianity," *Sewanee Theological Review* 41 (1998): 130–35; Stephen T. Davis, "'Seeing' the Risen Jesus," and William P. Alston, "Biblical Criticism and the Resurrection," both in *The Resurrection: An Interdisciplinary Symposium on the Resurrection of Jesus*, ed. Stephen T. Davis, Daniel Kendall, and Gerald O'Collins (Oxford: Oxford University Press, 1997), 126–47, 148–83, respectively; Caroline Walker Bynum, *The Resurrection of the Body in Western Christianity, 200–1336* (New York: Columbia University Press, 1995); Raymond E. Brown, "The Resurrection of Jesus," *Jerome Biblical Commentary* 81:118–134 (1968): 1373–77; Joseph A. Fitzmyer, "The Resurrection of Jesus Christ according to the New Testament," *The Month*, 2nd n.s., 20 (November 1987): 408–9; William Lane Craig, *Assessing the New Testament Evidence for the Historicity of the Resurrection of Jesus* (Lewiston, N.Y.: Edwin Mellen Press, 1989), 117–48, 325–47; Ben Witherington III, "Resurrection Redux," in *Will the Real Jesus Please Stand Up? A Debate between William Lane Craig and John Dominic Crossan*, ed. Paul Copan (Grand Rapids, Mich.: Baker Books, 1998), 133–136; C. E. B. Cranfield, "The Resurrection of Jesus Christ," *Expository Times* 101 (1990): 170; Thomas C. Oden, *The Word of Life*, vol. 2 of *Systematic Theology* (Peabody, Mass.: Hendrickson, 1989), 464, 478–79; Norman Kretzmann, "Resurrection Resurrected," in *Hermes and Athens*, ed. Eleanore Stump and Thomas Flint (Notre Dame: University of Notre Dame Press, 1993), 149; Donald G. Dawe, *Jesus: The Death and Resurrection of God* (Atlanta: John Knox Press, 1985), 112–14; Norman L. Geisler, "The Significance of Christ's Physical Resurrection," *Bibliotheca Sacra* 146 (1989): 148–67; Paul Barnett in *Resurrection: Truth or Reality*, ed. Barnett, Peter Jensen, and David Peterson (Sydney: Aquila Press, 1994), 22, 28–33; Grant Osborne, *The Resurrection Narratives: A Redactional Study* (Grand Rapids, Mich.: Baker Books, 1984), 278–79, 292; Margaret Pamment, "Raised a Spiritual Body: Bodily Resurrection according to Paul," *New Blackfriars* 66 (1985): 380–81, 386; Roger E. Olson, "Resurrection, Cosmic Liberation, and Christian Earth Keeping," *Ex Auditu* 9 (1993): 123, 129.

28. Wright, "Early Traditions," 131.

29. As we have mentioned in earlier chapters, eternal life was still not synonymous with the Kingdom of God. Jesus affirmed that saints who lived before his time were alive (Mk 12:26–27; cf. Lk 16:19–31). An afterlife was a present reality, too (Lk 23:43; cf. Jn 11:25–26).

30. Peter J. Kreeft, *Everything You Ever Wanted to Know about Heaven . . . But Never Dreamed of Asking* (San Francisco: Harper and Row, 1982), 62.

31. Besides Kreeft, *Everything*, and Murray Harris, *Raised Immortal: Resurrection and Immortality in the New Testament* (Grand Rapids, Mich.: Eerdmans, 1983), just a few of the other scholars who also make some of these distinctions are John Hick, *Death and Eternal Life* (Louisville, Ky.: Westminster John Knox Press, 1994), 179–81; Jürgen Moltmann, *The Way of Jesus Christ: Christology in Messianic Dimensions*, trans. Margaret Kohl (Minneapolis: Fortress Press, 1993), 224–25; Wright, "The Resurrection of Resurrection," 63; Luke Timothy Johnson, *Living Jesus: Learning the Heart of*

the *Gospel* (San Francisco: Harper Collins, 1999), 101; Brian Hebblethwaite, "The Resurrection and the Incarnation," in *The Resurrection of Jesus Christ*, ed. Paul Avis (London: Darton, Longman and Todd, 1993), 162–63; John Drane, *Introducing the New Testament* (San Francisco: Harper and Row, 1986), 109; Gabriel Fackre, "I Believe in the Resurrection of the Body," *Interpretation* 46 (1992): 49; Meier, *A Marginal Jew*, 2:432; Francis X. Durrwell, *La Résurrection de Jésus: Mystère de Salut* (Paris: Les Éditions du Cerf, 1976), 255–62; Peter Stuhlmacher, *Was geschah auf Golgatha? Zur Heilsbedeutung von Kreuz, Tod und Auferweckung Jesu* (Stuttgart, Germany: Calwer Verlag, 1998), esp. 69–77.

32. Harris, *Raised Immortal*, 199. For further outstanding studies on these and other relevant terms, see 182–83, 199–201, 209–14, 232–36, 273–75.

33. Harris, "Resurrection and Immortality in the Pauline Corpus," in *Life in the Face of Death*, esp. 169. While Harris's conclusions here are related to Paul's view, he concludes the same about the other New Testament writers, as well (*Raised Immortal*, 232–36).

34. Gary R. Habermas and J. P. Moreland, *Beyond Death: Exploring the Evidence for Immortality* (Wheaton, Ill.: Crossway Books, 1998), esp. 269–72.

35. Fackre, "I Believe," 49.

36. G. B. Caird, *New Testament Theology*, ed. L. D. Hurst (Oxford: Clarendon Press, 1994), 277.

37. Francis Schaeffer remarked in regard to the Christian's imagination: "Christian man has a basis for knowing the difference between subject and object. The Christian is the really free man—he is free to have imagination. This too is our heritage. The Christian is the one whose imagination should fly beyond the stars" (*Art and the Bible* [Downers Grove, Ill.: InterVarsity Press, 1973], 61).

38. The image of God as a Shepherd caring for His people is a very common Old Testament theme (Pss 28:9, 37:3, 74:1, 79:13, 80:1, 95:7, 100:3; Is 40:11, 53:6).

39. The theme of God as the believer's Refuge, Shield, Rock, Fortress, Stronghold, Shelter, and Protector is a common idea in the Old Testament. See II Sm 22:3; Pss 3:3; 5:11; 9:9; 11:1; 16:1; 17:8; 18:2, 30; 25:20; 27:1; 28:7; 31:1–4, 19–20; 32:7; 36:7; 46:1–7; 144:2; Is 17:10; 25:4–5; 31:5; 57:13; Jer 16:19; 17:17.

40. C. S. Lewis, "The Weight of Glory," *The Weight of Glory and Other Addresses* (Grand Rapids, Mich.: Eerdmans, 1949), 13.

41. See examples in Ps 45; Is 54:1–10; Zec 14:16–19.

42. For a discussion of the imagery of heaven and an expanded treatment of heaven, see Habermas and Moreland, *Beyond Death*, chap. 13.

43. More than one translation of this difficult verse has been proposed. We are following the RSV reading.

44. C. S. Lewis said: "There have been times when I think we do not desire heaven but more often I find myself wondering whether, in our heart of hearts, we have ever desired anything else" (*The Problem of Pain* [New York: Macmillan, 1962], 145). For an excellent study, see Peter J. Kreeft, *Heaven: The Heart's Deepest Longing* (San Francisco: Harper and Row, 1980).

45. For a number of the many scholars who affirm this, at least as the New Testament position, see Crossan, "Rebuttal," in *Will the Real Jesus Please Stand Up? A Debate between William Lane Craig and John Dominic Crossan*, ed. Paul Copan (Grand Rapids, Mich.: Baker Books, 1998), 46; Hick, *Death and Eternal Life*, 178–84; Pannenberg, *Systematic Theology*, 2:350–51; Moltmann, *The Way of Jesus Christ*, 224–25, 259–62; Gordon D. Kaufman, *In Face of Mystery: A Constructive Theology* (Cambridge, Mass.: Harvard University Press, 1993), 378, 381; Walter Künneth, *Theologie der Auferstehung*, 6th ed. (Giessen, Germany: Brunnen Verlag, 1982), 291–92; Karl Rahner, *Foundations of Christian Faith: An Introduction to the Idea of Christianity*, trans. William V. Dych (New York: Seabury Press, 1978), 268; Brown, "The Resurrection of Jesus," 1373; Pheme Perkins, *Resurrection: New Testament Witness and Contemporary Reflection* (Garden City, N.Y.: Doubleday, 1984), 296–315; Caird and Hurst, *New Testament Theology*, 241, 267, 277; Michael Grant, *Saint Paul* (Glasgow: William Collins Sons, 1976), 89; Thomas Torrance, *Space, Time and Resurrection* (Grand Rapids, Mich.: Eerdmans, 1976), 102; Howard Clark Kee, *What Can We Know about Jesus?* (Cambridge: Cambridge University Press, 1990), 112–13; N. T. Wright in *The Meaning of Jesus: Two Visions*, by Marcus Borg and Wright (San Francisco: Harper Collins, 1999), 126–27; Johnson, *Living Jesus*, 100–105; Ben F. Meyer, *The Aims of Jesus* (London: SCM Press, 1979), 68; James D. G. Dunn, *The Evidence for Jesus* (Louisville, Ky.: Westminster Press, 1985), 76; Gerald O'Collins, *Jesus Risen: An Historical, Fundamental and Systematic Examination of Christ's Resurrection* (New York: Paulist Press, 1987), 179–87; Hebblethwaite, "The Resurrection and the Incarnation," 162–63; William Strawson, *Jesus and the Future Life* (London: Epworth Press, 1970), 230; Drane, *Introducing the New Testament*, 109; Dale C. Allison Jr., *The End of the Ages Has Come: An Early Interpretation of the Passion and Resurrection of Jesus* (Philadelphia: Fortress Press, 1985), 80, 100, 167, 171, 178; Thomas C. Oden, *The Word of Life*, vol. 2 of *Systematic Theology* (Peabody, Mass.: Hendrickson, 1989), 479–82; Clark Pinnock, "Salvation by Resurrection," *Ex Auditu* 9 (1993): 6–7; Ted Peters, *God—The World's Future: Systematic Theology for a New Era*, 2nd ed. (Minneapolis: Fortress Press, 2000), 321, 392; Witherington, "Resurrection Redux," 138; Stephen T. Davis, *Risen Indeed* (Grand Rapids, Mich.: Eerdmans, 1993), 202, 206–8; Charles H. Talbert, "The Place of the Resurrection in the Theology of Luke," *Interpretation* 46 (1992): 23–28; Fackre, "I Believe," 49; Meier, *A Marginal Jew*, 2:432, 435; Craig, *Assessing*, chap. 4; Richard Bauckham, "God Who Raised the Dead: The Resurrection of Jesus and Early Christian Faith in God," in *The Resurrection of Jesus Christ*, ed. Paul Avis (London: Darton, Longman and Todd, 1993), 145; Paul Badham, "The Meaning of the Resurrection of Jesus," in *The Resurrection of Jesus Christ*, 36; Janet Martin Soskice, "Resurrection and the New Jerusalem," in *The Resurrection*, 57; John Frederick Jansen, *The Resurrection of Jesus Christ in New Testament Theology* (Philadelphia: Westminster Press, 1980), 94–100; Donald Goergen, *The Death and Resurrection of Jesus, A Theology of Jesus* (Wilmington, Del.: Michael Glazier, 1988), 116, 147; Alan F. Segal, "Paul's Thinking about Resurrection in its Jewish Context," *New Testament Studies* 44 (1998): 412, 417–19; David Marshall, "The Resurrection of Jesus and the Qur'an," in *Resurrection Reconsidered*, ed. Gavin D'Costa (Oxford: Oneworld Publications, 1996), 175–77; Dawe, *Jesus*, 101;

Ladd, *I Believe*, 148–52; Joost Holleman, *Resurrection and Parousia: A Traditio-Historical Study of Paul's Eschatology in 1 Corinthians 15* (Leiden, Netherlands: E. J. Brill, 1996), 206–7; Muddiman, "I Believe in the Resurrection of the Body," in Barton and Stanton, eds., 129–37; Gundry, *Soma*, 176–83; Maier, *In the Fullness of Time: A Historian Looks at Christmas, Easter, and the Early Church* (San Francisco: Harper Collins, 1991), 205; Peter Selby, *Look for the Living: The Corporate Nature of Resurrection Faith* (Philadelphia: Fortress Press, 1976), 9–19; Donald G. Bloesch, *Essentials of Evangelical Theology: Life, Ministry, and Hope* (San Francisco: Harper and Row, 1979), 184; Thorwald Lorenzen, *Resurrection and Discipleship: Interpretive Models, Biblical Reflections, Theological Consequences* (Maryknoll, N.Y.: Orbis Books, 1995), 246–47, 257–58; Paul Barnett, *Jesus and the Logic of History* (Grand Rapids, Mich.: Eerdmans, 1997), 129; Donald Hagner, "Gospel, Kingdom, and Resurrection in the Synoptic Gospels," in *Life in the Face of Death*, 119; G. Walter Hansen, "Resurrection and the Christian Life in Paul's Letters," in *Life in the Face of Death*, 222; Harris, *Raised Immortal*, chap. 5; Durrwell, *La Résurrection de Jésus*, 212–14; Stuhlmacher, *Was geschah auf Golgatha?* esp. 69–77.

46. For several other evidences for life after death, see Habermas and Moreland, *Beyond Death*, chaps. 1–9.

PART TWO

THE RESURRECTION AND SOME PRACTICAL ISSUES

CHAPTER SEVEN

Challenging the Fear of Death

Have you ever been shocked by suddenly confronting the reality of your own mortality? Perhaps the catalyst was the funeral of a loved one, friend, or your own close brush with an accident or disease. Maybe the prompting came from a more simple source like a reminder of your age (however young), or even from a picture of a casket. At moments such as these, the whispered truth is that we, too, will die some day.

The dread that sometimes fills our hearts at the mere mention of the subject of death is a common experience for many humans. Often this anxiety lasts only for a moment; other times it initiates a downward emotional spiral. But whether the experience is spontaneous and short-lived or lingers for long periods of time, it is usually discomforting. Sometimes it is even traumatic.

Some pundits have said that the worst evils in life are death and taxes. But not everyone pays taxes. The ultimate fear is probably the dread of death. Believers are not exempt from this fear.[1] In one penetrating passage we are told that many people suffer bondage throughout their lives, due to the terror of death. However, Jesus came to release us from that fear (Heb 2:14–15).

We, too, frequently experience dread at the prospect of death, either our own or that of a loved one. Maybe we fight these emotions every time we undergo a painful or nagging illness, or even when we are threatened by such situations. Why do even believers experience such fears? Is it possible to successfully deal with at least the more painful, anxiety-producing portions of this fear? These are the practical areas of focus for this chapter.[2]

Why We Fear Death

There are several reasons we may experience anxiety at the thought of dying. For many of us, death is associated with pain or the loss of mental functions. We want to die quickly and painlessly. Many wish to "go" in their sleep. Or we often suffer trepidation at the idea of hearing a doctor predict our imminent demise. Some fear that every illness may be their last. It is almost as if we would rather deal with death itself than with its anticipation. We would rather have death come silently and swiftly so we will not have time to think about its arrival.

Of course, impending death limits or even ends our dreams and plans. It crushes our fondest hopes.

Another factor that causes a great deal of dread is the thought of saying good-bye to our loved ones on Earth. Ironically, this may even be the case with those who, because their priorities are properly placed, value relations with persons over their enjoyment of things. So they worry about the possibility of being separated from those they have loved so much. This emotion usually intensifies when the anxious individual is a parent with small children.

Still another worry comes from the fear of being alone. Nothing changes the basic fact that dying is something we all must do by ourselves. It is inevitable.

Perhaps our chief fear of death involves apprehension over the unknown. In spite of biblical teachings and beautiful images of the afterlife, believers muse in "what if" terms. What if Christianity is not true? What if an interpretation of a particular text is incorrect? Admittedly, it is so easy to wonder whether one is right after all.

Closely related is the horror of nonexistence. Visions of funerals, caskets, and bodily decomposition also encourage these fears. These stark reminders invade our private thoughts, a constant reminder of the Grim Reaper. Doubts arise concerning the reality of an afterlife—any kind—even though Scripture clearly affirms it. What if nothing exists after death? Few things are more violently opposed to the nature and desires of humans than the thought of utter extinction.

Some believers are even afraid of judgment, or the thought of standing before God. This fear can persist in spite of the biblical attestation that Christians will not be judged regarding their final destination, but only to determine their rewards.

It is doubtful if many human beings avoid experiencing one or more of these fears about death, and this includes Christians. Fancy talking will not remove these fears entirely, at least not in most cases. As long as we insist on allowing emotions to judge the facts, including entertaining visions of our most horrible anxieties and "what if" scenarios, such fears will plague us.

So where does this leave us? Hebrews 2:14–15 says that Jesus came to deliver believers from our fear of death. Even those who are tormented all their lives by this paralyzing anxiety may be freed from its most fearful aspects. Paul added that the death of loved ones need not cause believers to grieve as do persons who have no future hope (1 Thes 4:13).

Still, none of these passages claim that we will be totally free of the emotional struggles that arise periodically. We are told, however, that victory over at least the more crippling elements of this fear is possible. Let us see how this may be possible.

Pursuing Victory over Our Fears

The basic New Testament response is that the death and resurrection of Jesus, viewed along with the heavenly perspective that these events provide, ultimately supply the chief answer to our dilemma. This is the uniquely Christian response to death, and it provides the basis for handling our worst fears of death.

While granting that looking forward to the prospect of our death is unpleasant, it is also true that this says more about the state of our thinking processes than it does about our actual demise. An extremely important part of maintaining a heavenly perspective involves the ordering of our thoughts so we can replace unedifying ideas with truthful, encouraging ones. We must learn to not allow concentration on temporary conditions, however real, to supplant eternal truths. Certainly suffering is real and death will come, but these realities are not ultimate. But when we treat them as such, we blind ourselves to eternity's vantage point. In fact, we replace eternal reality with temporal vision. We must keep Paul's words before us, allowing them to clear our vision: "I consider that the sufferings of this present time are not worth comparing with the glory that is to be revealed in us" (Rom 8:18, RSV).

In Philippians 4:6–9, Paul also addressed the topic of worry and challenged his readers' anxious thinking (v. 6), commanding them to pray, give thanks, and, perhaps most importantly, exchange their anxious thoughts for edifying, truthful ones (v. 8). Then he exhorted his readers to practice this process until it became a way of life (v. 9). How can we do this?

It is best to apply these steps *precisely during* the time of anxiety. We must learn to cultivate disciplines like prayer and thanksgiving. Then we need to identify the things we tell ourselves that are not only misplaced, but merely contribute to our worry. Lastly, we must substitute anxious thoughts for godly ones. Practicing these truths during our roughest moments, whether we feel like it or not, is the key. As Paul says, constantly rehearsing this process until it becomes a habit will lead to peace.

We should also remind ourselves that this process of transforming our perspective is not a mind game meant to manipulate our thinking or con us into believing that reality is something else. This process is based firmly on the truths of Jesus's resurrection and eternal life. When we fail to participate in mind renewal based on truth, we actually fall prey to falsehood and illusion.[3]

This subject of redirecting our thinking patterns is much more than a nice-sounding, quickly stated suggestion to stem the tide of fear. It is thoroughly biblical, and for those interested in scientific verification, it is also based on demonstrated psychological methods. It has been tested in a variety of circumstances, demonstrating that it really, truly works.[4] What are some of the biblical thoughts that we can utilize to assist us in handling the fear of death for either ourselves or in advising someone else?

It is undeniable that pain frequently accompanies death. And yet Paul counsels believers to focus their attention on eternal life instead of their physical problems (2 Cor 4:7–18). He carefully explains that this perspective follows from the fact that the Christian's troubles are only momentary and terminal—they will not last long. On the other hand, the afterlife is eternal, blissful, and of inestimable value, so it warrants our concentration (vv. 17–18). The reality of Jesus's resurrection provides the firm ground for Paul's concept of eternal life in this passage. Believers will be resurrected by the same God who raised Jesus from the dead (vv. 14). This top-down, heavenly perspective can even lessen our pain associated with death, by removing the emotional element, which is often the worst portion.[5] Further, eternal life is true and is still a reality long after the pain actually does cease.

Impending death often curtails or ends our dreams. But as I pointed out in the last chapter, it also opens to us entirely new vistas—a new creation to enjoy, ongoing knowledge, peace, rest, security, beauty, and intimate fellowship with Jesus, our friends, and loved ones. No doubt, our hopes will be revitalized, and in quick order!

While we cannot escape the fact that earthly relationships temporarily cease at death, Paul explains that true knowledge of and fellowship with others will occur only in the future state (1 Cor 13:12). We will be reunited with believing family and friends, either by death or by the coming of the Lord (1 Thes 4:17–18). Jesus taught that our relationships will broaden and deepen in the afterlife (Mt 8:11; cf. 1 Cor 5:8). While the sting of death still separates us temporarily from loved ones, ironically it is also the only way to achieve true and lasting fellowship with them.

For similar reasons, we can rest assured that we will not be alone after death. As we just said, we experience fellowship, and that even more fully, after our passing to the next world. Further, Jesus exemplified this fellowship during his postresurrection appearances to his disciples. So there is no factual basis for the belief that the afterlife is a separate, lonely existence. The facts argue otherwise. The sooner we align our thinking with these facts, the sooner we will experience victory over the paralyzing aspects of the fear of death.

Although I do not deny that death embodies the chief unknown ever encountered by human beings, Jesus did experience it, and he conquered it by rising from the dead. While Jesus's resurrection does not tell us everything we may wish to know about the nature of eternal life, it does reveal enough that we need not be so fearful of death. Due to Jesus's experience, death and its aftermath are no longer a frightening mystery. We really can calm our sometimes raging fears. Earlier in this book I described a "Christmas morning" view of heaven. We have some specific ideas of what heaven will be like, as well as some highly suggestive biblical images. Therefore, although we know very little about what follows death, what we *do* know is abundantly able to soothe our worst fears if we will only allow it to do so.

From this we can also find reasons for calming our worries about the threat of nonexistence. We know certain details about heaven, including our immediate existence after death, because of Jesus's resurrection. Paul also confirms that we will still be alive after our bodies die (Phil 1:21–23; 2 Cor 5:1–8). So this is yet another place where practicing proper thinking is imperative. Nonexistence is simply an incorrect prospect, so why concentrate on it?

So while the fear of extinction may be fostered by visions of funerals, caskets, and bodily decay, this fear is directly due to improper thinking patterns that we can correct. It is also misplaced factually, because eternal life, not eternal extinction, is an evidenced reality. However unpleasant and scary these imaginings may be, they will not hinder us from experiencing immediate consciousness after death. We do, in fact, survive our own funerals and bodily decomposition. A blissful existence awaits believers.

Some philosophical considerations are worthwhile here, too. While our greatest fear may be experiencing nonexistence, a moment's reflection shows that this is *impossible*. By its very nature, we could never experience nonexistence, for if there is no experiencer, there is nothing to feel! Neither could someone else ever *experience* it and then report a state that *denies* that experience. So what many fear the most can never occur. Further, even in a worst-case scenario involving the nonexistence of the next life, *we could never know this* to be the case experientially. Those struggling with this fear should meditate on these truths.

Standing before Christ's judgment seat (see 2 Cor 5:10) is another worry for some Christians, but it should not be so. In the same context, Paul teaches that believers will be in the Lord's presence after death (v. 8; cf. Phil

1:21–23), not rejected by him. This follows from Jesus Christ's actions on our behalf, accomplished through his death and resurrection (Eph 2:4–7). According to the Fourth Gospel, Jesus confirmed that Christians will not be condemned (Jn 3:16–18, 36; 5:24–29). Anxieties to the contrary may dominate when we ignore texts that correct this fear. Only unbelievers need to fear condemnation (Mt 25:31–46). So the answer to worries about judgment is to trust the Lord in light of the Gospel facts. While the certainty of our future should not give us an excuse to be proud or calloused (1 Cor 10:12), it should help us realize that our eternal destiny is not at stake.

In 1 Corinthians 15:53–57, Paul explains that after our bodies are raised, death will finally be conquered. He taunts death and the grave, which will have lost their bite (vv. 53–56); they will maintain no more control over the destinies of human beings. And once again, the certainty of these events is a factual one: because of Jesus's resurrection from the dead (v. 57; 1 Cor 6:14; 2 Cor 4:14), our bodily resurrection and the defeat of death are assured (Phil 3:20–21). Other New Testament writers agree (1 Jn 3:2; 1 Pt 1:3–5).

None of this means that death is our friend. Death is an enemy, a consequence of our wrongdoing, a bitter pill that goes down hard. Thinking about it often hurts. And suffering through it as it claims loved ones tears at our hearts.

As painful as all this is, though, we can find hope and solace in the fact that death is not the end. It does not have the final say. For Christians, ultimate victory lies on the other side of death. There we will find the best in (eternal) life. God has turned death into the door that opens to the fullest possible joy—heavenly bliss (Ps 16:11). As believers, we can stare death in the face and see it as an evil from which God brings good. For us, it can even be a blessing to be at home with Christ (Phil 1:21–23; 2 Cor 5:8) and our loved ones (1 Cor 13:9–13). The more we can bring our thoughts into line with these truths, the greater will be our opportunity to conquer the most painful side effects of this fear.

Of course, we are not suggesting that we can ever progress to the place where even the thought of our own death or that of a loved one does not bother us at all. But this is not a defeat. The temporal separation and pain of death even affected Jesus after the death of his friend Lazarus. We are told that Jesus stood in front of Lazarus's tomb and wept (Jn 11:35). Feelings of loss and sadness are appropriate. But we do not have to fear death and what lies beyond it in any inappropriate, incapacitating way.

Like all human beings, Christians struggle with their emotions, but they do not have to be overcome by them. Believers can still achieve victory over the most painful aspects of their greatest fear. That is the example provided by Jesus, who wept over death, but came to free us from the bondage-creating elements of this king of anxiety (Heb 2:14–15). With Paul, we can grieve, but not as those who have no hope (1 Thes 4:13).

A Strategy for Facing Death

Perhaps we can move beyond the considerations in the previous section in order to suggest a more specific strategy for dealing with at least the most unruly elements of the fear of death. Here I outline three steps: internalizing the truth that eternal life is a reality, shifting our pattern of thinking to a heavenly perspective, and substituting our anxious thoughts of death with these truths. In other words, we need to be assured of eternal life, apply this truth to everyday life, and then allow these new attitudes to transform our fearful thoughts about death. This process seeks to apply psychological assurance to factual data.

Internalizing the Truth of Eternal Life

Throughout this book we have related the resurrection of Jesus to several doctrines of Christian theism. Although it is not the only evidence for an afterlife,[6] I have argued that Jesus's resurrection provides a twofold argument for the believer's eternal life. Directly, the very nature of his resurrection indicates an actual *example* of victory over death. When the disciples saw the risen Jesus, they beheld walking, talking eternal life. Heaven had broken into Earth and they witnessed it. Indirectly, Jesus's central message was the Kingdom of God and the necessary requirements for entrance into eternal life. So if any of Jesus's teachings were vindicated by the resurrection, his teachings about the afterlife would head the list, since they were his chief focus.

Although none of these evidences amounts to absolute proof or certainty, they do indicate strongly that eternal life is a reality. Practically, accepting this truth lays a sturdy foundation for treating fear. Since believers will live after the death and corruption of their earthly bodies, they have no *ultimate* reason to fear death's power. The glories of heaven can even produce an enjoyable longing for our future abode (Phil 1:21, 23; Heb 11:16). At the very least, while viewing death as an enemy and a necessary evil, we do not have to be overcome with worry over its reality.

Still, oftentimes it is not enough to know that eternal life is a reality. Being convinced will certainly help, but this is still too superficial. We must internalize this truth, working it deeply into our thoughts and actions. We need to meditate on its truth, reviewing it regularly. And we should discover additional ways to apply this on a personal level. After all, we can *never* experience personal extinction after death; we can only experience our afterlife. This truth needs to infiltrate our lives.

Shifting Our Thought Patterns to God's Heavenly Perspective
Once we embrace the reality of eternal life, we must learn to view life and death from God's eternal perspective. Here we need to actually think and behave on an everyday basis by bringing eternity to bear on our daily lives. This is another facet of seeking God and his Kingdom above everything else (Mt 6:33). We need to turn our thinking from suffering, pain, and death, however real and painful they may be, and redirect our thoughts toward eternal life (2 Cor 4:14–5:9; Phil 1:21–23).

This heavenly perspective is the theme of Hebrews 11. The heroes of the faith are extolled for having spent their entire lives in pursuit of their eternal home. This lifelong quest is far more meaningful than any earthly, mundane aspirations (vv. 8–10, 13–16, 24–27). Elsewhere believers are told not to pursue or be satisfied with physical gratification because their citizenship is already located in heaven (Phil 3:18–21).

This perspective involves a life-changing principle. It is perhaps even the most frequent motivational challenge in the New Testament. Living according to a heavenly perspective is radically liberating because it calms and frees us from life's usual worries to live for God and His Kingdom, our first love.

For example, what I have called the "top-down" perspective views life from an eternal vantage point. The "top floor" represents the eternal Kingdom of God. The "bottom floor" includes the myriad situations and items that occupy our daily lives. The main idea is to develop viewpoints and behaviors in every area of our lives according to how that particular aspect is affected and informed by the Kingdom. As Colossians 3:2 summarizes: "Set your minds on things that are above, not on things that are on earth" (RSV).

More specifically, in dozens of texts, the New Testament exhorts believers to apply this perspective to our anxieties and daily needs (Mt 6:19–34), social responsibilities (Lk 10:25–37), material possessions (Mt 16:26), suffering and persecution (1 Pt 1:3–9; 5:9–10), finances (1 Tm 6:17–19), and even death (2 Cor 4:16–5:8; Mt 10:28). In each of these texts, eternity is related to an area of life, each of which requires a strong dose of heaven.

Jesus taught that our desires determine where our treasures are accumulated (Mt 6:21). And heaven is worth all we own (Mt 13:44–45). By being centered on God and His Kingdom (6:19–20, 33/Lk 12:31–34), we cultivate an outlook that sifts everything through a heavenly filter. The result is a single-minded life that is simpler and less complicated, since it is devoted to a single master (Mt 6:24/Lk 16:13). Streamlining our lives in light of heaven gives Earth an entirely new perspective.

This approach counters the fear of death. God offers a meaningful life at present, one that can be best lived for Him and others by being directed toward eternity. Living the good life forever is the *best possible reward*. It is the treasure hidden in the field that is worth everything we own. The images of heaven that I pursued in the last chapter should further encourage us to desire and seek God and His Kingdom. These biblical texts do not just promote a problem-solving technique, as useful as that is, but an entire lifestyle. Its results are revolutionary.

This heavenly perspective ought to spur us to reorient our lives. What could be more invigorating than enjoying eternity with the God of the universe and other believers? So we should strive to change our perspective so that whatever does not fit the heavenly pattern is rejected. Why should we encourage thoughts that only cause us to get out of focus?[7]

Once believers are assured of eternal life, they need to think and act in light of that reality. By changing our vantage point to a top-down angle, we have actually prepared ourselves to practice the third step to defeating our worst fears.

Replacing Our Fearful Thoughts

Whenever we experience an anxious thought regarding death, we need to replace it with an edifying one. Maybe the corrective truth will involve Jesus's resurrection, or the reality or nature of eternal life. Perhaps God's promises about immortality or the biblical images of heaven will be the most comforting. Regardless, the point is to restructure our thinking by recalling key truths in the face of potentially debilitating fears (cf. Rom 12:2).

Another option is to argue against these fears. For example, we must forcefully remind ourselves that funerals, cemeteries, and caskets clearly do not represent *ultimate* reality. These images cannot annul the evidence for eternal life, for *that would be contrary to the data*. Fearful thoughts call for an *immediate* review of truths like those I have mentioned.

Even *before* the fears plague our imagination, topics such as the resurrection of Jesus or the biblical teachings concerning heaven are excellent themes for daily meditation. This practice provides "preventive therapy," encouraging a strong mind-set.

Of the many biblical texts that encourage such reframing practices,[8] Philippians 4:6–9 may be the clearest. Paul begins by giving advice for dealing with anxiety. He commands prayer (cf. 1 Pt 5:7) and thanksgiving to God (v. 6). After promising peace (v. 7), he instructs his readers to substitute edifying truths in place of the worries (v. 8). They were to continually practice these steps (v. 9). So prayer, thanksgiving, changing our worrisome thoughts, and practice were Paul's remedies for dealing with anxiety.

How do we substitute edifying thoughts for our fear of death? One method is to identify our misbeliefs, argue against them, and replace them with truthful counterthoughts. While truth frees us, lies always enslave.[9]

Weeding out unedifying thoughts can be difficult and demanding. But its rewards are incalculable. Not only can it correct our bad habits and allay our worst fears, but it can also revolutionize our entire lives. The key is to practice substituting truthful thoughts for misleading ones *every time we allow the latter to intrude into our thoughts* until our emotions are corrected. Believe it or not, it is possible to reach a stage where we are no longer dominated by these fears. The result can be enjoying a taste of heaven on Earth. This strategy for dealing with the fear of death can bring some of the nectar of heaven's fruit to lives dominated by the sting of death.[10]

Conclusion

Some brief comments on the subject of grief may also be appropriate here, since it is a close companion of death and our fears of the grave. Losing a loved one can be traumatic, no matter how the loss occurs. Feelings of disorientation, abandonment, resentment, anger, and despondency are all common. How can the truth of eternal life help us through such a loss? The Gospels tell us that Jesus dealt with this subject, too. More than once, Jesus counseled those grieving the death of a family member or close friend. He taught that something could be done about these emotions.

The Fourth Gospel narrates the story of the death of Lazarus, Jesus's close friend. Jesus comforted the sisters Martha and Mary after their brother's death (Jn 11:17–44). In response to Martha's grief, Jesus reminded her that Lazarus would be raised from the dead (v. 23). Martha misunderstood him at first. She thought he was just reminding her of Jewish theology: her brother would rise again at the final resurrection, along with all the other righteous dead (v. 24). Jesus gently corrected her and explained that he was the resurrection and the life, and that those who exercised faith in him will live even immediately after death (vv. 25–26a). Martha embraced these truths (vv. 26b–27).

Jesus was not questioning the future resurrection of the righteous dead. He was informing Martha that the resurrected state involves immortality—deathlessness. As a result, believers remain conscious after death and before their resurrection. Jesus taught her what he later said to the believing thief on the cross next to him (Lk 23:43) and what his disciples would learn much more clearly after witnessing Jesus's resurrection appearances: our consciousness does not cease at death.[11] Then to show both Martha and Mary that he was indeed the Lord of life, Jesus raised Lazarus from the dead (vv. 34–44).

So, with Martha and later with his own disciples, Jesus counseled grieving persons with the facts and their implications.[12] For Martha, the answer was found in the theological instruction concerning the true meaning of immortality: believers do not cease to exist after death and before the final resurrection of the body. The reality of personal life after death was the foundational truth on which Jesus's comments were based, and his counsel shows that comforting the bereaved is important, and it can be successful, even during stressful times.

Jesus's resurrection appearances were the chief answer for his disciples' grief. When Jesus spoke to his beleaguered followers after his death, we are told that his presence and comforting words changed their emotional state from doubt and fear to joy and faith (Jn 20:19–20, 27–29). The emphasis on his resurrection as the cure for grief, doubt, and fear is clear (Lk 24:36–46).[13] Just seeing and hearing their resurrected Lord was enough to calm the disciples' fears, and comfort their sorrowful hearts.

Not unlike my earlier treatment of death anxiety, then, we frequently find a cognitive approach being taken with those who grieve. Among the available healing balms drawn from these combined cases are the truth of Jesus's resurrection, the nature of eternal life, God's promises concerning the reality of immortality, or even the biblical images of heaven that so wonderfully address our deepest longings. Many lives were touched by these techniques.

Many have lost loved ones and still grieve the loss. Often we are not sure how to help these persons. Ironically, sometimes it is not even necessary to speak; our presence is enough.[14] Jesus intimately understood the grief, loss, and the sense of abandonment. He wept at the grave of his good friend Lazarus (Jn 11:35). And he promised that all those who follow him will join him in heavenly fellowship, reunited with their believing loved ones, feasting on the sweet, incorruptible fruit of eternal life. This does not presently make all the pain go away, but drawing often from this well of truth can bring healing balm to our aching wounds.

The reason I personally know that these biblical strategies work is that, several years ago, my wife died. Before the ordeal, I would have said that such a scenario would have been the very worst thing that could possibly have happened to me. But God brought our family through the suffering, teaching us some lessons along the way. Internalizing biblical truth brought me profound healing, even during the summer she died. This personal account is the subject for the next chapter.

Notes

1. For several examples from the Old Testament poetic writings, see Job 5:26, 30:20–23; Pss 6:3–5, 48:14, 55:4–8, 89:46–48; Prv 13:14, 14:27. Other passages, especially from the New Testament, will be discussed later.

2. An edited version of this chapter appeared in Gary R. Habermas and J. P. Moreland, *Beyond Death: Exploring the Evidence for Immortality* (Wheaton, Ill.: Crossway Books, 1998), chap. 16.

3. This subject is mutifaceted, and many different topics could be mentioned here. For a biblical discussion of several pertinent passages, including Phil 4:6–9, as well as other related subjects, see Gary R. Habermas, *Dealing with Doubt* (Chicago: Moody Press, 1990), esp. chap. 4.

4. For a popular but highly effective treatment, see William Backus and Marie Chapian, *Telling Yourself the Truth* (Minneapolis: Bethany Fellowship, 1980), esp. chaps. 1–3. For technical treatments, see Paul M. Salkovskis, ed., *Frontiers of Cognitive Therapy* (New York: Guilford, 1996), esp. chaps. 14–16, 19; Jan Scott, "Cognitive Therapy of Affective Disorders: A Review," *Journal of Affective Disorders* 37 (1996): 1–11.

5. For details on the application of Jesus's resurrection to some of these issues, see chapter 4, "Grief, Suffering, and Pain" in Gary R. Habermas, *The Resurrection: Heart of the Christian Life*, vol. 2 (Joplin, Mo: College Press, 2000), esp. 81.

6. For a number of other arguments, see Habermas and Moreland, *Beyond Death*, chaps. 1–9.

7. For many more details, including practical ways to apply this principle to specific situations, see: Habermas, *Dealing with Doubt*, chap. 9; Habermas and Moreland, *Beyond Death*, chap. 15; Gary R. Habermas, "Top-Down Thinking and the Problems on Earth," *Christian Counseling Today* 6 (1998): 26–28, 66–67; Habermas, *The Resurrection: Heart of the Christian Life*, chap. 6.

8. See Pss 42:5–6, 11; 43:5; 55:4–8, 16–17, 22; 56:3–4; 57:1–3; Lam 3:19–26; Rom 1:25; Jas 4:7–10.

9. Backus and Chapian, *Telling Yourself the Truth*, esp. chap. 1. Other methods and patterns work, too. The best approach is to study the subject and develop a pattern that may better meet one's individual needs.

10. This is neither a pie-in-the-sky suggestion nor a positive-thinking scheme. For more details, especially concerning the application of these ideas, see Habermas, *Dealing with Doubt*, esp. chap. 4–5. Many additional applications to both our thinking as well as our acting are included in Gary R. Habermas, *The Thomas Factor: Using Your Doubts to Draw Closer to God* (Nashville: Broadman and Holman, 1999), chaps. 6–8.

11. Murray Harris, *Raised Immortal: Resurrection and Immortality in the New Testament* (Grand Rapids, Mich.: Eerdmans, 1983), esp. 211–14.

12. In the discussion with Martha and Mary, the focus is on Jesus and the resurrection, not directly on the raising of Lazarus (Jn 11:25–26). Jesus dealt with the subject of immortality and resurrection before the sisters even knew that he intended to raise their brother from the dead.

13. Other New Testament passages that emphasize Jesus's resurrection in the context of discussions on death include 1 Cor 15:45–57; 2 Cor 4:7–18; 1 Thes 4:13–18; cf. Heb 2:14–15; 1 Pt 1:3–4.

14. See Henri J. M. Nouwen, *Our Greatest Gift: A Meditation on Dying and Caring* (San Francisco: Harper Collins, 1994), 103–4. This book contains much wisdom on this subject.

CHAPTER EIGHT

Suffering and Jesus's Resurrection: A Personal Account

Just a few years ago I had a personal encounter with the worst thing that could have happened to me. I experienced the horrifying sting of suffering and grief, face-to-face. I remember the physician's initial words as if they were said just minutes ago. "The bad news is, your wife has stomach cancer." He had just come out of surgery, where Debbie had been stitched up. Nothing could be done for her.

It is difficult to recount how the fear instantly rose to levels I could only have imagined until then. My stomach felt like it was in my throat. I had to pace. What was I going to do? One issue after another detonated in my mind. We had been married for almost twenty-three wonderful years. She was a mere forty-three years old. We had had a very close marriage and she was my dearest, closest friend. What about my four children, all still living at home? I immediately felt a double dose of pain. How would I tell them? *Could* I tell them? Would they ever recover? What about psychological scars—would they be forever wounded? Would they turn against the Lord?

Unfortunately, my questions had no answers. To this day, I am not sure how we lived the next few months. With the children, I simply allowed them to bring up any issues that they wanted to, and we discussed whatever was on their mind. I spent as much time as I could with Debbie, which was often all day long. I read her Psalms—chapter 91 was her favorite. We talked about something or nothing at all. Every minute was unspeakably precious. Then I read for hours at her bedside while she slept.

Church members brought meals nightly. I never realized the great friends I had, having tended to take them for granted. Family members regularly arrived from other states to help us out and share our burdens.

Four short months after her diagnosis, my beloved Debbie died. My first trip to the funeral home was devastating. The service was easily the toughest event in my life. Afterward, the heartache started as never before. The lack of companionship was devastating. How I missed her!

But still, through it all, the Lord was good. I said it then, and I still say it today. There were too many indications that He was at work in one situation after another. It may be trite to say that we lived one day at a time, but we had to do so. We had no other choice. My mother often reminded me, "God is leading us ever so gently." It became the watchword between us in our conversations together. The pain was enormous, but it was always endurable.

Many lessons were forthcoming. A few years earlier, I coauthored a book on death and the afterlife. I even dedicated my portion to Debbie.[1] I monitored my reactions, observing the classic signs of grief. I kept a journal, noting all sorts of items, both trivial and profound. Then, less than a year after Debbie's death, I wrote another book, my family's diary, dealing with our grief, our pilgrimages, and our triumphs. Its title, *Forever Loved*, is the epitaph we had placed on her gravestone.[2]

Usually while Debbie was sleeping, I had mused frequently about Christianity. What answers were there to our most intense suffering? I had made a lifelong study of the resurrection of Jesus. Did it have anything profound to offer those who grieve deeply? Did its truth even begin to touch the tremendous pain of such a loss? Or did it offer any balm to the other suffering that life sometimes brings our way?

My Friend Job

As strange as it may sound, during many painful days I sometimes felt as if I had befriended Job.[3] He had wrestled through a severe dose of suffering. His story had been a recurring meditation for me. I did *not* think that I had suffered in the same manner. But I was intrigued by this famous story of a man whose name is almost synonymous with pain.

I had said in print that the lessons found in Job really *worked* in real-life predicaments. Now I had the opportunity to prove it. Could I "put my money where my mouth was" now that my own dilemma had arrived? Frankly, I wanted to know if the lessons I found in Job could in any way be applied to my modern situation.

I started by recalling several of Job's problems. Perhaps this would make me more appreciative of any remedy that emerged. According to the text, Job had unquestionably suffered greatly, both physically and emotionally. To make it even worse, he could not understand why God did nothing to help him. Why was God silent? If God could heal him any time He wanted to, then why not do it? He had created the universe, so why did He refuse to do something? But now the situation seemed to have gotten out of control. Would his suffering ever end?

Yet, we are also told that, through his trials, Job learned some fantastic truths that completely transformed his life. How could this be? What secrets were hidden there?

Reading the pages once again, I reviewed his situation. Although he was a righteous man, Job had suffered numerous calamities. One was not enough. His herds of animals were either killed or stolen by outlaws. His livelihood had vanished. Then his servants were murdered. Lastly, the evil touched his own family; his children were killed in a desert storm.

Then phase two of Job's suffering kicked in, and his pain moved closer to home. Job developed painful sores over his entire body. From the itching or the oozing of the sores, he scraped himself with a piece of broken pottery. "Curse God and die," was his wife's counsel. In spite of all this, Job refused to charge God with the fault of these multiple tragedies. Job did not have the luxury of sitting in a college classroom and philosophizing about his dilemmas in some theoretical, detached fashion. And neither did I. He lived through his struggles and pain. So did I. Though I did not suffer like he did, I still felt comradery with him. Since he succeeded, his experience should be quite instructive for me. I gravitated toward the experience and advice offered by others who had lost either a spouse or a child. Maybe Job's lesson could be applied to my own situation with Debbie. I wanted to know how well it would actually work, in the real world where I lived.

After a while, Job challenged God. Several times he demanded his right to have a hearing before the Creator of the universe. He even requested a debate. Job's chief question was a very normal one: "Why am I suffering the way I am? How could these horrors possibly be justified?"

Then God responded. In what exact manner, we do not know. But we are told that God challenged Job to answer an entire host of questions—sort of like a final exam. More than once, God even asked if Job could solve the problems of pain and suffering. But Job did not have an answer. He finally responded by just keeping quiet.

Incredibly, God never answered Job's main question. It seemed like a fair request, one that almost everyone asks from time to time. But God never explained why Job suffered like he did. This is very crucial. I concluded that this might be a key to the entire issue. What if God had provided some heavy philosophical justification for evil, say, a discussion about free will, natural law, or soul making? Even if Job had understood it, would he have cared? Would a graduate school course have met his existential needs? While perhaps Job would at least have understood an undergraduate answer, would that have been what he most wanted or needed?

After all, our textbooks generally tell us the same thing. Philosophical discussions are rarely what grieving persons desire. Sometimes I did enjoy philosophical discussions with my friends during Deb's sickness. But usually I wanted no part in this sort of banter. It took time and patience that I did not have to offer. Ours was far more than a theoretical situation. I was not terribly interested in the leading theories. We were hurting. If I realized this, surely God must. By implication, God knew that such an answer was precisely what Job *did not* need.

Whatever the reason that God never provided an answer to Job's chief question, one thing is crystal clear. In the end, Job was completely satisfied. So why did he abandon his protest? What chief lesson had he learned?

After the dialogue, Job realized that God could do anything. This is evident in the first half dozen verses of the last chapter. So God could perform everything that He had just challenged Job to do, including solving the puzzle of evil. Next, Job recognized that the problem was actually his own inability to understand the things he was questioning. This realization must have stung. But he was honest enough to admit that he had lost the debate with God. After his "showdown," Job declared that the only thing left to do was to repent. He despised his previous position (42:1–6).

This was not simply some cerebral truce on Job's part, either. It had cost him. He had been humbled by his time in God's presence. He had to relinquish his stance. Moreover, he needed to act on his decision and repent. In all of this, God did not force him. Job did it willingly and ungrudgingly. What lesson could he have learned to possibly account for this revolution in his thinking? Why did he change his mind so drastically?

It seems that Job's encounter with the Lord led to an incredible insight, a conclusion that became the foundation for his liberation and peace. *Based on what he knew about God, Job realized that he could trust God even in those things that he did not know.* In other words, Job already knew enough about God to conclude that there were good reasons for his suffering, even if he did not understand all of them. Indeed, he could now trust the One who *did* know why it all had happened.

Therefore, Job was satisfied without ever knowing exactly why God had not answered his questions. He made these decisions during his afflictions, before God blessed him (42:10–17). The latter did not lead to Job's repentance; his new realization had occurred beforehand.

Back Home

There was a tremendous principle for me to learn here, as well. During times in my life when I thought I knew the specific reason for my suffering, so much the better. I was thankful for that knowledge.

But what about those items that I plainly did not understand? What could be done concerning my family's pain? I had not suffered on the scale that Job did, but I had wrestled with some of the same quandaries: Would Debbie survive? Did she have to suffer this much? What about my suffering and that of my children? I wondered about God's seeming silence.

But now I was about to add a crucial addendum. Even when I could not figure out everything, or when God seemed to be silent, I also knew that I still had to trust Him. Why did this follow? We at least have more information about God today than did the saints of ancient times. For one thing, the New Testament supplies some of this truth. Science helps to explain other matters. Psychology adds still more insights. Certainly there is much in this vast universe that we do not know. I had no problem realizing that I was finite. In fact, I never quite understood why people sometimes acted as if they have unlimited knowledge. So I had strong grounds for concluding that God knew what I did not, and for trusting God in the things that I did not understand—like Debbie's illness.

In my opinion, we clearly know more than Job did regarding the nature of suffering. Scripture also teaches some helpful lessons, such as Joseph's rejection by his brothers, David's trouble from his family and friends alike, as well as the prejudice against Daniel. We also read about John the Baptist's doubts, Jesus's struggles in Gethsemene, Paul's "thorn in the flesh" that went unanswered, and the persecution and death of early believers. We are not alone in our struggles.

How much did my family know about our troubles? We knew that pain and suffering often result from free choices, although we did not know the specifics regarding our own distress. I also knew some crucial truths about Jesus, and that the historical basis for Christianity was firmly established. I could not deny this, even during our troubles, and this gave me great comfort. Other times I reminded myself of things that I knew about God. This tactic could take several forms. Suitable subjects for meditation included

God's attributes, truths about heaven, or God's promises. Therefore, like Job, what I *did* know about God was sufficient for me to trust Him.

But could this approach really be applied to the numerous painful circumstances when I did *not* know why things happened the way they did? Given the many books that I had written on the subject of Jesus's resurrection, my thoughts almost always followed a very specific path. During previous troubles, the thought of Jesus's resurrection had nearly always given me relief. But could it have the same results in the worst situation I had ever faced, when I most needed answers? Or would even this great truth fail to produce the desired effects this time?

Often during Debbie's sickness, I took a tack with myself like this one: "I am unsure why things are happening the way they are, and I am suffering. But this is still the same world in which God raised Jesus from the dead. Eternal life for believers is the direct result of this great event. Therefore, I can still trust God that there is a sufficient answer here, even if I do not know what it is. At the very worst, I will see Debbie again in heaven."

Could Job's lesson be successfully applied precisely during the worst of Debbie's struggles? Could I build a bridge between good theory and good practice, even when I did not know all the answers?

I began to picture a situation similar to Job's—only with me asking the questions. How would God answer me? Would He then proceed as He did with Job, commanding me to answer Him (38:3)? If so, what would God ask? I thought I knew in an instant: He would undoubtedly pursue the subject of Jesus's resurrection, challenging me in the area of my own research.

I pictured the conversation going something like this:

> "Lord, I just do not understand why You are allowing these things to occur to my family. Why, especially when Debbie is so young, and all four kids are still at home?"
>
> "Gary, I will answer your question with one of My own. Did I raise My Son from the dead?"
>
> "Well, yes, certainly You did, Lord. But how does that help me solve *our* suffering?"
>
> "You do not seem to understand the intent of My question. Did I raise Jesus from the dead?"
>
> "Yes. But does it have to happen like this, to someone so young? Why *us*?"
>
> "I repeat My question: Did I raise Jesus from the dead?"
>
> "Sure, but . . ."
>
> "Then since you know that this is a world where I raised Jesus, would you also say that His teachings are true?"
>
> "Yes, I have always thought that would follow as the best explanation."

"So do you have good reasons for thinking that I am still in control of the universe?"

"Yes. . . . You are, Sir. I have no good reason to question that."

"Then is it also the case that, although you do not know why your family is suffering, I do?"

"Well, certainly, I suppose that is true."

"Do you know that, in spite of your suffering, I have chosen you and Debbie in My Son? You will be with Me in heaven for eternity. I promise, you will see her again."

"Lord, I could not even imagine a more glorious truth."

"Does it not follow from the truth of the resurrection?"

"Yes, it would seem to do so. . . ."

"Then what remains? Since you know these things, do you think you can also trust Me in those areas where you do not know all of the answers?"

(Silence)

"I repeat. Do you presently have enough information to trust Me through circumstances that you do not understand?"

"I think you made your points well, my Lord. You got me. I should be trusting You with all of my heart."

"Then review these truths often. And do not forget to practice them. Refuse to get sidetracked by other topics, no matter how painful they may seem. Stop carrying your heavy burden by trying to figure everything out. Trust Me with all of your heart."

Granted, my questions or worries were sometimes more stubborn than those in this dialogue. But an approach just as simple as this one actually sufficed in the majority of instances. Admittedly, I was a bit surprised. Why did this role-playing have such a powerful result? I am convinced that it was because of the truth of Jesus's resurrection and its application to real-life situations. In short, this event not only happened but it can meet our daily needs, too.

But sometimes I needed to be more forceful with myself. I learned a very useful lesson in these cases. Regardless of how badly I hurt, or how much I wanted to scream out in anguish, I had to *force* myself to *focus* on the factual issues alone. The result in these tougher times was, more often than not, that I had my answer. Relief almost always followed.

In these instances, I "turned up" both the volume and the force of the rhetoric as I got to the part about the resurrection:

"You do not seem to understand the intent of My question. Did I raise Jesus from the dead?"

"Sure, but that was almost 2000 years ago and . . ."

"Gary, just answer My question. I know you only have a Ph.D., so I'll try to speak more slowly. Did I raise My Son Jesus from the dead?"

"Well, yes, the evidence is truly exceptional but . . . what about today?"

Then, taking me gently by the collar: "Can we stay on track here? Gary, READ MY LIPS: Did . . . I . . . raise . . . Jesus . . . from . . . the . . . dead?"

"Yes, Lord."

"Then what kind of a world is this?"

More slowly: "The kind of world where You are in control, Lord."

"Good answer. Then what about today? Am I STILL in control? Is this *still* My world?"

"Yes, Lord. It is the same world that it was 2000 years ago."

"And in that world of long ago did I watch My own Son suffer horribly and then die?"

"Yes, Lord, I sometimes forget about His torturous pain and suffering."

"My child, suffering is a most insistent taskmaster. Since Jesus is your example, should your pain be removed when His remained? Do you demand better?

"Oh. . . . That really hadn't occured to me."

"But He was raised from the dead afterward. I heard his agonizing plea just before he died. The empty tomb was the answer to the cross."

"I hadn't looked at it from that angle, either."

"While suffering instructs, eternal life is the ultimate answer that conquers pain."

"Yes, I see that now."

"Then are there good reasons for allowing suffering even if I choose not to explain them?"

"Yes, Lord. I understand."

"Then relax, son. You will understand better one day when you enter My eternal Kingdom. Until then, keep up your work that I called you to do."

I cannot overemphasize the directness of these approaches. I simply could *not* allow myself to get sidetracked. It is amazing how *very few* issues *must* be addressed at this particular point. True, shifting the discussion back to Debbie's disease or to my pain were related and seemingly natural moves, but deceptively so. *The most direct cause of my suffering is what I was saying to myself about the situation.*[4] So I sometimes had to *forcefully* remind myself, "Not now. This is not the time to go back to this. Stay directly on the subject of the pain."

True, I could not heal the sickness. All I could do was deal with the immediate situation. But then the previous truth dawned on me with all of its force: If emotional pain is the worst sort of suffering, and the most direct cause of my emotional pain is what I was saying to myself, I could change that *immediately*![5]

Whenever my pain felt unbearable, I would try to sit down, often on my porch. Most frequently, I forced myself to work through and address directly each of the questions that I thought God would ask me. I could not refute this line of reasoning. The facts were true and the conclusion followed.

On each occasion, I made myself answer all of the questions as if I were hearing them for the first time. Over and over again, I had to decide. It was an exam. Do the facts indicate that God raised Jesus from the dead? (Yes or no?) So is eternal life a reality? (Yes or no?) Are Jesus's other teachings also true? (Yes or no?) Is God still in charge of the world? (Yes or no?) While other issues were also relevant, these were usually sufficient for me to know that everything would work out in the end, even eternally so. One day I would know the answers to my other questions, too. So I could wait, assured that there were, indeed, real answers to my toughest questions. Best of all, Debbie would be waiting for me in heaven, all smiles, for she already knew all of this!

Of course, this would not be the exact line of questioning that God would take with everyone. I suspect that the examination would be tailored differently, according to each person's situations and needs. Sometimes the chief question might be, "Did I not answer a major prayer request for you recently?" (Yes or no?) Or: "Did I not help you out of some rough circumstances?" (Yes or no?) Or, more like Job: "You have always appreciated my creation. So can you nullify the intricacies of my design—say, the secrets of DNA or enzyme development?" (Yes or no?) Or even tougher and also like Job: "Can *you* explain why there are pain and suffering in the world that I created?" (Yes or no?) Or: "What is the value of free will?"

Though the challenge might be different, the conclusion would be the same. Since we cannot explain or even understand God's ways, on what grounds can we justifiably "second-guess" Him? He created the world, raised His Son from the dead, made a path of salvation for us, answered our prayers, and prepared heaven for us. So why do we find it so difficult to trust Him in our present circumstances? We should realize and admit that He knows more than we ever could, and that includes knowing the reason for our pain and suffering.[6]

Intriguingly, Job was never told to believe something without a basis. God repeatedly directed him to facts in the real world, usually based on biology and physics. This may seem refreshing in an age in which science is frequently thought to oppose religious belief. For later believers, the historical resurrection of Jesus Christ is the key. God did not ask Job or us to believe in a vacuum.

So Job's conclusion led to victory over the incredible suffering in a life that has become synonymous with pain. *What he already knew about God was sufficient to trust Him in those things that he did not know.* And precisely this same truth should focus our thoughts on the most crucial matters in the Christian faith. Not only can we also deal with much of our own pain in a related manner, but it works in other circumstances, as well. For instance, we can be freed from the burden of always having to figure everything out.

Incidentally, even an unspoken insinuation that we have a right to know God's thoughts is ridiculous. Most would readily admit that they are certainly not God. Then why do we sometimes insist on thinking that we have a right to know all of these things? True, what seems to be an almost unbearable pain could influence us to think some of these things. Yet, this is precisely the signal we may need in order to make sure that our thinking is clear. In brief, *it is precisely because of the pain* that we must apply these truths. Further, we must do so forcefully! Do we truly want peace? It awaits our decision.

Conclusion

This was Job's lesson. He experienced some deep waters, suffering an extraordinary amount of pain. He responded by charging God with being unjust and challenging Him to a verbal dual. God's retort was a personal and direct challenge. In the end, Job confessed his rebellion, acknowledging that he was guilty of charging headlong into matters that he clearly did not understand. He affirmed that God could do anything. And he knew that he could trust God in the deep things of the universe, including his problem of pain and suffering.

I discovered with joy that Job's remedy would also work for my family. Precisely during my pain, I applied his lesson liberally, as many times as I needed it. During Debbie's sickness and afterward, it never once failed to provide relief. Every single time I reviewed God's challenge regarding Jesus's resurrection, I realized anew that Job's basic theme could answer my deepest questions about suffering. In fact, the process became easier with each application. It became unnecessary to grit my teeth as I rehearsed the procedure.

What, precisely, did God accomplish in me through this practice? Although I still did not know why Debbie was dying, it quickly became a moot point. The *reason* for our suffering was inconsequential. It would not change the situation anyway. The One who had raised His Son Jesus from the dead knew the reasons. Since I could not deny this, I would wait for the answer. Given my questioning mind-set, this was a revolutionary conclusion. But it brought peace.

I gained other benefits, as well. Since I no longer asked, "Why?" neither did I suffer the additional emotional pain associated with second-guessing God. This allowed me to deal with the daily issues directly before me, without adding the anxious stress that postulates other "what if" scenarios. This also allowed me to enjoy the tremendous truth that, whatever else happened, God was indeed in control. Lastly, I realized that I would be with Debbie in heaven, and for all eternity. I could rest in this promise, even during my suffering. It actually worked in the real world, too. The ensuing relief was immeasurable. God had answered my prayers.

Notes

1. Gary R. Habermas and J. P. Moreland, *Immortality: The Other Side of Death* (Nashville: Thomas Nelson, 1992).

2. Gary R. Habermas, *Forever Loved: A Personal Account of Grief and Resurrection* (Joplin, Mo.: College Press, 1997).

3. From this point on, my discussion follows more or less closely from chapter 9 of my work *Forever Loved*.

4. For details here, see William Backus and Marie Chapian, *Telling Yourself the Truth* (Minneapolis: Bethany Fellowship, 1980), chaps. 1–3; for example, see 17–22.

5. Backus and Chapian, *Telling Yourself the Truth*, 14.

6. The careful reader will realize that, in this chapter, we are applying some of the same cognitive principles that we outlined in the last chapter, although they are being aimed at a different emotional challenge.

CHAPTER NINE

The Testimony of the Holy Spirit and Evidence

I have said that there is more to Jesus's resurrection than the study of evidences. There are other ways to approach this subject than via historical arguments and the state of current scholarship, which are only one side of the issue. Nothing I have said militates against other paths to the truth and application of Christian theology. Besides my earlier pursuit of practical topics like the fear of death and existential suffering, another important avenue is the personal witness of the Holy Spirit to the believer (sometimes called the testimonium). This can additionally be related to earlier chapters in this volume. Comparatively little appears to be available on this subject, especially in recent decades.

The Nature of the Holy Spirit's Testimony

To those who judge, as I did for many years, that this topic is condemned to subjectivity and is therefore next to valueless, I plead only for a fair consideration.[1] And it still should be noted very carefully that reaching such a conclusion of subjectivity does not affect our previous discussions regarding the truth of Jesus's resurrection and Christian theism.

But if my conclusions here are essentially correct, then this subject provides an entirely different angle for approaching at least the issue of Christian assurance. Certainly, decisions on this topic are person specific, and will not appeal to everyone.[2] But it is addressed in the New Testament, and believers should not ignore this issue.

Perhaps the most difficult issue is simply attempting to delineate the nature of the Holy Spirit's witness. What should be included in such a concept? It may be helpful to begin our discussion by eliminating certain common notions concerning the nature of the Holy Spirit's testimony to the believer. In the New Testament, it is never associated with overt signs like an audible voice or extraordinary experiences. Neither is this phenomenon ever connected with human reason, sense experience, or emotions. It is not attributed to any sort of human origin.

In a study of major passages like Romans 8:15–17 and Galatians 4:6–7, Bernard Ramm identifies the witness of the Holy Spirit specifically as a "direct connection from the mind of God to the mind of the Christian." The specific subject of this direct testimony is the assurance of the believer's salvation. The process occurs at a level that is deeper than other information that we gain by reason or sense experience. In this sense, the Holy Spirit can impress redeemed individuals more profoundly than they can touch themselves.[3]

Arguing that the Holy Spirit's witness is actually intuitive in nature, Ramm asserts that such a concept ought not be problematic. All forms of knowledge require "an irreducible intuitive element." So this testimony is a direct confirmation of the believer's salvation, not a conclusion following from an argument.[4]

If this is the case, then should all Christians have the same experience? For Ramm, the expressions of this witness are as varied as are individuals. Different levels of intensity are also found. For example, one believer might express his assurance in a calm, settled manner while another may be more dogmatic. Still other Christians might experience more uncertainty and doubt, even though they certainly believe.[5] Just as in everyday life, people respond differently to the same stimuli.

So if Ramm is correct, the essence of the Holy Spirit's testimony is not outward phenomena like audible voices, extraordinary experiences, or even in spiritual gifts. It is not that these occurrences are absent from the New Testament, but this is simply not how the testimony is described.

Rather, passages like Romans 8:15–17, Galatians 4:6–7, John 14:16–17, and 1 John 3:24 and 4:13 indicate that this witness is the individual communion between the Holy Spirit and the redeemed individual. This conviction is therefore different from what is learned through other cognitive channels. There are variations in human expression and intensity. We need to investigate in more detail what the New Testament states concerning the chief purpose of this blessing.

The Major Purpose of the Holy Spirit's Testimony

Whatever else may be thought about the identification and nature of the Holy Spirit's testimony, the major New Testament texts affirm that this inner witness is a personalized testimony to the Christian that he or she is a child of God. The assertions are rather straightforward that the purpose of this testimony at least includes the subject of the individual's assurance of salvation.

Romans 8:15–17 refers to Christians being adopted as children, evoking our response of "Abba" (v. 15). So the new believer is a family member and now addresses God in a radically different and intimate manner. Further, the Holy Spirit provides a personal witness to the individual believers spirits that they are, indeed, children of God (v. 16). As if this were not amazing enough, Paul asserts that believers are entitled as coheirs with Christ himself! The result is sharing not only Christ's sufferings, but also his glory (v. 17).

The most crucial point for our discussion seems to be quite clear from this text. Romans 8:16 characterizes the Holy Spirit's testimony as a personal, firsthand communication with the believer's spirit, specifically informing the Christian of a familial relationship to God.

In another closely related text (Gal 4:6–7), Paul also explains that the Holy Spirit is sent into believers' hearts, crying "Abba" to God (v. 6). Paralleling the earlier passage, the apostle informs us that, accordingly, we are heirs of God (v. 7). The subject again concerns becoming a family member through salvation.

Other New Testament texts make similar claims. We are told that Jesus made a promise to his disciples that he would send the Holy Spirit to them (Jn 14:16). They would know the Spirit because he would indwell them (v. 17). Consequently, this indwelling would cause the disciples to realize their unity with Christ (v. 20). Again, the message seems clear: the presence of the Holy Spirit would be the means by which Jesus's disciples would obtain the knowledge and recognition of their union with God.[6]

Twice the epistle of 1 John further applies this promise to believers as a whole. They would similarly know that God resided in their lives, because of the presence of the Holy Spirit in them (1 Jn 3:24; 4:13).

So we find the same message in the New Testament's teachings of Jesus, Paul, and John. All agree that the Holy Spirit provides believers with the individual certainty that they are God's children and thereby participants in His family. This seems to be the major purpose of the witness.

This testimony specifically concerns truths related to the believers salvation, involving the knowledge of having become God's children and coheirs through the Holy Spirit's indwelling. There is no suggestion that the Holy Spirit's witness is given in order to judge the content of theological matters, or to decide between conflicting doctrinal positions. In other words, the testimony is not a hammer with which to beat others over the head, informing them of their errors. Not only is there a lack of textual support here,[7] but even in New Testament churches, some moral and theological differences were apparent (Rom 14:1–23).

Among commentators, the most notable exception to my position is the view that the witness is primarily the conviction that Scripture is God's Word (or even that there are two witnesses, one to the individual's salvation and one to the text). This appears to be found most frequently in those who are persuaded of the Reformed theological position.[8] But it should be noted that not all Reformed theologians agree with this interpretation.[9]

A passage often used to support the view that the Holy Spirit primarily testifies to the truthfulness of Scripture is 1 Corinthians 2:4–16. Yet this text seems, on the one hand, to refer to much broader aspects of the Holy Spirit's ministry, while, on the other, it does not appear to specify any mention of the witness at all. Ramm agrees with this assessment, remarking that the overall intent of these verses is Christological and soteriological, not being oriented toward the more specific subject of the Holy Spirit's testimony.[10]

Yet this is not to deny that there is a secondary sense in which the witness still confirms Scripture. If the witness primarily confirms the believer's salvation and place in the family of God (which seems to be quite clear), it will still lead to the ancillary recognition of a few other inclusive aspects of theology, as well. For example, if the chief confirmation is that the believer is a child of God, we also know that the Gospel data are true. After all, saving faith (in New Testament terms) is not exercised in a vacuum (Rom 10:9–10). Further, it would seem to follow as well that Scripture, which sets forth both the Gospel and the testimony of the Holy Spirit, is God's Word. But the *primary* focus seems clearly to be the Holy Spirit's witness to believers.

Is the Spirit's witness to the believer *indirectly* through Scripture or *directly* to the heart of the Christian? I have just said that this testimony is not independent of Scripture—it comes through the Word of God, by which we know the nature of this witness in the first place. Yet, texts like Romans 8:16–17 also teach that the Holy Spirit testifies to the believer's spirit. It can hardly be denied that this confirmation is intensely personal.[11]

Ramm is particularly adamant that too many commentators insist on wandering to areas beyond the direct provision of this testimony. Ramm remarks: "it is a witness to individual participation in salvation; of the divine adoption. The intent of the witness is to bear witness to *our* participation in this redemption."[12] It does seem that the primary product of the Holy Spirit's testimony is the believer's certainty of salvation. This blessing is the possession of all believers and is independent of items like one's profession, schooling, or knowledge. Ramm concludes: "the humblest person enjoys the same certainty as the learned theologians."[13]

In sum, even if the witness of the Holy Spirit includes additional areas of confirmation, its chief purpose is to provide believers with the personal certainty and assurance of their own participation in God's eternal plan. The relevant New Testament texts agree on this central message. There are tremendous implications here in terms of this volume. Especially if this assurance is given directly from God to us, the knowledge that one is indeed a child of God should produce comfort and peace, especially for those who struggle with these issues.

The Testimony of the Holy Spirit and Evidence

Can the Holy Spirit's testimony serve as an argument for the truth of Christian theism? What relation does it have to the major emphasis of this book—the death and resurrection of Jesus? If the witness is only subjective, why is it valuable? Can it really assist the believer who is tormented by questions about the truth of Christianity, for example?

We recognize that the Holy Spirit's witness cannot be proven. Neither can it, in turn, demonstrate Scripture or Christian theism to be true. To assert the opposite is to turn the process around backward. Evidences show that Christianity is true, as we have seen in this volume. The Holy Spirit provides personal testimony that the individual believer is a child of God.

Further, holding that the Holy Spirit's witness cannot be demonstrated fails to render it valueless. Initially, this witness is not proven by reason or sense experience, but neither can it be disproven by such methods.

But this is not to concede that the witness of the Holy Spirit is entirely subjective in nature. Ramm interestingly argues that it is both subjective and objective. The former aspect is characterized by the private, inward features of the testimony. "The *testimonium* is at the very center of our being, where nothing can be deeper." This private aspect "is its very strength, for it is by the same token *immediate* and therefore *certain* and *sure*."[14] In addition to being unprovable, the Spirit's broader work with the believer cannot be experientially shared or communicated to an unbeliever (1 Cor 2:14). Thus, while this witness may be defined and experienced, it cannot be proven, and neither can it be explained so that an unbeliever can also experience it while remaining unchanged.

But Ramm asserts that there is also an objective component involved in the testimony of the Holy Spirit. It is shared by all believers, hence it can be reported as a common phenomenon among them (even though it is not necessarily experienced in the same manner). Further, the content on which this testimony is based, namely the facts of the Gospel message of Jesus Christ's death and resurrection, are highly evidenced. Even so, we should not mistakenly assume that these considerations objectivize the witness; rather, they point to an evidenced message.[15]

We might look from another angle at the relation between the witness of the Holy Spirit and evidences. For those who appreciate the confirmation of Christian theism by evidences, it may be argued that the New Testament teachings on the witness of the Holy Spirit are thereby given an even more substantial basis. So while this witness is not objectively proven, it is a reported experience of a great many believers, and it is firmly secured to a solid foundation.

What other strengths might be presented by a phenomenon that we have considered to be chiefly subjective and individually experienced? Must an individual's personal claims be questioned or even considered untrue simply on the grounds that they are private?

Roderick Chisholm has argued that one's personal, experiential claims,[16] as long as they are unopposed by conflicting evidence, ought to be considered trustworthy.[17] Similarly, Richard Swinburne refers to the "principle of credulity," according to which one's own experience constitutes evidence for a belief unless contrary data disprove it.[18]

Moving to the work of the Holy Spirit, philosopher Paul Moser maintains that the "Christian theory of knowledge must therefore give a central role to the immediate testimony and power of God's revealing Spirit."[19] Agreeing with Ramm, Moser continues: "This kind of knowing Christ is an intimate, loving, and transforming personal relationship. It is thus no mere intellectual matter. It is full self-commitment to a personal agent, not just to ideas or principles."[20] Moser, a specialist in epistemology, adds this intriguing conclusion: "We thereby receive God's personal assurance of our filial relationship with God. This assurance is more robust than any kind of theoretical certainty offered by philosophers or theologians. It liberates us from dependence merely on the quagmire of speculation, hypothesis-formation, or probabilistic inference about God. Such assurance yields a distinctive kind of grounded, firm confidence in God unavailable elsewhere."[21] Reminiscent of Ramm, though this is not ordinary knowledge, attained by evidences and arguments, it is personal knowledge of God.[22]

The witness of the Holy Spirit cannot be dismissed as some credulous belief, but I have also clearly said that it cannot be objectively proven, either. So it does not provide any arguments for the truth of Christianity, especially for unbelievers. I have developed the position that it is a personal indication from God to the believer that she has experienced salvation and adoption as a child of God. The witness of the Holy Spirit functions by indicating *the certainty of the individual's own belief and condition*. This conviction extends indirectly to the truthfulness of the Gospel message, since it grounds one's faith. This provides valuable comfort in matters of assurance.

We may view this subject from still another vantage point. Believers have solid reasons on which to base their faith. So why should they be *surprised* if their own personal experience matches what the Scripture attests? In other words, several texts declare that the Holy Spirit would produce His personal testimony in our lives. Should not the realization of just such an internal witness be considered *normal* (and perhaps even exciting)?

Some Questions

This topic often generates questions. I attempt to single out a few of the more prominent issues.

Some Christians might wonder why they have not felt such a witness at all. If the chief focus here concerns the *feelings*, we should not be surprised if it goes unnoticed. While the Holy Spirit's testimony can certainly affect one's feelings, and frequently does so, the witness is not an emotion at all, so we should never look for it there. I have said that this is an area where individual personality variances may well account for the differences. Besides, emotions often seem to disappear when placed under a microscope. So we should not pace ourselves by either the presence or the absence of feelings.

Further, there can be many hindrances to realizing that the witness is present in our lives. The work of the Holy Spirit can be stifled or restrained (1 Thes 5:19; Eph 4:30). While sin can more obviously suppress the recognition of God's presence, so can the simple denial of the New Testament teaching on the subject. For example, if one rejects the biblical reports of the Holy Spirit's testimony, how can it then be complained that one does not appear to experience it?

Religious doubt can also develop into a vicious circle. Tough questions or the lack of assurance may lead a Christian to look suspiciously at the Holy Spirit's testimony, perhaps because it is not objectively known. But then this very suspicion can itself keep one from recognizing the presence of this witness, which may be the single item that is most needed to quell these questions. The Holy Sprit's testimony could be there all the time! A subtle denial of this teaching can thus effectively cut off the assurance that the Holy Spirit could have provided. So there are several possible reasons that believers may not be able to identify the Holy Spirit's witness in their own life. Sin, the subtle or blatant denial of the testimony, or simply a misidentification of its nature are probably the chief obstacles.

Thankfully, these barriers can be removed. Ramm states it this way: "The remedy consists in the restoration of spiritual vision and sight, of the opening of ears and eyes resulting in an intuition of the truth of God."[23]

Personal questions should not keep the Christian from recognizing a crucial truth: Scripture does, in fact, teach the witness of the Holy Spirit. One's inability to recognize it is insufficient to deny its reality.

A more serious challenge of another sort might come from those who might claim a similar witness or conviction with regard to a "liberal" or non-Christian version of salvation. What prevents others from saying that they are also totally convinced or assured that they also believe the right things? Several responses need to be made here.

It is not the Christian's job to classify members of other groups or judge who ultimately belongs under each label. Beyond this initial caution, Ramm argues a further, potentially crucial point. In a detailed discussion, he asserts that these other groups basically do not hold any specific doctrine of the witness.[24] Regardless, we need to grant that others may still claim to experience assurance concerning their beliefs. It could even turn out that they really are Christians, in spite of their theological differences. Still, as I have said repeatedly, assurance can be accounted for several ways, including being a product of one's personality type.

When we get beyond these few caveats, we are asking questions about the truth of the belief systems making the claims, Christian or otherwise. Since claims to personal assurance are not directly open to demonstration, we must investigate the systems themselves in the context of the philosophies from which they emerge. We have said throughout this book that a strong case can be made for Christian theism. Then the witness of the Holy Spirit moves beyond this case, persuading the individual believer concerning his or her personal participation in salvation. In other words, more than a *claim* to assurance is required at this point. Biblical teachings concerning the Holy Spirit's testimony are built upon a firm basis. Then we must examine the rival system in order to ascertain if it is evidenced. If Ramm is correct, there may be few challenges to the Christian position on assurance, anyway.

Some may think I am claiming that the testimony of the Holy Spirit demonstrates Scripture to be true, only to have the Bible justify this witness, in return. But there is no circular argument here, for I have said without hesitation that the witness does *not* prove Scripture to be true. In fact, the testimony gives no external verification at all. While the Holy Spirit may convince a believer in a secondary sense that Scripture is God's Word, this is just what it is: a conviction. It is not really an *argument* for the truth of Scripture. So there is no circularity here; the witness in not an evidential argument at all.

The reader could then retort that the witness of the Holy Spirit is really totally subjective, after all. Thus it has no value. I have already responded in much detail to this sort of challenge. The inward testimony of the Holy Spirit is highly personal, but it is not totally subjective. Even if all the witness did was to build further on the truth of the Christian message by providing private assurance to the believer that she was a child of God, this is still exceptionally crucial, especially for the doubting believer.

Some might object that this doctrine prompts too much emotionalism. While these convictions *may* affect one's emotions, often they do not. At any rate, the doctrine itself says nothing directly about the emotions. The fact that it *could* affect one's emotions is no indictment against it, however, for so could many other Christian teachings that are not thereby labeled as being perilous. God certainly knew all this when He created us with emotions!

Perhaps similarly, others may still say that this understanding of the Holy Spirit's witness is dangerous because it may lead to strange teachings being revealed by the Holy Spirit. But I have already said that we find no encouragement for those who think that this testimony produces independent teachings or interpretations. The *only clearly stated function* of the Holy Spirit's witness is to testify to Christians concerning their own inclusion in the body of Christ.

Some Christians may fear the teaching that the Holy Spirit's testimony is given independently of Scripture. But I have said that the Holy Spirit works *through* the text, not in ways that are contrary to it. By providing a private conviction that the believer is a child of God, we have a secondary witness both to the nature of the Gospel message, as well as to the truth of the texts that record it. This is the sense in which, while occurring *through* Scripture, the witness comes *directly* to the believer in a one-to-one manner. If this interpretation is correct, then in order to be true to the New Testament teaching, the message must be an individualized one.

Ultimately, it is a moot point whether someone thinks that this teaching might be misused in some sense. For the believer, the primary issue concerns the *nature* of the Holy Spirit's testimony, as taught in Scripture.

Last, it may be asked if the witness of the Holy Spirit can be explained in psychological terms. What if it is only a personal endorsement of one's private beliefs, culture, and environment? It must be remembered that the

Spirit's testimony is more than just the internal state of being reassured that one's beliefs are true. Some believers, like Ramm and Moser, might attest that the witness is much deeper and stronger than simple assurance; the witness seems to be almost part of oneself, as if it were woven into the fabric of one's innermost being. The witness prevails when normal assurance is assaulted almost to the point of despair. It is the deepest conviction regarding one's salvation, since it proceeds from God directly to the believer.

An illustration might be helpful. An adequately strong chain, with an anchor that is firmly embedded in rock, can hold a ship in place. As the boat drifts, the slack in the chain is used up. But the ship reaches a point where it can drift no further than is allowed by the anchor. On many occasions, believers may witness their "chain" being stretched to the furthest point, only to discover that they could not deny Jesus Christ or give him up for another savior, where this did not seem due to the Christian's own faith or stamina. This might be described as the work of the Holy Spirit's witness. That others think they have not experienced this does not affect those who heed the internal conviction.

In addition to indications that the testimony of the Holy Spirit is essentially different from mental certitude, psychology cannot explain the strong evidences on which Christian theism is based. So *the nature of the Holy Spirit's witness is soteriological in character and its basis in the Gospel facts is firmly attested.* The primary function of this witness is to convince a believer of her personal salvation. The cornerstone of salvation, the Gospel data, can be historically verified. These facts remain untouched by psychological inquiry. Since this basis is firm, we should not be surprised if we do, indeed, experience the witness of the Holy Spirit, just as the New Testament authors promised.

The matter can be summed up briefly. Christians are justified in making the assertion that the Holy Spirit provides a witness to them that they are, indeed, God's children. While this claim does not constitute any sort of external proof, neither is it disproven by methods like reason or sense experience. Further, the claim is based on a firm foundation. So the Christian may even *expect* to experiences this testimony, since it is just what Scripture attests. The discovery that this witness is present in the believer's life should be considered quite normal.

Conclusion

Comparatively little has been written on the personal testimony of the Holy Spirit, especially in regard to the truth of the Christian Gospel. Christians seem frequently to have ignored its place in the believer's life, perhaps because of difficulties like those I have discussed in this chapter. Even defining this doctrine and identifying its domain are difficult.

But this subject needs to be carefully addressed. While it is difficult, its contribution, especially on the issues of Christian doubt and the secondary witness it provides to the truth of the Gospel message, is indispensable. The Holy Spirit stands alongside the believer, going beyond the subject of evidences and providing direct testimony to Christians of their salvation. In short, the evidence shows that Christianity is true. The witness of the Holy Spirit marks those who belong to the truth.

Notes

1. For a much more detailed version of this chapter, see Gary R. Habermas, "The Personal Testimony of the Holy Spirit to the Believer and Christian Apologetics," *Journal of Christian Apologetics* 1 (1997): 49–64. In that article, the section "A Personal Odyssey" (49–51) details some of my struggles with doubt and my newly discovered appreciation of this important subject.

2. On the importance of person specificity in argumentation, see George I. Mavrodes, ed., *The Rationality of Belief in God* (Englewood Cliffs, N.J.: Prentice-Hall, 1970), 5.

3. Many of the insights in this chapter are drawn from the excellent text by Bernard Ramm, *The Witness of the Spirit: An Essay on the Contemporary Relevance of the Internal Witness of the Holy Spirit* (Grand Rapids, Mich.: Eerdmans, 1959). For Ramm's conclusion here, see 54; cf. 36, 52, 84, 86, 116. Cf. George Eldon Ladd's agreement in *A Theology of the New Testament* (Grand Rapids, Mich.: Eerdmans, 1974), 461, 491.

4. Ramm, *The Witness of the Spirit,* 84.

5. See Ramm, *The Witness of the Spirit,* 74, 76, 82.

6. Ladd, *Theology of the New Testament,* 296.

7. Some could insist that 1 Jn 2:20, 26–27 is an exception, where the testimony of the Holy Spirit imparts a broader menu of doctrines for Christian certainty (beyond the witness to one's salvation), to the extent that believers do not even need teachers of doctrine. While a broader range of theology might be very convenient for resolving theological differences of opinion, it is a problematic interpretation of this passage on several fronts. (1) This view favors an interpretation that is not at all clear from the text. For example, although Raymond Brown believes that this passage refers to the Holy Spirit, he develops a case for those expositors who think that the reference is to the anointing and teaching of the Word of God, rather than that of the Spirit. See Raymond E. Brown, *The Epistles of John,* The Anchor Bible (Garden City, N.Y.: Doubleday, 1982), 30:345–47. The difficulty of determining an accurate meaning makes dogmatism difficult. (2) The epistle would hardly be saying that the Holy Spirit nullifies the need for teaching theology, since the author was obviously a theological teacher! Further, the writer would be refuted by the very fact that the teaching in his letter was needed to communicate this truth in the first place.

(3) If teachers are no longer needed, then this interpretation might also vilify the rest of Scripture, too. Few would be willing to say that this is the intended message. (4) Most importantly for our study, the immediate context still appears to indicate that the doctrine concerning which Christians do not need further teaching (vv. 26–27) is precisely that of salvation, which would agree with the interpretation that we have favored concerning the testimony of the Holy Spirit. The readers are being warned about those who deny the deity of Christ, an integral portion of the Gospel (vv. 18–23), and encouraged to pursue eternal life (vv. 24–25). This discussion of salvation immediately precedes the text in question. (5) Whatever is concluded about these difficult verses, assurance of salvation *is* included in the remainder of 1 John as knowledge that is imparted by the Holy Spirit to the believer (1 Jn 3:24; 4:13; cf. 5:13). So at least this portion of our thesis would remain intact.

8. Cunningham contends that the most prominent view among the Reformers was that the Holy Spirit's witness was to Scripture being God's Word. There were theological reasons for this interpretation——this position strictly avoided any claims to either independent revelation or to the testimony of the church (118), both obviously being rejoinders aimed at the Catholic views. See William Cunningham, *The Reformers and the Theology of the Reformation* (1852; reprint, London: Banner of Truth Trust, 1967). Ramm agrees with this reasoning, noting that the Reformers' interpretation sought to avoid both personal experience and any reliance on the church (*The Witness of the Spirit*, 102; cf. 98–105). Brown's discussion above (*The Epistles of John*, 346–47) shows that this is not exclusively a Reformed position.

9. Even John Calvin notes clearly that the witness includes the believer's salvation and adoption: "He does not simply say that the Spirit of God is a witness to our spirit. . . . Paul means that the Spirit of God affords us such a testimony that our spirit is assured of the adoption of God . . . for while the Spirit testifies to us that we are the children of God, He at the same time pours this confidence into our hearts, so that we dare invoke God as our Father" (*The Epistles of Paul the Apostle to the Romans and to the Thessalonians*, Calvin's Commentaries, trans. Ross MacKenzie, ed. David W. Torrance and Thomas F. Torrance [Grand Rapids, Mich.: Eerdmans, 1979], 170).

Concerning another of our passages, 1 John 3:24, Calvin holds that there is a difference of emphasis between Paul and John. Nevertheless, John's "statement verbally agrees with Paul's, when he says that the Spirit testifies to our hearts that we are God's children and through Him cry to God, 'Abba, Father'" (*The Gospel According to John 11–21 and The First Epistle of John*, Calvin's Commentaries, trans. T. H. L. Parker, ed. David W. Torrance and Thomas F. Torrance [Grand Rapids, Mich.: Eerdmans, 1979], 282).

10. Ramm includes an enlightening discussion of this topic (*The Witness of the Spirit*, 99–105; cf. 60–61, 68, 94).

11. Calvin's quotations in note 8 above show how freely he mentions the theme of the Holy Spirit witnessing to the spirit and heart of the believer.

12. Ramm, *The Witness of the Spirit*, 51.

13. Ramm, *The Witness of the Spirit*, 113; cf. 82.

14. Ramm, *The Witness of the Spirit*, 52.

15. Ramm, *The Witness of the Spirit*, 52, 75–76, 82, 117–19.

16. While the testimony of the Holy Spirit does not consist of feelings, reason, or sense experience, it does impinge on all three, for it affects the entire person.

17. Roderick Chisholm, *Theory of Knowledge*, 2nd ed. (Englewood Cliffs, N.J.: Prentice-Hall, 1977), 26–33. Ramm agrees here (*The Witness of the Spirit*, 76).

18. Richard Swinburne, "The Evidential Value of Religious Experience," in *The Sciences and Theology in the Twentieth Century*, ed. A. R. Peacocke (Notre Dame: University of Notre Dame Press, 1981), 182–96.

19. Paul Moser, *Why Isn't God More Obvious? Finding the God Who Hides and Seeks* (Norcross, Ga.: RZIM, 2000), 23.

20. Moser, *Why Isn't God More Obvious?* 55.

21. Moser, *Why Isn't God More Obvious?* 48.

22. Moser, *Why Isn't God More Obvious?* 55.

23. Ramm, *The Witness of the Spirit*, 84.

24. Ramm, *The Witness of the Spirit*, 49, 106–7; esp. chap. 5.

CHAPTER TEN

Jesus and the Authority of Scripture

Near the heart of Christian theism is the conviction that Scripture, both the Old and New Testaments, comprises God's Word to us. It is our chief source for doctrine. It also grounds our practical pursuits like teaching, counseling, ethics, and social responsibility. Are these and other practices based on a solid foundation? In this chapter, I produce two arguments in favor of this doctrine, the second of which may be the strongest. Then I ask how this basis may be helpful in several areas of application, such as study, ministry, and meeting the needs of others. This is more than a scholastic enterprise; it affects all of life.

Throughout this book, I have argued that a strong case can be made in favor of the principle that God verified Jesus's teachings by raising him from the dead. If Jesus taught that Scripture was God's message to us, then this would constitute a powerful reason for believers to do the same. And if Jesus utilized Scripture for his own ministry to others, believers should likewise do the same.

Many have argued that the Gospel texts are generally reliable documents when they report Jesus's teachings.[1] Even more debated aspects, such as certain historical elements of Jesus's miracle stories, have been largely vindicated in recent studies.[2] From such a general basis I outline our initial path for Jesus's view of the authority of Scripture. Then I pursue a second avenue that does not build on trustworthy Gospel texts.[3]

Jesus's Teachings on the Authority of Scripture

Jesus's Teachings on the Old Testament

If God verified Jesus's message by raising him from the dead, then the chief issue concerns whether Jesus taught that Scripture was inspired. Certainly the Gospels agree on a variety of fronts that Jesus had total confidence in the text of the Old Testament. We are told that Jesus made many statements regarding the trustworthiness and even the inspiration of Scripture. An examination of Jesus's teachings provides a clear indication of this.

One of the strongest statements concerning the Old Testament was Jesus's reported affirmation that heaven and Earth would pass away before even the smallest portion of the Law (Mt 5:17–18). In a very similar comment, Jesus taught that these minute morsels of the Law would never fail (Lk 16:17). Jesus cited a particular text from Psalm 82:6, then we are told that Jesus stated that Scripture could not be nullified (Jn 10:35). These comments are striking reminders regarding the extent to which Jesus thought that Scripture spoke the truth.

Regularly, Jesus also demonstrated his trust in the Old Testament by utilizing it as his source for solving theological disputes. On more than one occasion, his argument in the Gospels turned chiefly on the significance of a single word in the text. In Mark 12:35–37, Jesus based an important theological point on the second usage of the word "Lord," arguing that the Messiah was more than just the son of David. In the English text of Mark 12:18–27, Jesus largely built his case against the Sadducees on the word "am" in order to teach the doctrine of the resurrection of the body, which they rejected.[4]

On many other occasions, Jesus cited Scripture passages as "proof texts" while debating his adversaries. During the wilderness temptation, Jesus quoted Old Testament texts in opposition to Satan (Mt 4:4, 7, 10/Lk 4:4, 8). Elsewhere, Jesus responded to his detractors by asking them, "Have you not read . . . ?"[5] or "It is written . . ." or a similar comment serving to refute an opposing view.[6] In Mark 12:24, Jesus remarked that an ignorance of Scripture caused the Sadducees to a make a theological error. It seems clear from uses of Scripture such as these that Jesus considered its contents to be the definitive authority in solving theological issues.

In yet another debate with Jewish leaders, after citing portions of the Law and prophets, Jesus appears to be referring to the entire Old Testament Scripture as "the commandment of God" and "the Word of God" (Mk 7:9–13). Jesus thought that God was the Authority behind these texts. It was an inspired writing, given for our edification. As such, these words must be fulfilled (Mt

26:54; Lk 4:21; Jn 7:38). Jesus used the Old Testament as God's blueprint for correct theology and behavior. It disproved contrary positions. Jesus did not doubt its authority.

Jesus referred to the entire Old Testament both as the Law and the prophets (Mt 5:17), as well as adding the Psalms (Lk 24:44). Referring to these sections, Jesus commented that each was the Word of God. Moses (Lk 16:31; 24:44) spoke God's words in Exodus 3:6 (Mk 12:26). David wrote by the inspiration of the Holy Spirit in Psalm 110:1 (Mk 12:36). The prophets also spoke God's words, because their prophecies of the Christ had to be fulfilled (Lk 24:27, 44).

So Jesus based arguments on specific words of the Old Testament text. He indicated his trust of even small portions of the texts; not even a portion could fail. The whole, as well as the individual sections, received his positive endorsements. Jesus referred to the Old Testament not simply as a time-honored human document. Rather, he called it the very commands and words of God. True, humans like Moses and David penned the text, but God still spoke through them. In citing the Scripture, Jesus believed that he was reporting the message of God. The Word of God was the expression of God's truth. Viewed from various angles, this is indeed a high view of inspiration. We conclude that Jesus definitely accepted the inspiration of the Old Testament. It is difficult to draw other conclusions.[7]

Jesus's Teaching on the New Testament

A case for the inspiration of the New Testament is more difficult to establish, since it was not penned until after Jesus's death. Jesus *approved* the already-written Old Testament. The best path for the New Testament is to argue that Jesus *provided* for it by his comments before it was written. Again, by raising Jesus from the dead, God placed his stamp of approval on his teachings. Similar endorsements are found in various New Testament texts (Rom 1:3–4; Acts 2:22–24, 17:31). I point out four particular considerations.

First, Jesus chose, trained, and taught his disciples. They were his designated witnesses and spokespeople (Lk 24:48; Acts 1:8; Jn 15:27). As his students, they learned his teachings so that they, in turn, might impart these principles to others. This was even true to the extent that those who believed and obeyed the disciples' words would actually be receiving Jesus Christ himself (Mk 6:11; Mt 10:40; Jn 13:20).

Second, the Fourth Gospel reports that Jesus also promised his disciples that the Holy Spirit would inspire and guide them. He would teach them the truth on several additional matters (16:12–13), causing them to remember Jesus's words (14:26), and revealing to them the future (16:13b).

From a critical perspective, the second point is more suspect, since it is drawn completely from the Fourth Gospel. Yet, it would seem that it is not a major extension of the initial consideration. Jesus elevated his teachings above those of the Law (Mt 5:17–48). And after all, he did choose his disciples to learn and carry on his teachings. As Jesus's chosen spokespeople, they represented him. Given Jesus's stance on the authority of the Old Testament writings, we could hardly expect less from any writings produced by his immediate or secondary followers, especially given Jesus's view that he was God's authoritative revelation.

We could reasonably expect the New Testament writings to be the result of these considerations alone. Jesus's instruction of the disciples and their designation as his spokesmen, as well as any further teaching by the Holy Spirit, would naturally pave the way for the authority of any writings that they produced. From a more minimal perspective, even *without* Jesus's promises, if those who sat at his feet and were closest to him, or their own students, were to produce writings that represented his teachings, it is not at all surprising that these products became authoritative. In fact, something like this seems to have occurred.

Third, as the writers of what became the New Testament books penned their words, they often recognized that what they produced was authoritative. They claimed Jesus's twofold promise for themselves. This is especially evident in Paul's epistles.[8] These authors thought that their teachings were based on the foundation that Jesus provided (Eph 2:19–22; 2 Pt 3:2; Heb 2:3–4). They taught that their words were inspired (1 Pt 1:12b). They were convinced that the Holy Spirit empowered both their teaching and their writing.

Fourth, a few New Testament writers recognized that Jesus's promises extended to Jesus's own words, as well as to the words of others of their own generation. For instance, 1 Timothy 5:18 notes two citations, referring to both as Scripture. The first is obviously drawn from Deuteronomy 25:4. Although the second is similar to certain Old Testament texts, it is nowhere quoted. This saying of Jesus is the same as the one recorded in Luke 10:7/Matthew 10:10. Comparing a quotation from the Law to one found in the sayings of Jesus, and calling them both Scripture, is certainly significant. At least some writers thought that the Old Testament was not the end of God's revelation. As I have said, if any writings were considered to be inspired, the words of Jesus definitely should be included!

Another example is found in 2 Peter 3:15–16, where Paul's epistles are placed alongside earlier Scripture, apparently being given the same status. Additionally, Jude 17–18 seems to cite 2 Peter 3:3 (or a common text) as the words of an apostle, again recognizing writings beyond the Old Testament.

We should be cautious about making extrapolations from a few examples to a theory. But by placing the sayings of Jesus and the teachings of his first- and second-generation disciples on a par with Old Testament Scripture, we get a glimpse of the growing conviction that the Old Testament was not the sum of God's revelation. His word extended to other writings, too. The canon was not closed, since other works needed to be included.

So the chief impetus for believing the authority of the New Testament writings rests on the teachings of Jesus. He promised his disciples both that they were his special witnesses and that they would be guided by the Holy Spirit. Some of the New Testament authors claimed this promise for their own writings, and they sometimes extended this promise to other qualified authors. Although I cannot pursue the issue here, we also have an abundance of New Testament texts that recognize the inspiration of various Old Testament figures and passages.[9]

Accommodation or Limitation?

Some question whether Jesus may have promoted a concept of inspiration that he, personally, did not accept. Perhaps he merely accommodated himself to the views of his contemporaries. According to this view, Jesus did not accept the doctrine, but spoke as if he did in order to avoid upsetting or undermining his listeners' religious beliefs. It is sometimes also charged that Jesus genuinely thought that Scripture was inspired, but he was mistaken. However, there are several major reasons to reject each of these suggestions.

Jesus's resurrection indicated that God approved his teachings. But for God to do so either on the assumption that Jesus accommodated his hearers' mistaken beliefs, or that Jesus was mistaken, would present problems. In either case, God would have approved Jesus's incorrect teachings. Such an approval is a difficult hurdle for the accommodation or limitation theories to overcome. Granted, Jesus's teachings here are not as central as his message about the Kingdom of God, but he still considered them to be important.

Further, the Gospels indicate that Jesus never accommodated his hearers with any of his teachings. To the contrary, he did precisely the opposite by undermining the incorrect views held by those who heard him. This is obvious, for instance, in his Sermon on the Mount, where in Matthew 5:21–48 he repeatedly challenged the beliefs of his contemporaries, correcting their understanding of the Old Testament. We have seen how he frequently debated the Jewish leaders, making it clear that they were mistaken (as in Mk 12:18–27). Jesus also spoke often against false prophets (as in Mk 13:21–23; Mt 7:15, 24:11). Other examples of correction abound in the records of Jesus's teachings.[10]

So Jesus did not accommodate his message to his hearers, but challenged incorrect beliefs. It should also be mentioned that the repeated ways in which Jesus emphasized the nature of Scripture and wielded its authority is much more compatible with his trust in its contents.

Regarding the view that Jesus's knowledge was limited and that he was simply mistaken when he taught that the Scripture was inspired, this approach is also laden with severe difficulties. As I said, it is difficult to imagine that the resurrection indicated God's affirmation of Jesus's false and misleading teachings. This alone favors the view that Jesus's testimony was not in error due to any limitation. To the contrary, his resurrection argues that Jesus's teachings were authoritative and truthful, as God's stamp of approval on his message.

Another problem with the limitation thesis is that even *after* Jesus's resurrection he presumably would have largely overcome his human limitations. Yet, at least Luke 24:25–27, 44–48 attest that Jesus still taught the same view of Scripture as before his death. Further, the Gospels teach that Jesus exercised supernatural knowledge on other occasions, too.[11] So it would seem that the limitation thesis is also highly problematic.

Using either accommodation or limitation theories to explain Jesus's teachings on inspiration is confronted by a number of serious obstacles. God's approval of Jesus's teachings as indicated by his resurrection would strongly oppose both hypotheses. Further, the Gospel texts provide many other reasons for rejecting both hypotheses. The manner in which Jesus used the Old Testament strongly indicates his firm approval, rather than either appeasement or ignorance.

Critical Scholarship and the Authority of Scripture

Strangely enough, addressing another potential objection actually points us to what is probably an even stronger argument for the authority of Scripture than the path I have so far pursued. How do we know that the Gospel references I have used here actually represent Jesus's view of Scripture? Could it be that, whatever the Gospel authors thought, Jesus never held such a view, and thus he never taught it? Maybe the reports of Jesus's view on this subject are simply inaccurate. Asked another way, how do we know that our entire argument is not simply a case of circular reasoning that *assumes* that Jesus really taught the inspiration of Scripture, as the Gospels report, without knowing that he actually did so?

Initially, I mentioned that there are some good arguments for the general reliability of the Gospels. If this is the case, and especially if some of the particular texts regarding Jesus's view of inspiration are well attested on other grounds, then one response to this objection would be to argue that we have a strong basis for claiming that Jesus at least really said what the Gospel texts report. Then, if God raised Jesus from the dead, Jesus's teachings on this subject would still be confirmed. But apart from such an initial response, are there any other grounds for addressing this objection?

Intriguingly, even critical scholars usually acknowledge that Jesus believed that Scripture was God's Word.[12] Ladd states that Jesus "regarded the Old Testament as the inspired Word of God and the Law as the divinely given rule of life."[13] On what is such a view based for scholars who do not think that the text is inspired in the first place? Scholars frequently reject the reliability of even the Gospels. Since these responses do not assume either the inspiration or the general reliability of the Gospel texts, to learn their reasons may actually provide additional grounds for accepting Jesus's belief in inspiration.

For example, Rudolf Bultmann asserts, concerning Jesus's view of the Old Testament: "Its authority stands just as fast for him as for the scribes." Bultmann points out Jesus's belief that God spoke and made known his will through the Old Testament writings which were the believer's sources for faith and practice. They were Jesus's text for both answering questions and challenging the errors of those who opposed him. Besides, that Jesus accepted the authority of Scripture "is proven by the course later taken by his Church." Interestingly, Bultmann lists texts like some of those mentioned above to support his position.[14]

More recently, Bart Ehrman provides some additional specifics regarding Jesus's view of Scripture. Not surprisingly, Jesus shared with his fellow Jews many religious ideas and theological doctrines, including the belief that the Old Testament Law was the special revelation of God's will. Actually, the majority of Jesus's teachings are drawn from these sacred texts. They were the basis that grounded his religious contentions.[15]

Then Ehrman addresses how critical scholars ascertain that this actually was Jesus's teaching. Even though Ehrman's "point is *not* that each and every one of these accounts must be historically accurate exactly as it is reported" regarding the authority of Scripture, he still thinks that we can arrive at Jesus's teachings on this subject. Ehrman argues that Jesus's position can be obtained from the "multiple layers of our traditions, scattered throughout a range of independent traditions." Ehrman finds Jesus's key teachings on the Law in four of the major Gospel sources: Mark, Q, M, and John. So our knowledge that Jesus did hold this view of Scripture "is thoroughly rooted in our tradition. It is therefore to be trusted as historical." This multiple testimony is strong evidence that Jesus held firmly to a high view of Scripture.[16]

We may actually strengthen Ehrman's points here. The two most critically acclaimed independent Gospel traditions are Mark and the Q material. In each of these, there is a wealth of citations indicating that Jesus held to the authority of the Old Testament. Perhaps the more crucial comments are found in Mark.[17] The so-called Q texts also include numerous instances where Jesus clearly showed his trust of many Old Testament passages.[18]

Critical scholars like Bultmann and Ehrman frequently argue something like this: Jesus was clearly a first-century Jew, so it is no surprise that he agreed with the common Jewish view regarding the nature and authority of the Old Testament as God's Word. That the early church continued this same view further confirms this teaching. But the strongest argument is that, even though critics do not know for sure which specific Gospel statements Jesus really made and which ones he did not, that he taught the authority of Scripture is still firmly established by the presence of many such comments across multiple, independent source traditions.

Ladd adds that, since Jesus thought that his words were just as divinely authoritative as the Law, and because the disciples had not yet understood everything that he had taught them, it would be natural for him to conclude that there was "a larger revelation yet to be given" by God. This revelation would be the domain of God's Spirit through his followers.[19]

The strength of these arguments that Jesus taught the authority of Scripture rests on a minimal amount of well-attested data, and is therefore generally granted by critical scholars. Further, it does not require an argument for the reliability of Scripture, or for each of the relevant texts.

So critical scholars have also added some worthy considerations for holding that Jesus did teach the authority and inspiration of Scripture. This is more intriguing when these scholars do not hold to the doctrine of inspiration, and frequently even deny the general reliability of Scripture. Yet, they still think that there is a solid foundation to assert that Jesus believed these doctrines.

Although the doctrine of the inspiration of Scripture is usually rejected by critical theologians, in spite of Jesus's view, I have some solid grounds on which to assert it. Using both traditional and critical paths to determine that Jesus firmly taught it, if God raised Jesus from the dead, then the most likely reason was to confirm the truthfulness of Jesus's teachings. If I am correct in this, then the authority of Scripture follows, affirmed by God when He raised Jesus from the dead.

Conclusion: Applying Scripture's Authority

But Scripture is not given to believers simply to beat on others or just to satisfy our private extravagances. It ought to change our lives. It is our manual for life and practice. It is a guideline for ethics. And since it is God's Word, it ought not be ignored, but obeyed. A number of eminently practical considerations follow from these considerations. If applied, Scripture's guidelines should make an incredible difference even today, especially in ministry and social situations.

First, Jesus frequently used Scripture as the text from which he confirmed his views, answered the improper outlooks held by others, and encouraged a life of following God. He relied on Scripture for what it was—God's Word to us. While it is true that Christians do not have the same divine authority as the Son of God, and while we often overstep the authority we do have (unfortunately, even grossly so at times), this benefit is also extended to us. Based on Jesus's example, we can likewise build our teachings carefully on the truth of Scripture, as well as use it as our guide for evaluating other positions, and for living a practical Christian life. This conclusion should strengthen the faith and assurance of Christians. In spite of modern challenges, there are good reasons for holding that there is a textual basis for our beliefs and practices.

Second, Scripture provides the necessary groundwork for Christian theology. The benefits of having such an underpinning are tremendous. Given a firm foundation, believers are free to build a Christian worldview, being careful to base their ideas on the same footing laid by Jesus himself.[20]

Third, Scripture regularly teaches good cognitive principles in order to shape a healthy life. In the Old Testament, the antidotes to worry, despondency, and dejection were prayer (Pss 18:1–6; 34:4–8; 55:4–8, 16–17, 22; 57:1–3; Lam 3:55–57), praise and thanksgiving (Pss 13:1–6; 42:1–6, 11; 43:5; 56:3–4; 68:19), a cheerful heart (Prv 12:25; 15:13–15; 17:22; 18:14, 21), meditation (Jos 1:6–8; Pss 27:1–9, 37:7–8, 143:1–6), recalling God's mighty actions (Pss 73:25–28; 77:11–15; 106:6–7, 21–22), and remembering His promises (Jos 1:1–9; Pss 91:14–16; 119:103, 139–40, 148; Lam 3:19–33).

The New Testament continues the emphasis on godly thinking to counteract life's problems. Properly directing our thoughts is also a remedy for worry (Mt 6:19–34; 1 Pt 5:7), a recipe for avoiding sin (contrast Rom 1:25 with 12:1–2; Jas 4:1–10), and a change of perspective during times of suffering and persecution (2 Cor 4:7–18; Jas 1:2–4; 1 Pt 1:3–9). I have already discussed the key text in Philippians 4:6–9, in which prayer, thanksgiving, praise, and changing our thoughts are Paul's advice for anxiety.[21]

Fourth, Scripture also supplies believers with a personal guide for the pursuit of growth and holiness. It is wonderful to know that Christianity is true. But Christianity consists of far more than simply giving arguments and quoting texts in order to defend one's view. As C. S. Lewis reminds us, "one must train the habit of Faith. . . . Neither this belief nor any other will automatically remain alive in the mind. It must be fed." Lewis's remedy is to exercise the classic Christian disciplines.[22]

Scripture prescribes steps for growing closer to God (2 Pt 1:5–11). This includes practicing the Christian disciplines that are grounded in Scripture.[23]
The purpose here is to develop a lifestyle of communion with the Creator of
the universe. Beyond knowledge alone, Scripture calls believers to disciplines
such as prayer (Mt 6:5–13/Lk 11:2–4; 1 Thes 5:17), fasting (Mt 6:16; 9:15),
meditation (Pss 27:4–8; 63:1–8), solitude (Mk 6:31; Lk 5:16), study (Ps 1:2;
1 Tm 3:14–17), worship and praise (Ps 148; Phil 4:6, 8), and to the single-
minded pursuit of God and his eternal Kingdom (Mt 6:19–24/Lk 12:33–34;
Mt 13:44–45). The result is a life attuned to God and others.

Fifth, Scripture also commands believers to be radically involved in the
lives of others, and provides a guidebook with many practical suggestions on
how this may be done. The Old Testament overflows with mandates to provide for those in need, from the Year of Jubilee (Lv 25:8–55), to leaving food
in the fields for the poor to eat (Lv 19:9–10, 23:22; Dt 19:19–20), to a pro-
hibition against charging interest to fellow Jews (Dt 23:19–20). The third
year of the tithe was even to be used to assist the poor (Dt 14:28–29). Justice
is to be administered to those who are oppressed (Dt 10:18, 27:19; Ps 103:6;
Prv 22:22, 29:7, 31:8–9). Food and other needs should be donated to the
needy (Prv 3:27–28, 11:24, 14:31, 21:13, 22:9, 28:27, 31:20; Is 58:6–7).[24]

Jesus taught that the second greatest command is to love others as
much as we love ourselves (Mk 12:28–31). The parable of the Good
Samaritan (Lk 10:29–37) teaches that we should sacrifice our time, goods,
and finances to assist those who are hurting. Jesus's ethic also involved
selling our belongings in order to assist the poor (Lk 12:33–34), feeding
those in need (Lk 14:12–14), and the willingness to forsake all our possessions in order to follow Jesus (Mk 10:29–30; Lk 14:33).

The other New Testament writers continue the same radical ethic. The
ideal is to give ourselves first to God, and then to others (2 Cor 8:1–15, esp.
v. 5). If we fail to share our material possessions with others, how can we
claim to love God (1 Jn 3:17–18; cf. Jas 2:16)? Pure religion involved meeting the needs of orphans and widows (Jas 1:27) and not mistreating the poor
(Jas 2:1–10). In actual practice, the early Christian community at Jerusalem
shared their possessions (Acts 2:44–45; 4:32–37). Paul collected offerings to
assist poor believers (1 Cor 16:1–4).[25]

In short, the doctrine of the authority of Scripture is anchored to the
teaching of Jesus Christ, and grounded in his resurrection. Scripture, in turn,
serves as the textual basis for Christianity and provides our theological
primer. Further, it is our guide both for developing healthy thinking habits
and for living the Christian life. It also commands us to reach out to others,
loving them even as we love ourselves.

Notes

1. We cannot provide details here. For examples, see Craig L. Blomberg, *The Historical Reliability of the Gospels* (Downers Grove, Ill.: InterVarsity Press, 1987); Paul Barnett, *Is the New Testament Reliable? A Look at the Historical Evidence* (Downers Grove, Ill.: InterVarsity Press, 1986); Paul Barnett, *Jesus and the Logic of History* (Grand Rapids, Mich.: Eerdmans, 1997); John Wenham, *Christ and the Bible* (Grand Rapids, Mich.: Baker Book House, 1984).

2. Two major studies are John Meier, *A Marginal Jew: Rethinking the Historical Jesus*, 3 vols. (New York: Doubleday, 1987–2001), see 2:967–70 for his conclusions; Graham H. Twelftree, *Jesus the Miracle Worker: A Historical and Theological Study* (Downers Grove, Ill.: InterVarsity Press, 1999), see chap. 17 for his conclusions.

3. An edited version of this chapter appeared as Gary R. Habermas, "Jesus and the Inspiration of Scripture," *Areopagus Journal* 2 (2002): 11–16.

4. As mentioned in chapter 6, John Meier provides many arguments for the historicity of this text (*Marginal Jew*, 3:411–44).

5. See the examples in Mk 2:25; 12:10, 26; Mt 19:4; 21:16.

6. Some instances are found in Mk 9:12–13; 11:17; 14:21, 27.

7. Other options will be discussed below. For a detailed study of Jesus's attitude toward Scripture, see Robert P. Lightner, *The Saviour and the Scriptures* (Philadelphia: Presbyterian and Reformed, 1966).

8. See esp. 1 Cor 2:13, 14:37; Gal 1:8–12; 1 Thes 2:13; cf. Eph 3:1–6.

9. The following are just some of the examples: Rom 3:1–2, 21; 9:17; 15:4; 16:25–27; Gal 3:8–18; 2 Tm 2:15; 3:16; Heb 1:1–2; 4:12; 10:15–17; 1 Pt 1:10–12; 2 Pt 1:2; Acts 1:16; 2:29–35; 3:18–20; 4:25–26; 26:22–23; 28:23–28. For the importance of texts like these, see Rudolf Bultmann's comments below regarding the early church agreeing with Jesus concerning the authority of Scripture.

10. For other examples, see Mk 7:6–16; Mt 12:9–14, 15:1–14, 23:1–39; Lk 6:24–26.

11. Examples can be found in Mk 8:31, 9:31, 10:33–34, 13:1–2; Lk 5:4–8; Jn 1:47–51, 2:24–25, 4:16–19, 6:64, 11:11, 18:4.

12. G. B. Caird and L. D. Hurst extend this view to the early Christians, as well (*New Testament Theology* [Oxford: Clarendon Press, 1994], 57–58). Cf. also Emil Brunner, *Dogmatics*, 3 vols., trans. Olive Wyon (Philadelphia: Westminster Press, 1950–79), 1:106–7.

13. George Eldon Ladd, *A Theology of the New Testament* (Grand Rapids, Mich.: Eerdmans, 1974), 124.

14. Rudolf Bultmann, *Theology of the New Testament*, 2 vols., trans. Kendrick Grobel (New York: Scribner's Sons, 1951, 1955), 1:15–18.

15. Bart D. Ehrman, *Jesus: Apocalyptic Prophet of the New Millennium* (New York: Oxford University Press, 1999), 164–67.

16. Ehrman, *Jesus*, 165 (emphasis added).

17. Of the many passages above from Mark, perhaps the major ones are 2:23–28; 7:5–13; 11:15–17; 12:10; 12:24–27; 12:36–37.

18. Compare Mt 3:7–10/Lk 3:7–9; Mt 4:1–11/Lk 4:1–13; Mt 10:15/Lk 10:12; Mt 12:38–42/Lk 11:29–31; Mt 23:32–36/Lk 11:49–51; Mt 23:37–39/Lk 13:34–35; Mt 11:10–15/Lk 7:27–28 and Lk 16:16; Mt 24:37–39/Lk 17:26–30.

19. Ladd, *Theology of the New Testament*, 296.

20. See Gary R. Habermas, *The Resurrection: Heart of New Testament Doctrine*, vol. 1 (Joplin, Mo.: College Press, 2000), for some thoughts on making the resurrection the center of Christian theology, a spot it clearly occupies in the New Testament.

21. See William Backus and Marie Chapian, *Telling Yourself the Truth* (Minneapolis: Bethany Fellowship, 1980), esp. chaps. 1–6; Gary R. Habermas, *The Thomas Factor: Using Your Doubts to Draw Closer to God* (Nashville: Broadman and Holman, 1999), esp. chaps. 7–9.

22. C. S. Lewis, *Mere Christianity*, rev. ed. (New York: Macmillan, 1952), 124.

23. See Dallas Willard, *The Spirit of the Disciplines: Understanding How God Changes Lives* (San Francisco: Harper and Row, 1988); Richard J. Foster, *Celebration of Discipline: The Path to Spiritual Growth*, rev. ed. (San Francisco: Harper and Row, 1988).

24. Foster, *Celebration of Discipline*, chap. 2; Craig L. Blomberg, *Neither Poverty nor Riches: A Biblical Theology of Material Possessions* (Grand Rapids, Mich.: Eerdmans, 1999), chaps. 1–3; Craig L. Blomberg, *Heart, Soul, and Money* (Joplin, Mo.: College Press, 2000), chaps. 1–2.

25. On Jesus and the New Testament, see Foster, *Celebration of Discipline*, chap. 3; Blomberg, *Neither Poverty nor Riches*, chaps. 4–7; Blomberg, *Heart, Soul, and Money*, chaps. 3–9.

Selected Bibliography

Alsup, John. *The Post-Resurrection Appearance Stories of the Gospel Tradition: A History-of-Tradition Analysis with Text-Synopsis*. Calwer Theologische Monographien 5. Stuttgart, Germany: Calwer Verlag, 1975.

Backus, William, and Marie Chapian. *Telling Yourself the Truth*. Minneapolis: Bethany Fellowship, 1980.

Barth, Karl. *Church Dogmatics*. Vol. 4, part 1. Edited by G. W. Bromiley and T. F. Torrance. Edinburgh: T. and T. Clark, 1961.

Bartsch, Hans Werner. "Der Ursprung des Osterglaubens." *Theologische Zeitschrift* 31 (1975): 16–31.

———. "Inhalt und Funktion des Urchristlichen Osterglaubens." *New Testament Studies* 26 (1980): 180–96.

Beasley-Murray, G. R. *Jesus and the Kingdom of God*. Grand Rapids, Mich.: Eerdmans, 1986.

Blomberg, Craig L. *Neither Poverty nor Riches: A Biblical Theology of Material Possessions*. Grand Rapids, Mich.: Eerdmans, 1999.

Bock, Darrell L. *Blasphemy and Exaltation in Judaism and the Final Examination of Jesus*. Vol. 106 of *Wissenschaftliche zum Neuen Testament*, 2nd series. Tübingen, Germany: J. C. B. Mohr (Paul Siebeck), 1998; Grand Rapids, Mich.: Baker Books, 1998.

Bonhoeffer, Dietrich. *Christ the Center*. Translated by John Bowden. New York: Harper and Row, 1966.

———. *The Cost of Discipleship*. 2nd ed. Translated by R. H. Fuller. New York: Macmillan, 1959.

Borg, Marcus J. *Jesus: A New Vision: Spirit, Culture, and the Life of Discipleship*. San Francisco: Harper Collins, 1987.

Bornkamm, Günther. *Jesus of Nazareth*. Translated by Irene and Fraser McLuskey with James M. Robinson. New York: Harper and Row, 1960.

Brown, Raymond E. *The Death of the Messiah*. Garden City, N.Y.: Doubleday, 1994.

———. *An Introduction to New Testament Christology*. New York: Paulist Press, 1994.

———. "The Resurrection and Biblical Criticism." *Commonweal* (1967): 232–36.

———.*The Virginal Conception and Bodily Resurrection of Jesus*. New York: Paulist Press, 1973.

Brunner, Emil. *Dogmatics*. 3 vols. Translated by Olive Wyon. Philadelphia: Westminster Press, 1950–79.

Bultmann, Rudolf. *History and Eschatology: The Presence of Eternity*. New York: Harper and Row, 1957.

———. *Jesus Christ and Mythology*. New York: Scribner's Sons, 1958.

———. "New Testament and Mythology." *Kerygma and Myth*. Edited by Hans Werner Bartsch. New York: Harper and Row, 1961.

———. *Theology of the New Testament*. 2 vols. Translated by Kendrick Grobel. New York: Scribner's Sons, 1951, 1955.

Caird, G. B. *New Testament Theology*. Edited by L. D. Hurst. Oxford: Clarendon Press, 1994.

Craig, William Lane. *Assessing the New Testament Evidence for the Historicity of the Resurrection of Jesus*. Lewiston, N.Y.: Mellen Press, 1989.

———. "The Bodily Resurrection of Jesus." *Gospel Perspectives*. Vol. 1. Edited by R. T. France and David Wenham. Sheffield, England: JSOT Press, 1980.

———. "The Historicity of the Empty Tomb of Jesus." *New Testament Studies* 31 (1985): 39–67.

Crossan, John Dominic. *The Historical Jesus: The Life of a Mediterranean Jewish Peasant*. San Francisco: Harper Collins, 1991.

———. *Jesus: A Revolutionary Biography*. San Francisco: Harper Collins, 1994.

Cullmann, Oscar. *The Christology of the New Testament*. Rev. ed. Translated by Shirley C. Guthrie and Charles A. M. Hall. Philadelphia: Westminster Press, 1963.

Davis, Stephen T. *Risen Indeed: Making Sense of the Resurrection*. Grand Rapids, Mich.: Eerdmans, 1993.

Davis, Stephen T., Daniel Kendall, and Gerald O'Collins, editors. *The Resurrection: An Interdisciplinary Symposium on the Resurrection of Jesus*. Oxford: Oxford University Press, 1997.

D'Costa, Gavin, editor. *Resurrection Reconsidered*. Oxford: Oneworld Publications, 1996.

Dembski, William A. *Intelligent Design: The Bridge between Science and Theology*. Downers Grove, Ill.: InterVarsity Press, 1999.

Dodd, C. H. *The Apostolic Preaching and Its Developments*. 1936. Reprint, Grand Rapids, Mich.: Baker Books, 1980.

———. *The Parables of the Kingdom*. London: Nisbet and Company, 1935.

Doré, Joseph. "Croire en la Résurrection de Jésus-Christ." *Études* 356 (1982): 525–42.

Dunn, James D. G. *The Evidence for Jesus*. Louisville, Ky.: Westminster Press, 1985.

Durrwell, Francis X. *La Résurrection de Jésus: Mystère de Salut*. Paris: Les Éditions du Cerf, 1976.

Edwards, William D., Wesley J. Gabel, and Floyd E. Hosmer. "On the Physical Death of Jesus Christ." *Journal of the American Medical Association* 255 (1986): 1455–63.

Elliott, J. K. "The First Easter." *History Today* 29 (1979): 209–20.

Evans, C. Stephen. *The Historical Christ and the Jesus of Faith.* Oxford: Oxford University Press, 1996.

Fitzmyer, Joseph A. "Crucifixion in Ancient Palestine, Qumran Literature, and the New Testament." *The Catholic Biblical Quarterly* 40 (1978): 493–513.

Flew, Antony, and Alasdair Maclntyre, editors. *New Essays in Philosophical Theology.* New York: Macmillan, 1964.

Foster, Richard J. *Celebration of Discipline: The Path to Spiritual Growth.* Rev. ed. San Francisco: Harper and Row, 1988.

———. *Freedom of Simplicity.* San Francisco: Harper and Row, 1981.

Fuller, Reginald H. *The Formation of the Resurrection Narratives.* Philadelphia: Fortress Press, 1980.

———. *The Foundations of New Testament Christology.* New York: Scribner's Sons, 1965.

Funk, Robert. *Honest to Jesus.* San Francisco: Harper Collins, 1996.

Geivett, R. Douglas, and Gary R. Habermas, editors. *In Defense of Miracles: A Comprehensive Case for God's Action in History.* Downers Grover, Ill.: InterVarsity Press, 1997.

Gill, David. "Radical Christian: Rethinking our Financial Priorities." *Right On* 12 (1976): 12.

Gourges, M. *À La Droite de Dieu: Résurrection de Jésus et Actualisation du Psalm 110:1 dans Nouveau Testament.* Paris: J. Gabalda et Cie Editeurs, 1978.

Grant, Michael. *Jesus: An Historian's Review of the Gospels.* New York: Scribner, 1977.

Grass, Hans. *Ostergeschehen und Osterberichte.* 2nd ed. Göttingen, Germany: Vandenhoeck and Rupert, 1962.

Griffith, Stephen. "Could It Have Been Reasonable for the Disciples to Have Believed That Jesus Had Risen from the Dead?" *Journal of Philosophical Research* 21 (1996): 307–19.

Guillaume, Jean-Marie. *Luc Interprète des Anciennes Traditions sur la Résurrection de Jésus.* Etudes Bibliques. Paris: J. Gabalda et Cie, 1979.

Gundry, Robert H. *Soma in Biblical Theology with Emphasis on Pauline Anthropology.* Cambridge: Cambridge University Press, 1976.

Habermas, Gary R. "Explaining Away Jesus' Resurrection: The Recent Revival of Hallucination Theories." *Christian Research Journal* 23 (2001): 26–31, 47–49.

———. *Forever Loved: A Personal Account of Grief and Resurrection.* Joplin, Mo.: College Press, 1997.

———. "The Late Twentieth Century Resurgence of Naturalistic Responses to Jesus' Resurrection." *Trinity Journal*, n.s., 22 (2001): 179–96.

———. *The Resurrection: Heart of New Testament Doctrine.* Vol. 1. Joplin, Mo.: College Press, 2000.

———. *The Resurrection: Heart of the Christian Life.* Vol. 2. Joplin, Mo.: College Press, 2000.

Habermas, Gary R., and Antony Flew. *Did Jesus Rise from the Dead? The Resurrection Debate*. Edited by Terry L. Miethe. San Francisco: Harper and Row, 1987.

Habermas, Gary R., and J. P. Moreland. *Beyond Death: Exploring the Evidence for Immortality*. Wheaton, Ill.: Crossway Books, 1998.

Harris, Murray. *Raised Immortal: Resurrection and Immortality in the New Testament*. Grand Rapids, Mich.: Eerdmans, 1983.

Hengel, Martin. *The Atonement: The Origins of the Doctrine in the New Testament*. Translated by John Bowden. Philadelphia: Fortress Press, 1981.

———. *Crucifixion*. Translated by John Bowden. Philadelphia: Fortress Press, 1977.

Hick, John. *Death and Eternal Life*. Louisville, Ky.: Westminster John Knox Press, 1994.

Holland, R. F. "The Miraculous." *Logical Analysis and Contemporary Theism*. Edited by John Donnelly. New York: Fordham University Press, 1972.

Hume, David. "On Miracles." *An Enquiry Concerning Human Understanding*, in *Hume on Religion*. Edited by Richard Wollheim. Fontana Library of Theology and Philosophy. London: Collins Sons and Company, 1963.

Johnson, Luke Timothy. *Living Jesus: Learning the Heart of the Gospel*. San Francisco: Harper Collins, 1999.

———. *The Real Jesus: The Misguided Quest for the Historical Jesus and the Truth of the Traditional Gospels*. San Francisco: Harper Collins, 1996.

Kasper, Walter. *Jesus the Christ*. New ed. Translated by V. Green. Mahweh, N.J.: Paulist Press, 1976.

Kee, Howard Clark. *What Can We Know about Jesus?* Cambridge: Cambridge University Press, 1990.

Kierkegaard, Søren. *Attack upon "Christendom."* Translated by Walter Lowrie. Princeton: Princeton University Press, 1968.

Kloppenborg, John. "An Analysis of the Pre-Pauline Formula in 1 Cor 15:3b–5 in Light of Some Recent Literature." *Catholic Biblical Quarterly* 40 (1978): 350–67.

Kremer, Jacob. *Die Osterevangelien—Geschichten um Geschichte*. 2nd ed. Stuttgart, Germany: Verlag Katholisches Bibelwerk, 1981.

Künneth, Walter. *Theologie der Auferstehung*. 6th ed. Giessen, Germany: Brunnen Verlag, 1982.

Ladd, George Eldon. *I Believe in the Resurrection of Jesus*. Grand Rapids, Mich.: Eerdmans, 1975.

———. *The Pattern of New Testament Truth*. Grand Rapids, Mich.: Eerdmans, 1968.

———. *The Presence of the Future: The Eschatology of Biblical Realism*. Grand Rapids, Mich.: Eerdmans, 1974.

———. *A Theology of the New Testament*. Grand Rapids, Mich.: Eerdmans, 1974.

Lapide, Pinchas. *The Resurrection of Jesus: A Jewish Perspective*. Minneapolis: Augsberg Publishing, 1983.

Lehmann, Karl. "Zugang zum Ostergeschehen Heute: Am Beispiel der Emmauserzählung." *Internationale Katholische Zeitschrift* 11 (1982): 42–50.

Léon-Dufour, Xavier. *Resurrection and the Message of Easter*. Translated by R. N. Wilson. London: Chapman, 1974.

Lewis C. S. *Miracles: A Preliminary Study*. New York: Macmillan, 1947.

Lightner, Robert P. *The Saviour and the Scriptures*. Philadelphia: Prebyterian and Reformed, 1966.

Longenecker, Richard, editor. *Life in the Face of Death: The Resurrection Message of the New Testament*. Grand Rapids, Mich.: Eerdmans, 1998.

Lorenzen, Thorwald. *Resurrection and Discipleship: Interpretive Models, Biblical Reflections, Theological Consequences*. Maryknoll, N.Y.: Orbis Books, 1995.

Lüdemann, Gerd. *What Really Happened to Jesus*. Louisville, Ky.: Westminster John Knox Press, 1995.

MacDonald, William. *True Discipleship*. Kansas City: Walterick, 1962.

Marshall, I. Howard. *The Origins of New Testament Christology*. Updated ed. Downers Grove, Ill.: InterVarsity Press, 1990.

Marxsen, Willi. *Jesus and Easter: Did God Raise the Historical Jesus from the Dead?* Translated by Victor Paul Furnish. Nashville: Abingdon Press, 1990.

———. *The Resurrection of Jesus of Nazareth*. Translated by Margaret Kohl. Philadelphia: Fortress Press, 1970.

Mavrodes, George I. "David Hume and the Probability of Miracles." *International Journal for Philosophy of Religion* 43 (1998): 167–82.

Meier, John. *Mentor, Message, and Miracles*. Vol. 2 of *A Marginal Jew: Rethinking the Historical Jesus*. New York: Doubleday, 1994.

Merk, Otto. Review of *The Anastasis* by J. Duncan M. Derrett. *Gnomon-Kritische Zeitschrift für die Gesamte Klassische Altertumswissenschaft* 59 (1987): 761–63.

Merklein, Helmut. "Die Auferweckung Jesu und die Anfänge der Christologie (Messias bzw. Sohn Gottes und Menschensohn)." *Zeitschrift für die Neutestamentliche Wissenschaft und die Kunde der Älteren Kirche* 72 (1981): 1–26.

Moltmann, Jürgen. *Theology of Hope*. Translated by James W. Leitch. New York: Harper and Row, 1967.

Moser, Paul. *Why Isn't God More Obvious? Finding the God who Hides and Seeks*. Norcross, Ga.: RZIM, 2000.

Moule, C. F. D. *The Origin of Christology*. Cambridge: Cambridge University Press, 1977.

Murphy-O'Connor, Jerome. "Tradition and Redaction in 1 Cor 15:3–7." *Catholic Biblical Quarterly* 43 (1981): 582–89.

Neirynck, Frans. "Marc 16,1–8: Tradition et Rédaction." *Ephemerides theologicae Lovanienses* 56 (1980): 56–88.

O'Collins, Gerald. *Jesus Risen: The Resurrection—What Actually Happened and What Does It Mean?* London: Darton, Longman and Todd, 1987.

———. "On Raising Venturini." *Gregorianum* 75 (1994): 241–65.

———. *What Are They Saying about the Resurrection?* New York: Paulist Press, 1978.

O'Donavan, Oliver. *Resurrection and Moral Order*. Grand Rapids, Mich.: Eerdmans, 1986.

Orr, James. *The Resurrection of Jesus*. Grand Rapids, Mich.: Zondervan, 1965.

Pannenberg, Wolfhart. "Die Auferstehung Jesu: Historie und Theologie." *Zeitschrift für Theologie und Kirche* 91 (1994): 318–28.

———. *Die Auferstehung Jesu und die Zukunft des Menschen*. München-Gladbach, Germany: Minerva-Publikation, 1978.

———. *Jesus: God and Man*. 2nd ed. Translated by Lewis L. Wilkins and Duane A. Priebe. Philadelphia: Westminster Press, 1977.

———. *Theology and the Kingdom of God*. Edited by Richard John Neuhaus. Philadelphia: Westminster Press, 1969.

———, editor. *Revelation as History*. Translated by David Granskou. New York: Macmillan, 1968.

Parrish, Stephen E. *God and Necessity: A Defense of Classical Theism*. Lanham, Md.: University Press of America, 1997.

Perkins, Pheme. "I Have Seen the Lord (John 20:18): Women Witnesses to the Resurrection." *Interpretation* 46 (1992): 31–41.

———. *Resurrection: New Testament Witness and Contemporary Reflection*. Garden City, N.Y.: Doubleday, 1984.

Perret, Jacques. *Ressuscité? Approche Historique*. Paris: FAC Éditions, 1984.

Perrin, Norman. *The Resurrection according to Matthew, Mark, and Luke*. Philadelphia: Fortress, 1977.

Pesch, Rudolf. "Materialien und Bemerkungen zu Entstehung und Sinn des Osterglaubens." *Wie kam es zum Osterglauben?* Edited by Anton Vögtle and Rudolf Pesch. Düsseldorf, Germany: Patmos-Verlag, 1975.

———. "Zur Entstehung des Glaubens an die Auferstehung Jesu." *Theologische Quartalschrift* 153 (1973): 219–26.

———. "Zur Entstehung des Glaubens an die Auferstehung Jesu: Ein neuer Versuch." *Freiburger Zeitschrift für Philosophie und Theologie* 30 (1983): 73–98.

Ramm, Bernard. *The Witness of the Spirit: An Essay on the Contemporary Relevance of the Internal Witness of the Holy Spirit*. Grand Rapids, Mich.: Eerdmans, 1959.

Remus, Harold. *Jesus as Healer*. Cambridge: Cambridge University Press, 1997.

Robinson, James M. "Jesus from Easter to Valentinus (or to the Apostles' Creed)." *Journal of Biblical Literature* 101 (1982): 5–37.

Sanders, E. P. "But Did It Happen?" *The Spectator* 276 (1996): 11–13, 16–17.

———. *The Historical Figure of Jesus*. London: Penguin Books, 1993.

Schleiermacher, Friedrich. *The Christian Faith*. 2 vols. Edited by H. R. Mackintosh and J. S. Stewart. New York: Harper and Row, 1963.

Schweitzer, Albert. *The Quest of the Historical Jesus*. Translated by W. Montgomery. New York: Macmillan, 1968.

Sloyan, Gerard S. *The Crucifixion of Jesus: History, Myth, Faith*. Minneapolis: Fortress Press, 1995.

Stein, Robert H. "Was the Tomb Really Empty?" *The Journal of the Evangelical Theological Society* 20 (1977): 23–29.

Strauss, David Friedrich. A New Life of Jesus. 2 vols., 2nd ed. No translator given. London: Williams and Norgate, 1879.

Strawson, William. Jesus and the Future Life. London: Epworth Press, 1970.

Stuhlmacher, Peter. "The Resurrection of Jesus and the Resurrection of the Dead." Translated by Jonathan M. Whitlock. Ex Auditu 9 (1993): 45–56.

———. Was geschah auf Golgatha? Zur Heilsbedeutung von Kreuz, Tod und Auferweckung Jesu. Stuttgart, Germany: Calwer Verlag, 1998.

Stump, Eleonore. "Visits to the Sepulcher and Biblical Exegesis." Faith and Philosophy 6 (1989): 353–77.

Swinburne, Richard. The Concept of Miracle. New York: St. Martin's Press, 1970.

———, editor. Miracles. New York: Macmillan, 1989.

Taylor, Vincent. The Atonement in New Testament Teaching. 3rd ed. London: Epworth Press, 1963.

Tillich, Paul. Systematic Theology. 3 vols. Chicago: University of Chicago Press, 1951, 1957, 1963.

Torrance, Thomas. Space, Time and Resurrection. Grand Rapids, Mich.: Eerdmans, 1976.

Twelftree, Graham H. Jesus the Miracle Worker: A Historical and Theological Study. Downers Grove, Ill.: InterVarsity Press, 1999.

Verwer, George. Come! Live! Die! The Real Revolution. Wheaton, Ill.: Tyndale House 1972.

Verweyen, Hansjürgen. "Die Ostererscheinungen in fundamentaltheologischer Sicht." Zeitschrift für Katholische Theologie 103 (1981): 428–45.

Vollenweider, Samuel. "Ostern—der denkwürdige Ausgang einer Krisenerfahrung." Theologische Zeitschrift 49 (1993): 33–53.

Wedderburn, A. J. M. Beyond Resurrection. Peabody, Mass.: Hendrickson, 1999.

Williams, Rowan. Resurrection: Interpreting the Easter Gospel. London: Darton, Longman and Todd, 1982.

Witherington, Ben III. The Christology of Jesus. Minneapolis: Fortress Press, 1990.

———. Jesus, Paul, and the End of the World: A Comparative Study of New Testament Eschatology. Downers Grove, Ill.: InterVarsity Press, 1992.

Wright, N. T. "Christian Origins and the Resurrection of Jesus: The Resurrection of Jesus as a Historical Problem." Sewanee Theological Review 41 (1998): 107–23.

———. "Early Traditions and the Origin of Christianity." Sewanee Theological Review 41 (1998): 125–40.

———. "The Resurrection of Resurrection." Bible Review 16 (2000): 10, 63.

Zias, Joseph, and James H. Charlesworth. "Crucifixion: Archaeology, Jesus, and the Dead Sea Scrolls." Jesus and the Dead Sea Scrolls. Edited by James M. Charlesworth. New York: Doubleday, 1992.

Index

About the Author

Gary R. Habermas (Ph.D., Michigan State University) is distinguished professor and chair of the Department of Philosophy and Theology at Liberty University. He has served as a visiting or adjunct professor at a dozen different seminaries and graduate schools in the United States and elsewhere. He has authored or coauthored twenty-five books, eleven on the subject of the resurrection of Jesus, including *Did Jesus Rise from the Dead? The Resurrection Debate* (with Antony Flew), *The Historical Jesus: Ancient Evidence for the Life of Christ, Beyond Death: Exploring the Evidences for Immortality* (with J. P. Moreland), *The Resurrection of Jesus: A Rational Inquiry, The Resurrection of Jesus: An Apologetic, The Resurrection: Heart of New Testament Doctrine, The Resurrection: Heart of the Christian Life, The Thomas Factor,* and *Dealing with Doubt*. He has contributed twelve chapters to other books, in addition to dozens of journal articles. He and his wife, Eileen, have seven children.

Milton Keynes UK
Ingram Content Group UK Ltd.
UKHW031313150224
437896UK00011B/54